THEME AND STRUCTURE

in

SWIFT'S *TALE OF A TUB*

by

RONALD PAULSON

Archon Books   1972

Library of Congress Cataloging in Publication Data

Paulson, Ronald.
   Theme and structure in Swift's Tale of a tub.

     Original ed. issued as v. 143 of Yale studies in English.
     Based on the author's thesis, Yale.
     Includes bibliographical references.
     1. Swift, Jonathan, 1667–1745. A tale of a tub.
I. Title. II. Series: Yale studies in English, v. 143.
[PR3724.T33P3 1972]   823'.5   72-6570
ISBN 0-208-01133-1

158878

TO MY MOTHER

AND THE MEMORY OF MY FATHER

PREFACE

This study of Swift's *Tale of a Tub* grew
out of a projected study of Swift's prose style. But because
the *Tale* offered a whole spectrum of stylistic problems itself and seemed to stand off from the rest of Swift's writings,
I limited myself for the present to that work. Style is not,
ultimately, an isolable quality, and so this has become a
more general study of theme and structure: I have tried to
show just what the *Tale* is and what it means.

My text is the excellent Guthkelch-Smith edition of *A
Tale of a Tub* (Oxford, Clarendon Press, 1920, 2d ed. 1958),
which will be referred to hereafter as G-S; page references
to it will ordinarily be designated simply by a number in
parentheses, e.g. (38). Although the pagination of the first
and second editions is virtually the same (by the time the
Mechanical Operation is reached there is only a difference
of two pages between the two editions), I use that of the
second edition, revised by D. Nichol Smith. The changes in
the text of Smith's edition, which generally go back to Swift's
first edition (1704), do not affect my study; in a few cases,
however, such as Smith's correcting of "retro" to "tetro" in
an intentional misquotation Swift makes from Lucretius
(100), I have used the original reading. Although in general
I have followed the typography of G-S, I have printed in
roman type italicized passages in which no distinction is
intended between roman and italics. I wish to thank the
Clarendon Press for permission to quote from the edition.

Several important works have laid the groundwork for
such Swift studies as the present one: Emile Pons, *Swift:*

Les Années de jeunesse et le "Conte du Tonneau," Stras-
bourg, Librairie Istra, 1925; Ricardo Quintana, *The Mind
and Art of Jonathan Swift,* London, Oxford Univ. Press,
1936; John M. Bullitt, *Jonathan Swift and the Anatomy of
Satire,* Cambridge, Harvard Univ. Press, 1953; and William
Bragg Ewald, Jr., *The Masks of Jonathan Swift,* Cambridge,
Harvard Univ. Press, 1954. Among critical studies I would
particularly single out Martin Price's *Swift's Rhetorical Art*
(New Haven, Yale Univ. Press, 1953) as containing certainly the sanest account we have of the *Tale.* While I have
consciously gone a separate way, I have found myself, like
Jack who keeps running into Peter, frequently meeting
Price's conclusions. Another excellent study which treats the
Tale perceptively is Kathleen Williams' *Jonathan Swift and
the Age of Compromise,* Lawrence, University of Kansas
Press, 1958. Although this study appeared too late to do
more than corroborate some of my views, one of Miss Williams' essays was most useful to me: " 'Animal Rationis
Capax,' A Study of Certain Aspects of Swift's Imagery,"
ELH, 21 (1954), 193–207, which discusses Swift's general
tendency to present moral problems in terms of a physical
body.

An exceptionally penetrating essay on the *Tale* appears
in Robert M. Adams' *Strains of Discord: Studies in Literary
Openness* (Ithaca, Cornell Univ. Press, 1958), pp. 146–79.
Unfortunately Mr. Adams' essay reached me after my manuscript had left my hands, or I might have benefited from his
insights. His scheme for the *Tale* is a simple and useful one:
he sees the *Tale* controlled by two images: wind, or spirit,
and the machine (see pp. 150–7).

Aubrey Williams' chapter "Of Wisdom and Dulness" in
his *Pope's Dunciad* (Baton Rouge, Louisiana State Univ.
Press, 1955) was suggestive and directed me to H. M. Mc-
Luhan's articles and his unpublished Cambridge University doctoral dissertation, "The Place of Thomas Nashe

in the Learning of his Time" (1943), which he kindly lent me. These essays have provided me with basic assumptions concerning the tradition of the ancient-modern quarrel and its connection with the grammar-dialectic-rhetoric conflict. In the text I have cited the articles of Walter J. Ong, S.J., concerning Ramus, but his thorough study of Ramist theory has now appeared and should be consulted for further information: *Ramus, Method, and the Decay of Dialogue,* Cambridge, Harvard Univ. Press, 1958.

An appointment by Yale University as a Sterling Fellow for 1957–58 permitted me the leisure to write the doctoral dissertation upon which this book is based; a grant from the University of Illinois Research Board provided for the typing of the final draft; and the Yale Fund for Young Scholars has provided welcome assistance in publication.

I am indebted to Benjamin C. Nangle, Frederick W. Hilles, and Cleanth Brooks for reading all or part of the original draft and offering encouragement; to Mr. Nangle for his advice and assistance in getting it ready for publication; to Robert Haig for reading the final draft, offering useful suggestions, and securing me the microfilm of Dunton's *Voyage round the World;* and to Jack Stillinger for his assistance with galley proofs. I owe an exceptional debt of gratitude to Maynard Mack, who directed the dissertation from which this study evolved, and who, from draft to draft, played Swift to my Grub Street Hack; and, most of all, to my wife who read and suffered with me from the start.

R.P.

Champaign, Illinois
May 1959

CONTENTS

CHAPTER ONE

THE PARODY OF ECCENTRICITY

And, Oh, it can no more be questioned,
That beauties best, proportion, is dead.
——Donne, "First Anniversary"

1. The Characteristic Tone

Swift's *Tale of a Tub* is one of the "eccentric" books of English literature. From it the mind moves naturally back to the anatomies of Rabelais and Montaigne in France or of Nashe, Burton, Browne, and Urquhart of Cromarty in England. Such phenomena, it can be argued, are best left alone by Reason with his "Tools for cutting, and opening, and mangling, and piercing." The result of analysis may be to exorcise the characteristic tone, or at least the one for which the book is famous; when all puzzles are solved the book, being no longer a puzzle, is no longer the same.

My justification for analyzing the *Tale of a Tub* lies in the evident need for a close reading, which Swift himself made a gesture toward sanctioning when he wrote his "Author's Apology" to meet the accusations of irreligion that were promptly leveled at his book. Over and over through the years since its publication, and largely because of its form, the *Tale of a Tub* has been accused of being (1) an outright attack on religion, (2) an expression of disorder which is nihilistic, or (3) an elaborate joke which disregards over-all unity for the hilarity of momentary incongruities.

Most Swift criticism before the twentieth century deals with the *Tale's* supposed religious deficiencies. It is on religious grounds that its first (rather prejudiced) critics, Wotton, Dennis, and Blackmore, attack it.[1] Dr. Johnson agrees that it is "certainly a dangerous example," [2] and Scott, De Quincey, Thackeray, and other nineteenth-century critics generally follow this line. All of them manage to steer clear of an actual examination of the text, perhaps because they do not expect to find order beneath the surface of disorder; such a discovery would disturb the characteristic tone. The idea of the disrespectful theme is such a strong preconception that the critics who see admirable qualities in the *Tale* either talk about Swift the man as a damned titan,[3] or, like Hazlitt, they praise its style, calling it "one of the most masterly compositions in the language, whether for thought, wit, or style," but altogether ignore the problem of what the "thought" may be.[4] Scott, while praising the brilliance of expression, admits that it "was considered [by contemporaries], not unreasonably, as too light for a subject of such grave importance," and "in some parts of the *Tale*" Swift's

1. See, e.g., John Dennis' vituperation in a letter *"To the* Examiner. *Upon his wise Paper of the Tenth of* January, 1710/1" (1712), in *The Critical Works of John Dennis,* ed. Edward Niles Hooker (Baltimore, Johns Hopkins Press, 1939), *2,* 397–8. See also William Wotton, *Observations upon The Tale of a Tub* (1705), in G-S, pp. 313–24; and Sir Richard Blackmore, "Essay upon Wit," in *Essays upon Several Subjects* (London, 1716), pp. 217–18.

2. Samuel Johnson, *Lives of the English Poets,* ed. G. B. Hill (Oxford, Clarendon Press, 1905), *3,* 10.

3. William Makepeace Thackeray, *The English Humourists of the Eighteenth Century* (London, 1858), pp. 1–57; Thomas De Quincey, "A Review of Schlossler's Literary History of the Eighteenth Century," in *The Collected Writings of Thomas De Quincey,* ed. David Masson (Edinburgh, 1889), *11,* 14–15.

4. William Hazlitt, "Lectures on the English Poets," Lecture VI, in *The Miscellaneous Works of William Hazlitt* (London, 1887), *3,* 131. Johnson also praises the fertility of invention: *Lives, 3,* 51.

wit has "carried him much beyond the bounds of propriety." [5]

In our own day John Middleton Murry has continued the tradition of religious criticism: "This cannot be merely a careless fling that strikes St. Paul by accident," he says. "Swift must have aimed it." [6] And for William Empson the *Tale* is a reduction of Christian terminology and imagery to their grossest physical equivalents.[7] F. R. Leavis believes that the *Tale's* ironic intensity is purely destructive, and that it is "essentially a matter of surprise and negation; its function is to defeat habit, to intimidate and to demoralize." [8] A well-meaning critic like Henry Craik has tried to dispel the religious bugaboo by pointing out that only one-third of the text pertains to religion, while two-thirds is devoted to the abuses of learning. But he settles for a harmless book at the expense of unity, for he admits that these two elements divide the work.[9] George Sherburn implies that in the *Tale* Swift is sometimes "not clear as to just what he wants to do, and allows himself a virtuosity of witty effervescence that delights or wounds by turns." [1] Criticism thus runs the gamut from seeing the *Tale* as consciously irreligious to seeing it as lacking a positive philosophy, and finally to seeing it as uncertain of intention. Murry, for example, finds it "primarily a manifestation of the comic spirit"—it is not possible to take it seriously, except at our peril (p. 86). Even Herbert Davis, who has noted Swift's employment of literary parody, tends to take the *Tale* as a

5. Sir Walter Scott, *The Works of Jonathan Swift* (Edinburgh, 1814), *1*, 85.

6. *Jonathan Swift: A Critical Biography* (London, Jonathan Cape, 1954), p. 79.

7. *Some Versions of Pastoral* (New York, New Directions, n.d.), p. 60.

8. *The Common Pursuit* (New York, George W. Stewart, 1952), p. 75.

9. *The Life of Jonathan Swift* (2d ed. London, Macmillan, 1894), *1*, 132.

1. "The Restoration and Eighteenth Century," *A Literary History of England*, ed. Albert C. Baugh (New York, Appleton-Century-Crofts, 1948), p. 869.

jeu d'esprit, impatient of too much analysis; while Leavis thinks that "this savage exhibition is mainly a game, played because it is the insolent pleasure of the author." [2]

We can conclude that closely allied to this preconception of the characteristic tone and the disrespectful theme is the belief that satirists like Swift did not seek unity or consistency in their works; that Swift in his major works was the same sort of journalist he was in his *Examiners* and party pamphlets. All apparent inconsistencies can thus be explained as either the satirist's roving fire or Swift's playfulness.

More recent critics have devoted themselves to seeking consistency and unity in Swift's works—more successfully with *Gulliver's Travels,* however, than with the *Tale.* The rhetorical critics of the last few years have cleared up such crucial misunderstandings as the relationship between Swift and the speaker of the *Tale,* but they tend to slight the religious question, demonstrating instead the brilliance of Swift's persuasion. [3]

It is my contention that one must try to come to terms with the *Tale* and determine what its particular kind of unity is, assuming that a work of art (in order to be one) must be in some way unified. There are, of course, different kinds of unity, for each work of art, as it creates its own world, has its own laws and logic. The question of whether Swift consciously sought unity in his works can best be answered by remembering that Swift, Pope, and their group were conscious inheritors of the Renaissance-Christian

2. Davis, *The Satire of Jonathan Swift* (New York, Macmillan, 1947), pp. 9–48; Leavis, p. 80.

3. See Robert C. Elliott, "Swift's *Tale of a Tub:* An Essay in Problems of Structure," *PMLA, 66* (1951), 441–55; Elliott finds the *Tale's* unity in its point of view (a Jamesian treatment). An example of the rhetorical approach carried to extremes is Harold D. Kelling, "Reason in Madness: *A Tale of a Tub,*" *PMLA, 69* (1954), 198–222; Kelling believes that the subject of the *Tale* is rhetoric.

ideals, an important one being the ideal of unity and harmony of proportion.

To cope with Swift's *Tale of a Tub* the critic can neither
ignore technical considerations of structure and satiric
method nor reason away the religious accusations. The defender of Swift must accept the fact that, whatever statistics
can be produced to the contrary, the religious theme is the
crucial one to an understanding of the *Tale*. A misunderstanding which lies at the bottom of the accusation of irreligion is brought to light in a comment of Scott's. He
refers to the *Tale's* being "recommended by Voltaire to his
proselytes, because the ludicrous combinations which are
formed in the mind of the peruser, tend to lower the respect
due to revelation." [4] Such juxtapositions appear to be disrespectful when aimed at revelation. The misunderstanding
implicit here is between two views of religion and two views
of man. One of these sees "ludicrous combinations" as destroying man's dignity, while the other sees them as holding
him down to his natural size. These two views are irreconcilable as to man's relation to God and, accordingly, as to
the nature of revelation. Our look at the *Tale of a Tub* will
demonstrate why they are irreconcilable and why and how
Swift accepts the less optimistic of the two views.

Because its theme is so closely connected with its form,
we shall approach the *Tale* through the eccentricity we
noted at the beginning of this section, the oddness which
has both fascinated and repelled Swift's readers.

II. Characteristics of Seventeenth-Century
    Form: A Possible Interpretation

We shall begin our inquiry by seeking a distinction between Swift's *Tale of a Tub* and the other anatomies whose

4. *Works of Swift, 1,* 86.

eccentricity brought them to mind; and so for our purpose
we must look on these works less with the reverence due historically important objects than with an inquiring eye to
the elements that make them eccentric and similar to the
Tale.[1]

Seen in this way, the anatomies of Nashe, Burton, and
Browne are at once compost heaps of information and
charming personal documents; and the list I have suggested
could be extended to include sermons and various other
forms which show the same characteristics, though on a
smaller scale. The sermon of a Donne or an Andrewes is as
exhaustive and personal on its given topic as is Burton on
his. The divine means to demonstrate the truth of his interpretation of Scripture by showing every bit of evidence
pointing to it, from the enumeration of authorities to the
exploitation of syntax and semantics.[2] Burton, on the other
hand, collects all the information he can find about theories
of the physiological causes of melancholy, but his object is
to show the disagreements and incongruities among these
theories in order to suggest the probability of psychological
causes. Burton and the divine have in common the desire
to prove something beyond the shadow of a doubt.

In the same way the anatomies of Montaigne and Browne
are similar in structure but aim at precisely opposite conclusions. Montaigne produces fact after fact, customs that
conflict, beliefs that do not agree, creating a great monument to the inconsistency and stubbornness of the human
mind and a triumphant proof that reason is inadequate,
from which proof he concludes, "O what a soft and easy
and wholesome pillow is ignorance and freedom from care

1. I am using "anatomy" in a broader sense than does Northrop Frye
when he equates it with Menippean satire, but in much the same sense he
employs in his title, *Anatomy of Criticism* (Princeton Univ. Press, 1957; see
pp. 308–14).

2. See Price, *Swift's Rhetorical Art*, p. 37.

to rest a well-screwed-on headpiece!" [3] Since reason is unreliable, one should examine the evidence but withhold
judgment. Browne accumulates his evidence, not unlike
Montaigne's; but having destroyed superstitions and having
proved that a reasonable man cannot possibly believe in,
for example, immortality, he concludes (with an "O Alti-
tudo!") that this is all the more reason for one to do so.

In each of these cases, however, the conclusion is all but
submerged in the evidence, which, one feels, exists as much
for its own sake as for that of the argument. What makes
these writers still interesting after three hundred years is, in
fact, the mass of detail with which they clutter their search
for an absolute. But seeking to establish universals, they
demonstrate a stronger probability of nominalism, and their
conflict between the validity of faith and the validity of
reason ends with the incidentals collapsing the main argument.

The Rabelaisian anatomy too is nominalist in method,
collecting all manner of stories, jokes, poems, songs, all the
paraphernalia of the medieval popular sermon. But, as
Erich Auerbach has pointed out, "Rabelais' entire effort is
directed toward playing with things and with the multiplicity of their possible aspects; upon tempting the reader
out of his customary and definite way of regarding things,
by showing him phenomena in utter confusion; upon tempting him out into the great ocean of the world, in which he
can swim freely, though it be at his own peril." [4] Every page,
by presenting the madness and inconsistency of men, be-
speaks freedom of choice and invites the reader to give way
to the natural man in him. The question of Rabelais' relation to Christian dogma is not important in the over-all ef-

3. "Of Experience," in *The Essays of Montaigne*, tr. E. J. Trechmann
(New York and London, Oxford Univ. Press, 1927), 2, 550.
4. *Mimesis*, tr. Willard R. Trask (Princeton Univ. Press, 1953), pp. 275–6.

fect of his work; rather the "imitation" of chaos is itself something at which the church tends to look askance, particularly when it appears to be urged upon the reader as a way of life. This is a far cry from the intention of either Montaigne or Browne—but it is a conclusion the reader may draw from them too if he is so inclined.

The first characteristic of these works, then, is an encyclopedic fullness in a protean disorder. The second is the personal quality. Rabelais is portraying the individual, free of restraint; and there is an equally striking autonomy in Montaigne's aloof and uncommitted "que sais-je?" Montaigne intends, by showing that man's only basis for certainty is his own subjective opinion, to prove man's inadequacy and need for the authority of tradition or common forms; but this emphasis is very easily shifted to an exaltation of the individual's subjective opinion. An underlying assumption in seventeenth-century literature that must not be discounted is the ever-growing interest in self, derived in part from Renaissance humanism and in part from the trend toward subjectivity manifested in all branches of the Protestant Reformation. At its logical extreme, this was the belief that everything one writes is interesting because it is self-expression. Although the seventeenth-century trend toward self-expression was only a whisper compared to what would come in the nineteenth century, it is safe to say that Montaigne was read as much for the revelation of an interesting mind as for his pyrrhonist epistemology.

In order to see how subjectivity was reflected in style and form we can begin with a passage from John Donne, who, speaking of the Metaphysical style of preaching, explains that

> the Holy Ghost in penning the Scriptures delights himself, not only with a propriety, but with a delicacy, and harmony, and melody of language; with height of

Metaphors, and other figures, which may work great
impressions upon the Readers, and not with barbarous,
or triviall, or market or homely language . . . and they
mistake it much that thinke, that the Holy Ghost hath
rather chosen a low, and barbarous, and homely style,
then an eloquent, and powerful manner of expressing
himselfe.[5]

Donne's God is unashamedly in his own image: to be God
—or the Holy Ghost—is to be grandiose and copiously creative, almost Rabelaisian. In the passage cited he piles "delicacy" upon "propriety," and "harmony" and "melody"
upon these—suggesting a great abundance rather than any
order or decorum an earlier generation might have associated with God. Donne's syntax is, in fact, disordered, and
each new adjective tries to go the last one better.

To see the norm from which a style like Donne's deviates
one need only turn back a few years to the writing of Richard Hooker:

The light would never be so acceptable, were it not for
that usual intercourse of darkness. Too much honey
doth turn to gall; and too much joy even spiritually
would make us wantons. Happier a great deal is that
man's case, whose soul by inward desolation is hum-
bled, than he whose heart is through abundance of
spiritual delight lifted up and exalted above measure.
Better it is sometimes to go down into the pit with him,
who, beholding darkness, and bewailing the loss of inward joy and consolation, crieth from the bottom of
the lowest hell, "My God, my God, why hast thou forsaken me?" than continually to walk arm in arm with
angels, to sit as it were in Abraham's bosom, and to

5. Sermon LV, "Preached at S. Pauls upon Christmas day. 1626," in *LXXX
Sermons* (London, 1640, folio), pp. 556(E)–557(C); cited in W. Fraser Mitch-
ell, *English Pulpit Oratory from Andrewes to Tillotson* (London, S.P.C.K.;
New York and Toronto, Macmillan, 1932), p. 189.

have no thought, no cogitation, but "I thank my God it is not with me as it is with other men." No, God will have them that shall walk in light to feel now and then what it is to sit in the shadow of death. A grieved spirit therefore is no argument of a faithless mind.[6]

This passage from Hooker's sermon "Of the Certainty and Perpetuity of Faith in the Elect" shows, in the control exerted by the periodic sentence, the employment of an external order. The first and second sentences, with their antitheses and point, could have been written by Donne or Andrewes. But the third sentence and then the fourth, pivoting on "Happier" and "Better . . . than," fill in their skeletons with clauses and phrases conveying information, each in an orderly relation to the central antithesis of the sentence. In the Ciceronian period the dependent members are arranged in climactic order, each directing the reader toward the principal member which, suspended until the end, acts as capstone to an almost architectural structure. The same can be said of the over-all form of Hooker's sermons or of the *Laws of Ecclesiastical Polity*. Every proof has its place in the argument, which moves forward like an army in review. The result is a "fixed" quality, a finality and forethought which are not apparent in Donne.[7]

In the loose (or anti-Ciceronian) style the function of the sentence as a sorter and arranger of information is lost. Its function is rather, as Morris Croll has written, "to express individual variances of experience in contrast with the general and communal ideas which the open design of oratorical style is so well adapted to contain." [8] The writer's indi-

6. *The Works of That Learned and Judicious Divine Mr. Richard Hooker*, ed. John Keble (Oxford, 1836), *3*, Pt. II, 590.

7. See Sister M. Stephanie Stueber, C.S.J., "The Balanced Diction of Hooker's *Polity*," *PMLA, 71* (1956), 808–26.

8. "'Attic Prose' in the Seventeenth Century," *Studies in Philology, 18* (1921), 88. See also Croll's "The Baroque Style in Prose," in *Studies in English Philology, a Miscellany in Honor of Frederick Klaeber*, ed. Kemp

viduality will not be fettered by the Ciceronian forms. "I shall here write down my thoughts without arranging them," wrote Pascal, "but not perhaps in deliberate disorder; that is the proper order, and it will convey my intention by its very want of order." [9] The sentence becomes a medium for showing the mind moving toward truth, rather than for presenting truth, and accordingly becomes so flexible as to be almost coextensive with the author's thought, in subtlety and duration. The larger structure of the work becomes similarly fluid, its most patent sign of freedom being the digression, its logical end the pile of notes that Pascal left behind him. There is no ordering from without; the sentences, paragraphs, and chapters record the thoughts the way—and in the order—they were thought.

The aesthetic which explains the trend we have been examining is summed up in Bacon's words: "There is no excellent beauty that hath not some strangeness in the proportion." [1] Its literary guides were the poets of the Roman Silver Age and their calculated disorder, instead of the ordered sanity of the Golden Age. Art historians call the period mannerist, and in Wylie Sypher's study, *Four Stages of Renaissance Style*, it is said to be characterized by "no logical focus for the composition," "no release; only tension," or by "techniques of disproportion and disturbed balance . . . with oblique or mobile points of view and strange—even abnormal—perspectives that yield approximations rather than certainties." [2]

Malone and Martin B. Ruud (Minneapolis, Univ. of Minnesota Press, 1929), pp. 427–56.

9. Blaise Pascal, *Pascal's Pensées, with an English Translation, Brief Notes and Introduction* by H. F. Stewart (New York, Pantheon Books, 1950), No. 27, p. 13.

1. Sir Francis Bacon, "Of Beauty," in *The Essayes or Counsels, Civil and Morall, 1597–1625*, in *Essays, Advancement of Learning, New Atlantis, and Other Pieces*, ed. Richard Foster Jones (New York, Odyssey Press, 1937), p. 125.

2. (Garden City, N.Y., Doubleday, 1955), pp. 111, 113, 116–17.

There is, however, more than one reason for aiming at the eccentric or unique: we have noticed its use as a presentation of the individual seeking self-knowledge; but it can also be a presentation of the self to catch attention, or it can become merely a device for moving an audience.

In our survey of seventeenth-century literature let us, for simplicity's sake, confine ourselves to the three areas Swift singles out for attention in the three "oratorial machines": the pulpit, the gallows, and the stage itinerant. Beginning with the pulpit, we can observe that in the seventeenth century both Puritan and Anglican preachers exploited the opportunities for brilliance inherent in a loose syntax, in vivid metaphors, and in the sudden outburst of rhetorical passion.[3] What followed was the great age of pulpit eloquence, when people crowded to hear their favorite preachers. It is possible to infer from this fact alone that expression became at least as important to congregations as the doctrine expressed. For example, schemata are used by Hooker as traditional patterns of expression—*parison, isocolon, homoioteleuton*—which organize and hold together the periodic structure of his sentences. In Andrewes' sermons there is a tendency—which becomes flagrant in his less scrupulous imitators—to use schemata for sheer word play; their contribution to the over-all structure is minimal. To take a

3. That the abuses were not limited to one party is evident from, for example, Robert South's attacks on both metaphysical and enthusiast modes of preaching. He attacks both in his sermon *The Scribe Instructed to the Kingdom of Heaven*, "Preached at *S. Mary's* Church in *Oxon*, before the University, on the 29th of *July* 1660. Being the Time of the KING's Commissioners meeting there, soon after the *Restoration*, for the Visitation of that University," in *South's Sermons* (Oxford, 1823), *3*, 34 ff. He preached against the Puritans again in *False Foundations Removed, and True Ones Laid for Such Wise Builders as Design to Build for Eternity*, preached "at St. Mary's, *Oxon*, before the University" (December 10, 1661), ibid., *2*, 346 ff. Another example is John Eachard, who, accused of having attacked only Anglican preachers in his *The Grounds and Occasions of the Contempt of the Clergy and Religion Enquir'd into; in a Letter written to R.L.* (London, 1670), was careful to attack Anglican, Puritan, and Catholic in his next book, *Some Observations upon the Answer to an Enquiry* (London, 1671).

well-known example, here is a passage from Andrewes' ninth
Nativity Sermon:

> For, if this Childe be *Immanuel*, GOD *with us;* then
> without this Childe, this *Immanuel*, we be without
> GOD. *Without Him, in this World* (saith the *Apostle;*)
> And, if without him, in this, without Him, in the next:
> And, if without Him there, if it be not *Immanu-el*, it
> will be *Immanu-hel;* and that, and no other place, will
> fall (I feare me) to our share. Without Him, this we
> are: What, with Him? Why, if we have Him; and GOD,
> by Him; we need no more: *Immanu-el* and *Immanu-*
> *all*. All that we can desire is, for us to be *with Him*,
> with GOD; and He to be *with us*. And we, from Him, or
> He from us, never to be parted.[4]

These members, for all the connected word play, give the
impression of being exploratory. The object is to present
the process of learning, or the process of Biblical exegesis,
rather than the accomplished fact.[5] The schemata have the
effect of drawing attention to a point being made, or
of awakening the congregation to a point about to be
made; but when used to excess, they direct attention to the
preacher himself. Accordingly, among the young and ambitious preachers the best way to attract attention was by employing the most extravagant, eye-catching wit.[6]

A chief criticism leveled at this style by the reformers of
the Restoration was that "the general sense of the [Biblical]

4. Launcelot Andrewes, "ɪxth Nativity Sermon," in *XCVI Sermons* (London, 1629; 3d ed. 1635), pp. 77–8; cited in Mitchell, p. 162.

5. Such use of pivotal words leads to a characteristic progression which,
like Andrewes' short, broken style, gives the sermon a piecemeal effect. The
Puritan sermon, consisting of innumerable subheadings, each with several
scriptural citations under it, has an equally broken effect.

6. Herbert Croft, Bishop of Hereford, writes that "in short, their main
end is to shew their Wit, their Reading, and whatever else they think is excellent in them": *The Naked Truth* (1675), ed. H. Hensley Henson, London,
1919; cited in Charles Smyth, *The Art of Preaching, A Practical Survey of
Preaching in the Church of England, 1747–1939* (London, Macmillan, 1940),

text was totally neglected, while every single word of it was separately considered under all its possible meanings." [7] One of the wittiest of these reformers, John Eachard, makes up an amusing example of the Metaphysical emphasis on individual words. Using the text, "But his delight is in the Law of the Lord," the preacher begins "BUT, *This* BUT . . . *is full of spiritual wine; we will broach it, and taste a little, then proceed.*" Eachard adds that he would have been happier if the preacher had "spoken in *Latin;* and told us, that this *sed* or *verum, enim, vero,* is full of *spiritual wine;* For then the *wit* would have been more admired for lying a great way off." [8] But if the Anglicans sometimes put too much emphasis on a word, the Puritans were "much in love with new-minted Words, in which they thought there were great Mysteries concealed." [9] While the Metaphysicals use learned words, Latin and Greek citations, and schemata, "so neither can the [Puritans'] whimsical Cant of *Issues, Products, Tendencies, Breathings, In-dwellings, Rollings, Recumbencies,*[1] and Scriptures misapplied, be accounted Divinity." [2]

Another eye catcher is metaphor, whose vividness depends largely upon the juxtaposition of a physical, sensory object with a spiritual concept, as in Andrewes' comparison of the Gunpowder Plot to the conception of a child: "there is not onely *fructus ventris,* there is *partus mentis:* the

---

p. 101. Eachard points out that it is "the joy of joys, when the parts jingle, or begin with the same letter; and especially if in Latin": *Grounds of Contempt,* p. 67.

7. Thomas Birch, *The Life of the Most Reverend Dr. John Tillotson, Lord Archbishop of Canterbury. Compiled Chiefly from his Original Papers and Letters* (London, 1752), p. 18; cited in Smyth, p. 106.

8. Eachard, *Some Observations,* p. 107.

9. Simon Patrick, *A Friendly Debate between a Conformist and a Nonconformist* (London, 1668, 4th ed. 1669), p. 27; cited in Smyth, p. 144.

1. A marginal note adds: "*Terms ofter and much used by one J*[ohn] *O*[wen] *a great Leader and Oracle of those Times.*"

2. South, *The Scribe Instructed,* in *Sermons, 3, 34.*

minde conceives, as well as the *wombe:* the word [conceiving] is like proper, to both. Men have their *wombe,* but it lieth higher, in them; as high as their *hearts;* and that which is there *conceived,* and *bred,* is a *birth.*" [3] The "Gunpowder sermons" contain Andrewes' most extravagant wit; here we find such phrases as "Through the Cisterne and Conduit of all *Thy mercies, Iesus Christ.*" [4] But this need only be compared with a metaphorical passage unfolded by a Puritan: "Christ can come by you suddenly in a blast of a whirlwind, in a preaching, and cast in a coal at the window of your soul, and leave it smoking, and slip His way. And He can shoot an arrow of love even to the feathers, and post away Himself, and say, 'Pack you out. Here is a bone for you to gnaw on.' " [5] Samuel Rutherford, the Scotch Presbyterian who wrote this, also advises "Thank God for the smell of Christ when ye cannot get Himself" (p. 103). Joseph Glanvill noticed that Puritan preachers "tell the people that they must roll upon *Christ,* close with *Christ,* get into *Christ,* get a saving interest in the Lord *Christ.*" [6] While the Puritans avoided the literary and the learned, the everyday images to which they resorted brought religion down either to the concrete level of wrestling matches and "a

3. Andrewes, vIIIth Sermon "Of the Gun-Powder Treason," in *XCVI Sermons,* p. 974; cited in Mitchell, p. 156.

4. Ibid., p. 970; cited in Mitchell, p. 155. However, we find a similar passage in Andrewes' sixth Nativity Sermon ("xIVth Whit-Sunday Sermon," ibid., p. 746): "The *Father,* the *Fountaine;* the *Sonne,* the *Cisterne;* the HOLY GHOST the *Conduit-pipe,* or *pipes* rather (for they are many) by and through which, they are derived downe to us." For Eachard's discussion of this kind of metaphor, see *Grounds of Contempt,* pp. 26 ff.

5. Samuel Rutherford, *Quaint Sermons of Samuel Rutherford, Hitherto Unpublished,* ed. Andrew A. Bonar (Ser. 5, London, 1885), p. 102; cited in Mitchell, p. 263.

6. *An Essay Concerning Preaching, Written for the Direction of a Young Divine, and Useful also for the People in order to Profitable Hearing,* London, 1678; in *Critical Essays of the Seventeenth Century,* ed. J. E. Spingarn (Oxford, Clarendon Press, 1908), 2, 277. South says the same in *False Foundations,* in *Sermons, 2,* 346.

busie Trade," or to the vagueness of "get into *Christ.*" [7]
What Andrewes' and the Puritans' sermons have in common is the use of the unexpected, of the momentary surprise.

Another characteristic of the seventeenth-century sermon
is a tendency to allow one of these momentary surprises to
grow, replacing more conventional structures with the logic
of a metaphor. The speaker, once committed to his vehicle,
begins to create meaning which may not be at every point
consonant with his intention. "The more I think of it," says
Andrewes, concerning the comparison of the Gunpowder
Plot to parturition, "the more points of correspondence do
offer themselves to me."

> 1. The *vessels* first give forth themselves, as so many
> *embrio's:* 2. The *vault,* as the *wombe,* wherein they
> lay so long: 3. They that conceived this device were
> the *mothers,* cleare: 4. the *fathers,* were the *fathers* (as
> they delight to be called) though, oft, little more than
> boyes; but here, *right fathers,* in that they perswaded,
> it might be, why not? might be *lawful;* nay, *meritori-*
> *ous,* then: so, it was they, that did animate, gave a
> *soule* (as it were) to the *treason.* 5. The *conception*
> was, when the *powder,* as the *seed* was conveighed in:
> 6. The *articulation,* the touching of them, in order,
> just as they should stand: 7. the *covering* of them, with
> *wood* and *fagots,* as the drawing a *skin,* over them:
> 8. The *Venerunt ad partum,* when all was now ready,
> *traine* and all: 9. The *Mid-wife,* he that was found
> with the *match* about him, for the purpose: 10. And

7. See William Haller, *The Rise of Puritanism,* New York, Columbia
Univ. Press, 1938, reprinted, Harper's, 1957. The Puritans, while holding
up "a perfectly arid and schematic dialectic as the ideal mode of discourse,"
knew better than to put their theory into general practice. "The preachers,"
Haller says, "if they wished to survive, had to find means to stir imaginations, induce emotional excitement, wring the hearts of sinners, win souls to
the Lord, in other words make themselves understood and felt" (p. 23).

partus, the *birth* should have bin upon the giving *fire.* If the *fire* had come to the *powder,* the *children had come to the birth.*[8]

As the Royal Society and modern semanticists have complained, a metaphor changes the thing itself, while the auricular figures employed by Hooker and the Elizabethans in general merely underline meaning.[9]

Sound itself often became divorced from meaning in this century of the sermon. There is evidence that the Anglican congregations liked to hear the sound of the Greek and Latin quotations in sermons when they were altogether unintelligible to them.[1] In 1668 Robert South, commenting on the problem in a sermon at Christ Church, Oxford, recognizes a sort of sensory appeal in the "fustian bombast" of these preachers, because "none are so transported and pleased with it as those who least understand it." He points out that "the greatest admirers of it are the grossest, the most ignorant, and illiterate country people, who, of all men, are the fondest of highflown metaphors and allegories, attended and set off with scraps of Greek and Latin."[2] The sensory

8. viiith Sermon, "Of the Gun-Powder Treason," in *XCVI Sermons,* p. 975; cited in Mitchell, pp. 156–7. "Touching" in the eleventh line is a printer's error for "couching."

9. When metaphors and similes were used, they were traditional and employed simply as illustrations or as coloring. For example, "Even as ye do provide indifferentlye for every parte of youre naturall bodye, by reason of the which, ye are bounde, and subiecte to corruption: So let no parte or member of your Christen bodye be unprovided for." In this sentence from Thomas Lever's *A Fruitful Sermon made in Poules Churche at London in the Shroudes the Seconde Daye of February* . . . (London, 1550), p. 47, the emphasis is rather on the neat opposition of "naturall bodye" and "Christen bodye" than on the simile. The simile is ordered by the syntax with transverse parison and the polyptoton of "provide" and "unprovided."

1. Mitchell tells how "Pococke, one of the most notable orientalists of his day, was complained of by his parishioners for insufficiency, since he did not choose to regale them with the unintelligible scraps of Greek and Latin to which they had been accustomed" (p. 106).

2. Sermon LIX, in *Sermons, 4,* 151; cited in Mitchell, p. 120.

element can be found in the Puritan preacher's coughs and hems; it appears to be a fact that dissenter preachers "looked upon coughing and hemming as ornaments of speech" to such an extent that they included them in the printed texts of their sermons.[3] Finally, there were, among the Puritans, "those strange new Postures used by some in the Delivery of the Word"—"Such as shutting the eyes, distorting the face, and speaking through the nose," which South noticed.[4] These sounds and motions have, of course, the two explanations we noticed earlier: they reveal the speaker's mind, and they can move an audience. For example, the visual gymnastics of dissenter preachers may convey the mind's agitation and suggest the inexpressible it is moving toward.

What we have said of the pulpit can be said of the second oratorial machine as well. The gallows, "the symbol of faction," represents the polemical writings dealing with church and state. It is, of course, always characteristic of a polemic to persuade at whatever cost to logic or consistency; but particularly so in the century that saw writers like William Prynne, whose pamphlets are simply a mad extension of the anatomies produced by Burton and Browne: "a torrent of unsorted, unconsidered precedents and citations. If one did not fit, another might." [5] Prynne's prestige, which gave authority to his most random erudition, depended largely on the figure of "Prynne the martyr" which accompanied, and played so large a part in, all of his pamphlets. The influence of Foxe's martyrology led not only to the spiritual autobiographies of Puritan sermons but also to the authority of martyrdom in the accounts of men like Burton, Lilburne, or Prynne in the pillory. Offering a possible source for Swift's pulpit which "exerts a strong influence on ears,"

3. Treadway Russel Nash, ed., *Hudibras*, by Samuel Butler (London, 1835), *1*, 12n., 43n.

4. *The Scribe Instructed*, in *Sermons, 3*, 37.

5. William Haller, *Liberty and Reformation in the Puritan Revolution* (New York, Columbia Univ. Press, 1955), p. 237.

Henry Burton (then earless) wrote that the pillory "was the happiest pulpett hee had ever preacht in." [6] Both Burton and Lilburne called the day of their martyrdom their wedding day, and capitalized upon it as an exemplum or *type* of the persecuted saint or the crucified Christ. The individual's experience has thus become an irrefutable piece of logic in the Puritan polemic; personality has replaced argument.

A more respectable example, however, is John Milton, who by Swift's time had become a great Whig-Dissenter prophet. Even Milton takes time off in the middle of his *Reason of Church Government* to insert a long autobiographical digression (as preface to the second part), and the *Apology for Smectymnuus* is essentially the continuation of this self-portrait. Although the *Apology* is strikingly digressive (a formal eulogy of the Long Parliament is inserted at one place between point-for-point confutations of Bishop Hall), the level of the sentence is perhaps most instructive as a gauge of Milton's form. The general tone of the syntax is consonant with the role Milton gives himself in the autobiographical parts: that of a prophet or seer, which requires rolling cadences and resounding periods. But this syntax, while often giving the impression of being Ciceronian, collapses into anacoluthon or rambles off into matters that are unrelated to the subject of the sentence. The frequent confusion of Milton's syntax is the result not simply of overloading a subordinated structure, but rather of the subordi-

6. *Documents Relating to the Proceedings against William Prynne*, ed. Samuel R. Gardiner, Camden Society Publications, new ser. *18* (1877), 87; cited in Don M. Wolfe's introduction, *Complete Prose Works of John Milton* (New Haven, Yale Univ. Press, 1953), *1*, 44. Roger L'Estrange's constant apologies (to which Swift alludes in his "Author's Apology," G-S, p. 7) are simply books in a tradition that goes back to the Book of Martyrs and to Prynne's *A New Discovery of the Prelates Tyranny* (1641), Bastwick's *The Confession of the Faithfull Witnesse of Christ* (1641), Burton's *Narration of the Life of Mr. Henry Burton* (1643), and Lilburne's *A Worke of the Beast* (1638).

nated matter's being not really subordinated as it would
appear to be; its grammatical links are belied by the erratic
order of the thought. In other words, we have here the employment of an ostensibly Ciceronian style without the
periodic turn of mind so important in the prose of a writer
like Hooker.. While Milton's periodic opening suggests a
kind of order and certainty, of the sort he is evoking in
Presbyterianism, the rest of the sentence demonstrates a
freedom that is associated with the anti-Ciceronian style;
and, as in the case of Prynne, reliance is placed on sheer
effect.[7]

In the branches of literature that are covered by the stage
itinerant (plays and Grub Street productions) the emphasis
on sheer effect was also carried to extremes. For example,
the characters of Fletcherian tragicomedy often change from
scene to scene, sacrificing dramatic consistency in order to
elicit "the maximum emotional response" contained in
every particular moment.[8] Commenting on the characters
of Beaumont and Fletcher, Dryden says "they are either
good, bad, or indifferent, as the present scene requires it." [9]
The tendency to minimize over-all significance for momentary effect is noticeable in many of the Jacobean plays, and
by the Restoration heroic drama has become little short of
operatic, employing set speeches like arias.

Since our object is to examine the exaggerated tendencies
of the period, we shall turn to *The Rehearsal* for our account of the heroic play. According to Buckingham and his
friends, the one aim of the heroic play is transport, at whatever cost. The search for novelty is epitomized by Bayes
(the Dryden of *The Rehearsal*) when he says, "I'll do noth-

7. Follow, e.g., the second sentence of *Of Reformation*.

8. Eugene M. Waith, *The Pattern of Tragicomedy in Beaumont and
Fletcher* (New Haven, Yale Univ. Press, 1952), p. 40.

9. John Dryden, "Preface to *Troilus and Cressida*," in *Essays of John
Dryden*, ed. W. P. Ker (Oxford, Clarendon Press, 1926), *1*, 217; cited in Waith,
p. 23.

ing here that ever was done before." [1] All his fancies are "new," and he "would not have any two things alike in this play" (IV.1; p. 70). Surprise is used for its own sake: "Here's an odd surprise," says Bayes; "all these dead men you shall see rise up presently, at a certain note that I have made, in *Effaut flat,* and fall a-dancing" (II.5; p. 63). "Songs, ghosts, and dances," as well as whole scenes, are introduced irrelevantly into the play to "surprise" (III.1; p. 65). Spectacle is accordingly a main objective, its most obvious form being size. Other characteristics of Bayes' play are complexity of plot and obscurity: "for to guess presently at the plot and the sense, tires [the audience] before the end of the first act" (I.2; p. 55): and the play's epilogue remarks that "The play is at an end, but where's the plot? / That circumstance our poet Bayes forgot" (p. 81). The plot, in fact, never manages to get under way, the effect of Bayes' technique being a distortion of the whole for the sake of local effect and of the ideal for momentary transport.

It should be apparent by now that a general trend in the art of the seventeenth century was casuist or opportunist.[2] Thus the digression, which destroys pattern on behalf of casual insight, becomes a prominent characteristic, and the most up-and-coming form is the essay—a tentative effort in some direction. Each of Dryden's prefaces embodies an attempt, Dryden's belief of the moment, but provides no over-all structure of critical theory; and the ideas—for example, those concerning rhyme and blank verse—change

1. *The Rehearsal* (1672), II.1, in *Plays of the Restoration and Eighteenth Century,* ed. Dougald MacMillan and Howard Mumford Jones (New York, Henry Holt, 1931), p. 58. "I tread upon no man's heels," Bayes says later, "but make my flight upon my own wings, I assure you" (III.1; p. 64). But earlier he has himself admitted plagiarism (I.1; p. 54).

2. See Sypher, *Four Stages of Renaissance Style,* pp. 131–40. He points out that it is difficult to define seventeenth-century style because there are hardly two paintings, plays, poems or palaces which are alike: each "is a special case, a personal manipulation of design, material, situation, language, response" (p. 120).

from essay to essay. When he writes one, it represents the
absolute truth of that moment; the next, though a reversal
of opinion, will be as valid to him because it represents the
truth of that moment, as he sees it.[3]

The critical demigod of the last quarter of the century
was "Longinus," another Silver Age figure, whom Dryden
ranked next to Aristotle.[4] It has been pointed out that the
figures recommended by Longinus for achieving sublimity
all "tend to have to do with abnormalities of syntax and
other peculiarities of structure," [5] and that "In the final
analysis . . . the supreme quality of a work turns out to be
the reflected quality of its author:—'Sublimity is the echo
of a great soul.' " [6] The idiosyncratic and personal, the distorted and extravagant are to be used for "not persuasion
but transport." [7] Longinus talks of the "spell" imposing
speech "throws over us," and emphasizes the "power and
irresistible might" the sublime exerts over the reader, as
well as the reader's loss of control.[8] The neo-Longinian
made "transport" into "enthusiasm" or "passion," which
extended upward to religious experience. John Dennis—
"Sir Longinus" as he was later called—felt the necessity for

3. Sir William Temple puts it this way: "though his opinions change every
week or every day, yet he is sure, or at least confident, that his present
thoughts and conclusions are just and true, and cannot be deceived": *An
Essay upon the Ancient and Modern Learning* (1690), in *The Works of Sir
William Temple, Bart.* (London, 1757), *3*, 460.
4. "Preface to *State of Innocence*," in *Essays, 1*, 179.
5. W. K. Wimsatt, Jr., and Cleanth Brooks, *Literary Criticism, a Short
Introduction* (New York, Knopf, 1957), p. 103. The figures are *"asundeton*
(absence of conjunctions), *huperbaton* (inversion), changes of number, person, tense, *periphrasis* (a roundabout way of saying something), rhetorical
question."
6. Meyer H. Abrams, *The Mirror and the Lamp: Romantic Theory and
the Critical Tradition* (New York, Oxford Univ. Press, 1953), p. 73.
7. *On the Sublime*, tr. W. Rhys Roberts, in *The Great Critics, An Anthol-
ogy of Literary Criticism*, ed. James Harry Smith and Edd Winfield Parks
(New York, Norton, 1932), p. 65.
8. Ibid.; also "carried away by enthusiasm" and "to stir the passions and
the emotion" (p. 82).

more emotion in poetry, a "fine frenzy" being the indispensable element. His solution was to infuse poetry with religious enthusiasm. From Longinus' theory and Milton's poetry he built a system which identified inspiration with passion and the highest poetry with the expression of religious enthusiasm.[9] Dryden's own critical defense of the heroic mode brings out the Longinian elements clearly:

> And if any man object the improbabilities of a spirit appearing, or of a palace raised by magic: I boldly answer him, that an heroic poet is not tied to a bare representation of what is true, or exceeding probable; but that he may let himself loose to visionary objects, and to the representation of such things as depending not on sense, and therefore not to be comprehended by knowledge, may give him a freer scope for imagination.[1]

Longinus has brought us back to the point we noticed in connection with Donne's apology for the Metaphysical style, that personal idiosyncrasy is raised to the level of a universal. As I said at the beginning of this section, we have developed one possible view of seventeenth-century forms of literature; we have looked at these supposed excesses from the point of view of the Restoration critics, of South, Glanvill, Eachard, and Marvell. But we can show that Swift agreed in general with these critics by glancing at the *Mechanical Operation of the Spirit,* where we find: "The Force, or Energy of this [modern] Eloquence, is not to be found, as among antient Orators, in the Disposition of Words to a Sentence, or the turning of long Periods; but agreeable to the Modern Refinements in Musick, is taken

---

9. See *Critical Works, 1,* 215–16: "Passion then, is the Characteristical Mark of Poetry, and, consequently, must be every where: For where-ever a Discourse is not Pathetick, there it is Prosaick."

1. "Essay of Heroic Plays," prefixed to *The Conquest of Granada* (1672), in *Essays, 1,* 153.

up wholly in dwelling, and dilating upon Syllables and Letters" (279).

In other of his writings we learn that he admired the style of Elizabethans like Hooker and Parsons for its "Simplicity which is the best and truest Ornament of most Things in human Life" and distrusted the complexity, and consequent lack of clarity, in the style of anti-Ciceronians like Sir Henry Wotton.[2] In his "Proposal for Correcting, Improving, and Ascertaining the English Tongue" (1711) he gives his account of literary history as regards prose style: "The period, wherein the English Tongue received most improvement, I take to commence with the beginning of Queen Elizabeth's reign, and to conclude with the great rebellion of forty-two. It is true, there was a very ill taste both of style and wit, which prevailed under King James the First." He believes this was corrected under Charles I (probably with the Laudian reform); but from the Civil War to the present, "I am apt to doubt, whether the corruptions in our language have not at least equalled the refinements of it; and these corruptions very few of the best authors in our age have wholly escaped. During the usurpation, such an infusion of enthusiastic jargon prevailed in every writing, as was not shaken off in many years after. To this succeeded that licentiousness which entered with the Restoration."[3]

What he attacks here, with a National Academy for standardizing the language in mind, are the Puritan jargon, the shortening of words, the "affected phrases" of plays, and the irresponsible creation of new words. The general trend of his thought is evident: new words are created to express new and odd states of mind. In the matter of preaching, Swift followed St. Augustine's aims: "ut doceat, ut delectet,

2. *The Tatler*, No. 230, Sept. 28, 1710; in *Bickerstaff Papers and Pamphlets on the Church*, ed. Herbert Davis (Oxford, Blackwell, 1940), p. 177.

3. *The Prose Works of Jonathan Swift, D.D.*, ed. Temple Scott (London, Bell, 1897–1908), *11*, 10–11.

ut flectat" (teach, delight, move).[4] In his "Letter to a Young Gentleman, Lately enter'd into Holy Orders" Swift makes it clear that teaching is the object of a sermon, and accordingly clarity and simplicity are the necessary qualities it must possess. "Where Men err against this Method," he says, "it is usually on Purpose, and to shew their Learning, their Oratory, their Politeness, or their Knowledge of the World."[5]

In our survey of the seventeenth century, then, we have seen that such different forms as the sermon, the polemical pamphlet, and the heroic drama have much in common with the anatomies with which our discussion began. In all of these forms detail takes on a greater autonomy than is always consistent with the over-all aim of the work, whether as a manifestation of the author's own individuality of purpose or as a device for moving the reader momentarily. There is a noticeable conflict between part and whole, each claiming the reader's undivided attention, and often not finally agreeing. In short, means—or method—may be said to have overwhelmed ends.

III. The *Tale* as Parody

We began by assuming that the *Tale* bears resemblances to the seventeenth-century writings we have been discussing. It will be well, however, to demonstrate this fact briefly before going on to see what it may mean.

Anyone opening *A Tale of a Tub* must be struck by the apparently pointless piling up of introductory sections and the tendency of the digressions to swamp the tale of the three brothers, which is the ostensible subject. Most sentences demonstrate a conscious search for the asymmetrical,

4. St. Augustine, *De Doctrina Christiana*, Bk. IV, 12; quoted in Mitchell, p. 52.

5. Swift, *Irish Tracts, 1720–1723, and Sermons*, ed. Herbert Davis (Oxford, Blackwell, 1948), p. 68.

an avoidance of forethought, an employment of whatever
happens to be at hand. Some sentences which sound most
portentous, and bristle with shows of order, simply flow off
into an endless linking of unsubordinated members. The
unemphatic sentence shows a mode of progression that
could be demonstrated as easily from paragraph to paragraph and from section to section. The *Tale's* preface, for
example, moves from an explanation of the book's purpose
and origin to a discussion of why the preface is not as long
as modern prefaces should be, to an explanation of why the
author has not attacked other writers, to clues as to how the
reader should read the book, to a discussion of satire. The
Tale itself wanders from critics to madmen in Bedlam,
from discussions of prefaces to discussions of digressions.[1]

The accumulation of information along the way—such
as the account of the macrocephali, the white powder that
kills without report, or the slitting of a stag's ear that
spreads through a whole herd—suggests that Swift wants
his book to recall a mound of erudition like Browne's
Pseudodoxia Epidemica.[2] We find here the same sprinkling
of Latin and Greek, the same references to learned authori-

1. Suggestions for an exact model upon which Swift based the *Tale* keep
turning up. See John R. Moore, "A Possible Model for the Organization of
'A Tale of a Tub,'" *Notes & Queries, 199* (1954), 288–90, where John Ray's
Miscellaneous Discourses Concerning the Dissolution of the World (1692) is
suggested; or J. M. Stedmond, "Another Possible Analogue for Swift's *Tale
of a Tub*," *Modern Language Notes, 72* (1957), 13–18, where John Dunton's
A Voyage round the World (1691) is put forward. It is difficult to decide
whether Dunton offered Swift a model or an object of satire. The *Voyage*
itself is so cheerfully presented as a piece of hack writing that we cannot
doubt that Dunton was being self-conscious; but whether he was satirizing
that kind of writing is another matter. At the least, the *Voyage* remains a
good example (particularly in its prefatory apparatus) of the sort of writing
Swift is parodying.

2. Swift specifically echoes Browne in these examples: G-S, pp. 268, 236,
201; Browne (cited by G-S, p. lix), *Pseudodoxia Epidemica*, in *The Works of
Sir Thomas Browne*, ed. Charles Sayle (Edinburgh, Grant, 1907), *2*, 376–7; *1*,
271; *2*, 377.

ties, the same abstruse speculations we encounter in the anatomy. We find suggestions of all manner of seventeenth-century forms in the *Tale*. The tour of Bedlam in section 9 is a convention of many a Jacobean play, as is the idea of the alternating plot and subplot, narrative and digression.[3] At the other end of the century we have the report of the Royal Society parodied in the report on oratorial machines and falling bodies (i.e. words) in the introduction, Restoration comedy parodied in the posturing fops of the allegory of the coats (section 2), and the etymological pursuits of the Bentleyan critic parodied in "A Digression concerning Criticks."[4] Judging by the briefest look at the *Tale*, it is safe to say, with Herbert Davis, that "in its outward shape and form it obviously resembles the work of those writers whom Swift repudiates, rather than the work of those like Hooker and Parsons, whose style he admired."[5] Swift admits in his "Author's Apology" appended to the fifth edition (1710) that there are, in the *Tale*, "what they call Parodies, where the Author personates the Style and Man-

3. Madness itself is associated with the Jacobean period rather than with the eminently sane Restoration and Augustan periods. The last act of *The Honest Whore*, Pt. 1, is laid in a madhouse, and a line of madmen—the lawyer, the alderman's son, the whore, the Puritan, the courtier—files across the stage, each offering an interview (as we go from one madman to another in sec. 9). The fourth act of *The Duchess of Malfi* shows madmen swarming over the stage to terrify the duchess, and ends in a dance of eight madmen "with music answerable thereunto" (IV. 2, following l. 120). In the fourth act of *The Changeling* the madmen who have enlivened the subplot impinge upon the main plot and dance at the wedding of Beatrice and Alsemero.

4. It is evident that the imitation of these forms graduates into allusions to forms, themes, and—from time to time—individual writers; for example, Donne's well-known compass image ("A Valediction: Forbidding Mourning," ll. 25–32) is echoed by the *Tale's* image of Jack and Peter as "two Pair of Compasses, equally extended, and the fixed Foot of each, remaining in the same Center" (199). Parallels to the employment of clothes imagery in sec. 2 can also be found in seventeenth-century plays, notably *King Lear* or *Volpone*; in Jacobean plays a Rosalinde is always dressing as a Ganymede or an Altofronto as a Malevoli, worse, a Euphrasia as a Bellario.

5. Davis, *Satire of Jonathan Swift*, p. 28.

ner of other Writers, whom he has a mind to expose" (7).

Like the seventeenth-century works we have examined, the *Tale* expresses a personal view of the universe; but it only *pretends* to be personal. It pretends to have "included and exhausted all that Human Imagination can *Rise* or *Fall* to" (129). It pretends to demonstrate exhaustive learning. It pretends to be eccentric. It satirizes works like those we have noticed, and so itself offers an implicit analysis of eccentricity. In short, the *Tale* is *about* eccentricity rather than an example itself.

Swift's parody is built around the vehicle of his theme, his speaker.[6] The queerness that is apparent in Swift's speaker has the same explanation as the other peculiarities we have noticed in the *Tale:* his mode of thought represents one aspect of the seventeenth-century sensibility. Having grasped the fact that the digressions and other eccentricities are manifestations of this sensibility, it is easier to see that one of the comic elements in the portrayal of the Grub Street Hack is his unabashed sacrifice of everything else for the effect of the moment—his willingness to collapse an argument for the sake of delicious details; or, in short, his casuistry. This aspect of the speaker is perhaps the key to the *Tale's* structure and to Swift's relationship to his material.

The word Swift uses to express his own relationship to the *Tale* is "Irony": "there generally runs an Irony through the Thread of the whole Book," he remarks in the "Author's Apology" (8). Doubtless written as an answer to those who assumed Swift himself to be the speaker of the *Tale,* the remark itself is an ironic understatement. But it is, of course, possible to take sentiments like the refusal to "de-

6. I am referring at present to the speaker of the *Tale* proper; I shall discuss the speakers of *The Battle of the Books* and *The Mechanical Operation of the Spirit* in Ch. 4, sec. v. I focus upon the *Tale* because it is the central, most puzzling part. The other two parts will be referred to from time to time, particularly as to imagery that runs through all three parts.

tract from the just Reputation of this famous Sect [the Aeolists]" (162) as the speaker's irony rather than his wide-eyed sincerity. If we accepted this view, we should conclude that the Grub Street Hack is himself being satirical and is not an instrument of Swift's satire, that there is no appreciable distinction between his views and Swift's. It is also possible to take the *Tale* as a sort of dialogue between two speakers, Swift sometimes coming through in his own voice. It is a fairly common view that the "whiplash" of "Fool among Knaves" is Swift's momentary dropping of his mask. More common yet is the critic's implicit acceptance of Swift as himself associated with the metaphor of dissection. Craik is guilty of this implication when he speaks of Swift's "marvellous strength and grasp with which the whole of human nature is seized, bound to the dissecting table, and made to yield, to his pitiless scalpel, the tale of its subterfuges, and pretences, and tricks." [7]

These views tend to lose their usefulness when we see that the Hack is an embodiment of the zeal, enthusiasm, and various kinds of eccentricity which he may *seem* to talk about satirically.[8] The parts that disturb readers most, however, are the quick reversals and non sequiturs, the most famous of which is in the "Digression on Madness," where one minute the Hack attacks Reason for being a dissector with claws, "for cutting, and opening, and mangling, and piercing" (173), and a few sentences later he is himself watching a woman flayed and ordering a beau stripped and dissected.[9] The latter is, accordingly, often taken to be Swift

7. Craik, *Life of Jonathan Swift, 1*, 131.

8. Kathleen Williams, in *Jonathan Swift and the Age of Compromise* (Lawrence, Univ. of Kansas Press, 1958), notices acutely that the speaker "is himself a style rather than a person" (p. 136); but she does not see any pattern in his presentation—he is "a mere bundle of unrelated qualities," "a conglomeration of incompatible attitudes, all equally important, or unimportant" (pp. 132, 133).

9. There are, of course, inconsistencies like that between the Bookseller's statement that he never saw the author (having gotten the MS from a friend

intruding. The inconsistency appears in the Hack's using a method he has just attacked; but in terms of the moment in which he speaks the Hack's position is perfectly consistent: to prove his point, that the outside (appearance) is lovely and should not be removed to seek the nasty reality, which is inside, he has to reveal the inside. In the same way, he is hired to write against the wits who pick at the "weak sides of Religion and Government"; but he defends the critics who make "many useful Searches into the weak sides of the *Antients.*" He can also attack these "penetrating" wits and praise the "penetrating Reader," or on one page defend the wits and on another attack them—one is on his side, one is not.[1]

In both the preface and the introduction an image of a crowd of milling people appears. In the former, we are told that the fat man who pushes and shoves, trying to get more room for himself, is not polite; in the latter, getting above the crowd is considered an ideal and we are approvingly shown ways of achieving it. The difference is in the context: in the first he is speaking of himself as one of the crowd, in the second he is one of the orators himself. But while the contexts are different, the metaphor is the same— as it was with the metaphor of dissection—and this irony, wholly outside the Hack's awareness, reveals to the reader an aggressive tendency in the Hack which he may not have been so conscious of before.

At other times, like some of the seventeenth-century divines we have seen, he commits himself to a metaphor

---

—28), and the Hack's reference to "the Bookseller who bought the Copy of this Work" from *him* (206). It might be argued that this too is casuistry, the inventing of a bookseller to illustrate his point of the moment. (See 206–7.)

1. See pp. 39, 96; 39, 69; 38, 40–1. Concerning the last two: one of his works "which will be speedily published" is *"A Character of the present Set of* Wits *in this Island,"* which he says is filled with "just Elogies [eulogies]" (38). But the *Tale* itself is a diversion to occupy the wits until they can be locked away permanently (40–1).

which, when its vehicle is carried out consistently, damages
the tenor he is trying to convey. In the "Dedication to
Prince Posterity" he chooses the metaphor of drowning for
the modern books which have disappeared. " 'Tis certain,"
he says, "that in their own Nature they were *light* enough
to swim upon the Surface for all Eternity" (32). He is trying
to prove that they would not naturally drown, by virtue of
their own properties, and so he uses "light." But to keep his
metaphor consistent he has admitted the lightness (i.e.
superficiality) of his books. Elsewhere, when he finds it
necessary to stress their sublimity, they are heavy, profound
and deep; they make a reader "descend to the very *bottom*
of all the *Sublime*" (44).

In the same section he defeats an intended meaning in
order to evoke the tone required at that moment. "Unhappy
Infants," he cries, "many of them barbarously destroyed, before they have so much as learnt their *Mother-Tongue* to
beg for Pity" (33). He has brought about a tone of sentimental pathos, but he has ended by admitting that modern
writers do not know their own language.[2]

Whatever the moment calls for, the Hack uses, in spite of
any general inconsistency. In fact, an obsessive quirk of the
Hack's style is his referring repeatedly to the moment in
which he is writing: "being just come from having the
Honor conferred upon me" (63), or "this Minute I am writing" (36), or "the very Garret I am now writing in" (169).
More often verb tenses emphasize the present moment:
"What *is* become of them?" (32), not "what became (or even
has become) of them?" And when he refers to the past it is
with specific dates or times, as with "Last Week I saw a
Woman *flay'd*," or "Yesterday I ordered the Carcass of a

2. Price points out that this may be a reference to Hobbes: "Children
therefore are not endued with Reason at all, till they have attained the use
of Speech." Thomas Hobbes, *Leviathan*, Pt. I, ch. 5; cited in Price, *Swift's
Rhetorical Art*, p. 58.

Beau to be stript" (173). By holding change down to "Last Week" or "Yesterday" he is trying to impose some sort of order on experience, although by a misplaced emphasis he overlooks the forest for the trees.

This casuistry is a notable link between the Hack and the seventeenth-century sensibility. His whole world, we shall see, is characterized by complete reliance on the momentary effect, forgetfulness of all that went before or that will come after.

The idea of the persona is itself typically seventeenth-century. The anti-Ciceronian writer automatically sets up a persona in his writings, whether it is the man Montaigne, the prophet Milton, or the companionable abstraction of a Dryden essay. Here the unity of idea or form is replaced by the unity of a "personality," maintained from essay to essay. What is more comic than the mind searching for order and oneness, in terms of the changeableness of mood, prejudice, and even intention? Donne and Browne and a host of others sought this order, demonstrating the process of their discovery; but nobody before Swift seems to have noticed the incongruity of end and means.

We shall discuss in Chapter 4 what principle directs the Hack's casuistry; but what these conflicting tendencies lead to in terms of the persona is an abstractness which tends to deny the Hack the individuality necessary if he is to be accepted as a fiction. There are points where the Hack's logic carries him to such an extreme of unawareness that the statement could be spoken as well by Swift. "But about this time it fell out, that the Learned Brother aforesaid, had read *Aristotelis Dialectica,* and especially that wonderful Piece *de Interpretatione,* which has the Faculty of teaching its Readers to find out a Meaning in every Thing but it self; like Commentators on the *Revelations,* who proceed Prophets without understanding a Syllable of the Text" (85). The passage, like an optical illusion, can be seen in two altogether different ways, though the pattern remains the same. It can be seen as a direct statement of the author's view of the Bentleyan interpreter of texts; it can also be seen as the words of the Hack, whose values have become so inverted that commentators do not need to "understand a Syllable of the Text."[3] The latter may be thought to show such fatuousness that the Hack tends to lose individuality. We may begin to think that there is some basic disagreement between the Hack and the reader on the meaning of words.

Whenever this coincidence takes place, it creates a moment of extraordinary intenstiy—for example, the "Fool among Knaves" statement (174)—unlike the passages where the Hack's view must be corrected by a reference to common sense. But the result is that, in terms of the *Tale* as a work of art, the rhetorical effect of the moment sometimes blurs the over-all effect of the work; to this extent, some of the seventeenth-century casuistry may be thought to have rubbed off onto Swift himself.[4]

Thus one of the facts about the *Tale* that contribute to its curiously unique air is that a reader is never wholly convinced of the fiction, nor unconvinced: if he were convinced, a passage like the above would be accepted without hesitation as the Hack's and enjoyed as such. But the Hack, in spite of all the details which can be shown to prove his psychological consistency and almost independent existence, never completely detaches himself from Swift. It is not easy

3. The Hack has shown himself to be one of these commentators; see the introduction (68) and his project for annotating the Grub Street writings.

4. An example of Swift's casuistry appears in the *Battle of the Books*, which, we shall see (Ch. 4, sec. v), depends for much of its effect on the supposed objectivity of its historian. But the reader is certainly made doubtful of his detachment when his statement that he is "possessed of all Qualifications requisite in an *Historian*, and [is] retained by neither Party" is immediately followed by his description of Bentley as "a Person of great Valor, but chiefly renowned for his *Humanity*" (224). The juxtaposition is witty but mars the larger effect of the section.

to see why; but the critical evidence of two and a half centuries (discounting prejudice and willful misunderstanding) shows that most readers find the ambiguity there. I suspect that the reason is that he, unlike Lemuel Gulliver, is too symbolic, or doctrinaire, too much the apologist and not enough the autobiographer.

Therefore, the question which remains is the extent to which the eccentricity we have observed is in some way reordered by the *Tale* so as to receive perspective and criticism. We have seen already an indication of how that reordering can be done: while the Hack is concerned with his individual moments the reader who seeks consistency will put the moments together and arrive at some of the tentative meanings we have suggested in this section. In the next chapter we shall examine some ways of reordering and see what sort of a theme is implied by the relationship we are outlining between order and disorder.

CHAPTER TWO

THE QUIXOTE THEME

> "God help us!" exclaimed Sancho, "did I not tell
> your Grace to look well, that those were nothing
> but windmills, a fact which no one could fail to see
> unless he had other mills of the same sort in his
> head?"
>
> —*Don Quixote,* tr. Putnam (1949), *1,* 63.

1. The Reordering of the Parodist

The basis for the *Tale's* reordering of the
opportunist chaos it imitates can be found in three areas of
seventeenth-century literature. First, there are the works
of the parodists who preceded Swift in the attempt to dis-
credit the forms we have discussed. But, second, there are
the writings parodied; for we shall see that the parodists
draw our attention to the possible ways of achieving order
in the anti-Ciceronian forms. Finally, there are the cases of
which to say that Swift merely parodied is to oversimplify;
these are models for his use of the eccentric, works which
achieve order out of the materials of nominalist perception
and suggest to us the theme such a process may embody.
The *Tale* will thus be seen to represent a curious mixture of
attack from without and imitation from within; even as it
attacks it draws its sustenance from the enemy. In this section we shall discuss the attackers, and see to what extent
the *Tale* belongs in the area of polemics.

During the Restoration a number of writers attacked the abuses we observed in the last chapter, among them men like John Eachard and Andrew Marvell of both Anglican and Puritan allegiance. The common ground for their different attacks is the mishandling of language, or the creation of a Quixotic reality which they feel it is their duty to see through. They represent a second strain of seventeenth-century literary thought, which, beginning with Bacon and Hobbes, had been busy searching for the tangible and definite in the vague and rhetorical.[1] "Wit," "fancy," and "imagination" had become words which evoked the Quixotic reality, as we can see in Locke's distinction between wit and judgment:

> wit [lies] most in the assemblage of ideas, and putting those together with quickness and variety, wherein can be found any resemblance or congruity, thereby to make up pleasant pictures, and agreeable visions in the fancy; judgment, on the contrary, lies quite on the other side, in separating carefully, one from another, ideas, wherein can be found the least difference; thereby to avoid being misled by similitude, and by affinity to take one thing for another.[2]

Wit is a combining and judgment a separating, a creative as opposed to a critical function. The beauty of metaphor, Locke adds, "appears at first sight, and there is required no labour of thought to examine what truth or reason there is in it" (p. 136).

In the seventeenth century a closer look was rendered necessary by two factors. One, we have seen, was the advocation of reform in language, a reaction against the excesses of both Metaphysical wit and nonconformist zeal, which, in

---

1. For a discussion of this trend, see Price, *Swift's Rhetorical Art*, pp. 1–14.

2. John Locke, *An Essay Concerning Human Understanding* (1690), Bk. II, ch. 11, sec. 2, in *The Works of John Locke* (London, 1794), *1*, 135–6.

their different ways, emphasized *words* to such an extent that the reaction against them was itself compelled, in order to defeat them, to put a similar emphasis on words. The second factor is related to the nature of controversial writing in the period. When an answerer reproved or refuted a work he made the form of his rebuttal largely dependent on that work, following it argument for argument, sometimes page for page. Enough quotation had to be given from the work under attack to guide a reader.[3] With these treatises giving themselves up to the form of the catalogue, rather than allowing meaning to evolve a form of its own, it would appear that an anatomy had been produced to end all anatomies. But, in fact, the result sometimes only bore the appearance of an anatomy.

The method employed by Eachard was to pick up some words of the enemy—often submerged metaphors—and run away with them, thereby, first, showing their absurdity and, second, drawing from them his own meaning, which would at least appear to have been implicit in the enemy's original words. Then in the ensuing pages, while Eachard continues the ostensibly plodding pursuit of the enemy's argument, the metaphor he has unloosed is playing around it with its own sharp comment.

The critique in question is Eachard's *Observations upon the Answer* (1671) to his *Contempt of the Clergy,* which, significantly, dealt with the problem of language and meaning.[4] Having pointed out the deficiencies in the education and preaching of the clergy, he was accused by John Bramhall of breeding contempt for Anglican divines. This being

3. Cf. Price, pp. 11–12, who attributes this to the need for holding the opponent down to his words, with the ideal form the dialogue. This practice of following the opponent's argument was not, of course, originated in the seventeenth century.

4. The book he answered was John Bramhall's *An Answer to a Letter of Enquiry into the Grounds and Occasions of the Contempt of the Clergy,* London, 1671.

the basis of argument, it is natural that he pounces upon Bramhall's use of language. Eachard begins his answer remarking, "What Service You or I should do to Church or State, by *cracking of Nuts,* I do not understand." [5] The italics announce that he has picked up some words of his opponent's, and he immediately adds, "excepting the case of *Chesnuts,* upon which, as it has been reported, the Kingdom of *Naples* has some mysterious Dependence" (p. 1). A few pages later he picks up the submerged metaphor again, interpreting it literally: "e're he closes up his *Preface,* [Bramhall] sets my unwilling Teeth to the difficult Task of *cracking Nuts*" (p. 5). But just before this, he has turned an abstraction used by Bramhall into a sensory image which picks up another of Bramhall's submerged metaphors: "he falls into such a commendation of me, for *joyning the Credit and the Serviceableness of the Clergy together,* as if he would have fed me with nothing but *Sugar-Sops* and *soft Jellies.*" [6] This, followed directly by the reference to "*cracking Nuts,*" implies that the sugar-sops and soft jellies are to soften and weaken his teeth in order to catch him short with the nuts. Accordingly, Eachard succeeds in not only pointing out the casualness of his opponent's language but also in drawing from his metaphor a meaning of his own. The new implication can be either a logical conclusion the enemy had not foreseen when he set the metaphor going, or, since any metaphor allows a number of possible interpretations, the recognition of a different point of analogy.

The second function of Eachard's technique, then, is to

5. Eachard, *Some Observations,* p. 1. Bramhall had remarked that "if all were true, unless the Author could probably think he might do some good Service to the Church in this Essay, he had better have been cracking of Nuts all the while, they would not so much have hurt his teeth, as his teeth have hurt us" (*An Answer,* preface, page unnumbered).

6. A little earlier he had slipped into another submerged metaphor when he remarked that Eachard's book "possibly . . . hath been accounted none of the most unsavory Sawces to [the] late Christmas Chear" of the unchurchly (Bramhall, ibid.). As we see, Eachard joins the two metaphors.

impose his own form upon the form of his opponent, which he ostensibly follows. While along the surface he is laboriously meeting his opponent's arguments, one after the other, the nutcracking image is allowed to lead into the metaphor of dining, as we have seen, which blossoms luxuriantly when Eachard quotes Bramhall as inviting him *"very kindly to hear him preach . . . one of the best of his Sermons"* (p. 61). He fears that Bramhall will tell him "that *his Text is like a spiritual Sack-posset,"* and he ends by pouring out a cascade of dining images (pp. 62–3), the effect of which is not simply to throw back at Bramhall with interest his metaphor, but rather to demonstrate the appropriateness of the metaphor to the kind of preaching they are discussing, where the congregation's senses are more aroused than its intelligence.

Meaning advances in a different way here than in an ordinary treatise. Eachard may take a particular point of his opponent's, like his employing Homer as an authority, and spend a long amusing digression playing on the fabulous nature of this Homer (pp. 44ff.). The digression reflects contempt for the opponent's emphasis on Homer; but whereas in the original such a digression carries away the author's thought, in the parody it advances the satirist's theme. And this action is, of course, necessary, because these writers—whether directly like Eachard or indirectly like Marvell—are writing against abuses of language, and however much they parody their opponent, they must present an ideal of proper rhetoric themselves. Eachard's ideal is the preacher who "has the Command of true and useful *Rhetorick;* discerning what Words are most proper and intelligible" (p. 24).

Marvell's *Rehearsal Transprosed* (1672; Part II, 1673) is important in this connection because it carries the method we are examining further than Eachard's work does, and also because it takes a step away from dialectic toward

dramatization. Whereas Eachard addresses himself to an
"Answerer," Marvell makes something of a character out
of his anonymous opponent (Samuel Parker, Archdeacon
of Canterbury), whom he calls Bayes after the playwright
in *The Rehearsal.*

First, as to the analysis of Bayes' language, Marvell's development of metaphor is far more elaborate than Eachard's.
He quotes Bayes as saying of the Calvinists, "There sprang
up a mighty bramble on the south side the Lake Lemane,
that (such is the rankness of the soil) spread and flourished
with such a sudden growth, that partly by the industry of
his agents abroad, and partly by its own indefatigable pains
and pragmaticalness, it quite over-ran the whole Reformation." [7] Examining this metaphor, Marvell notices that the
"bramble" has "agents abroad," and is itself an "indefatigable bramble." "But straight our bramble is transformed to
a man, and he 'makes a chair of infallibility for himself'
out of his own bramble timber: yet all this while we know
not his name; one would suspect it might be a Bishop Bramble." [8] Having shown that the metaphor's denotative meaning is something not at all intended by its author, he develops its "true" meaning. Bayes should have continued,
he says, that

> upon that bramble "reasons grew as plentiful as black-
> berries," but both unwholesome, and they stained all

7. Andrew Marvell, *The Rehearsal Transprosed: or, Animadversions upon
a late Book, intituled, A Preface, shewing What Grounds there are of Fears
and Jealousies of Popery,* in *The Works of Andrew Marvell, Esq., Poetical,
Controversial, and Political,* ed. Edward Thompson (London, 1776), 2, 37.

8. Ibid.: "Bramble" is a pun on Bramhall. Swift himself employs this exact
method upon occasion, as in his essay on Dr. Burnet: "However, he 'thanks
God there are many among us who stand in the breach:' I believe they may;
'tis a breach of their own making, and they design to come forward, and
storm and plunder, if they be not driven back" (*A Preface to the B - p of
S - r - m's Introduction to the Third Volume of the History of the Reformation of the Church of England, by Gregory Misosarum,* in *Prose Works,* ed.
Scott, *3,* 159). The passage continues, taking Burnet's phrases one by one
and analyzing them. Price has discussed this process, pp. 36–56.

the "white aprons so" that there was no getting of it out. And then, to make a fuller description of the place, he should have added, that near to the city of roaring lions there was a lake, and that lake was all of brimstone, but stored with over-grown trouts, which trouts spawned Presbyterians, and those spawned the Millecantons of all other fanaticks; that this shoal of Presbyterians landed at Geneva, and devoured all the bishops of Geneva's capons, which are of the greatest size of any in the reformed world. And ever since their mouths have been so in relish that the Presbyterians are in all parts the very canibals of capons: insomuch, that if princes do not take care, the race of capons is in danger to be totally extinguished [pp. 40–1].

Marvell's imagination runs on and on, and it is a pity to stop here, but the point is that his metaphor is like a funnel, moving out in ever larger circles. He has accepted the active implications of "bramble" and ignored the less pleasant ones which Bayes intended; thus, from a parasitical and prickly shrub the Calvinists become the active defenders of Protestantism and destroyers of Roman Catholics.

Marvell no longer even requires the opponent's words— instead he examines a cliché like "to rise in the world," which expresses his view of Bayes' motive for writing his book. When Bayes is freed from "the narrowness of the university," "coming out of the confinement of the square-cap and the quadrangle into the open air," he begins to "rise" —his body grows and, accepting another cliché (heads swell with pride), his head swells "like any bladder with wind and vapour." His legs grow until he is so "elevated" "that he could not look down from top to toe but his eyes dazzled at the precipice of his stature" (pp. 45–7). Marvell exploits the similarity between *rising* "in the world" and *rising* in spiritual ecstasy, until at last Bayes "was seen in his prayers to be lifted up sometimes in the air, and once particularly so

high that he cracked his scull against the chappel ceiling"
(p. 47).

As these examples suggest, Marvell also carries the unifying use of metaphor further than Eachard. One such
metaphor finds its origin in Bayes' hatred of the printing
press as a device for stirring up sedition (p. 5). Marvell
asks why Parker-Bayes has himself written so many books,
considering this hatred. Lust, he concludes, is the answer:
"when a man's fancy is up, and his breeches are down; [9]
when the mind and the body make contrary assignations,
and he hath both a bookseller at once and a mistress to
satisfie; like Archimedes, into the street he runs out naked
with his invention" (p. 10). The lust is, accordingly, for
power and position, with a book the progeny; on the next
page the metaphor is developed as a conflict of love and
honor, and when passion for advancement joins the visual
metaphor of growth and expansion we have followed, it
turns out that, in terms of love, he is his own minion. Marvell builds to a dazzling climax:

> For all this courtship had no other operation than to
> make him still more in love with himself; and if he
> frequented their [the ladies'] company, it was only to
> speculate his own baby in their eyes. But being thus,
> without competitor or rival, the darling of both sexes
> in the family and his own minion; he grew beyond all
> measure elated, and that crack of his scull, as in broken
> looking glasses, multiplied him in self-conceit and
> imagination [p. 48].

Thus, the metaphor of love contributes to the metaphor of
expansion, and expansion leads to the cracked skull when
it is confined by natural limits. Then the crack in the skull

9. Cf. G-S, p. 78: "a *Pair of Breeches*, which . . . is easily slipt down for
the Service of [Nastiness and Lewdness]." The rhythm of the sentence suggests the passage which begins "But when a Man's Fancy . . ." (G-S, p. 171).

leads to crack-in-mirror, and the mirror, representing vanity, when broken suggests madness; and madness is what follows in the next pages (pp. 48–9). Finally, the metaphor of love continues intermittently until it is implied that the affair has given Parker a venereal disease (p. 96) and that the book is an illegitimate child (p. 98).

Another unifying element in Marvell's book is the figure of Bayes and the continued, if sketchy, filling in of his grotesque portrait. Not content merely to quote the opponent's solecisms, Marvell builds up the image of the corrupt imagination itself in the character he addresses. He names him Bayes, he explains, "chiefly because Mr. Bayes and he do very much symbolize [i.e. resemble each other], in their understandings, in their expressions, in their humour, in their contempt and quarrelling of all others, though of their own profession" (p. 14). As we have seen, Bayes largely represents opportunism and casuistry. When asked the plot of his last play he answers, "Faith, sir, the intrigo's now quite out of my head: but I have a new one in my pocket." [1] Bayes comes to Marvell as an example of the imagination run wild, with but a single assumption upon which all his creation is built: divert and hold the attention of the audience.[2] Thus, once Bayes is established as the opponent, and to some extent dramatized, he comes to *represent* the solecism, and any cliché becomes a manifestation of Bayes.

While the name "Bayes" wears out its usefulness before Marvell has finished with it and his reiteration of "Holla, Mr. Bayes" becomes tiresome, it is nevertheless important to notice a line of descent for Swift's Grub Street Hack. For the Hack is a sort of Bayes, who is trying to create a diver-

---

1. *Rehearsal*, I. 1, in MacMillan and Jones, *Plays of the Restoration*, p. 53.
2. Parker, too, is made to appear an opportunist and a turncoat: Marvell claims that he was a nonconformist before the Restoration, and thereafter a staunch Anglican. Cf. the Hack, G-S, p. 70 ("perpetual turning").

sion which, like Bayes' play, never really gets under way.
Marvell's transprosing of Bayes is an intermediate step
which may have suggested to Swift that the logical end was
to let Bayes speak for himself.

What we have seen in writers like Eachard and Marvell
is an awareness of language, a preoccupation with metaphor,
and a sharp eye for cliché, which remorselessly sees through
the shabby pretenses of language—through language as
a cloak for nonmeaning or false meaning. Bayes best demonstrates the intention behind the practice of both Eachard
and Marvell, which is either to absorb the enemy into a
fiction of their own making or to create such a fiction around
him like a cocoon; in either case the satirist has put him
into a special world which does not work on his assumptions, in which his words and actions make him appear the
fool. The preoccupation with language can be seen, in this
light, as a way of taking a cornerstone from the enemy himself, and so implying that it is really his own world that is
defeating him.

Putting the enemy in an alien context is, of course,
the general method which characterizes Augustan satire,
whether Roman or English. The enemy is made to appear
an outsider, against all of *us,* and so we judge him by the
standards of the *insiders*. But the particular techniques we
have examined in Eachard and Marvell are Swift's most immediate source for the linguistic-type satire of the *Tale of
a Tub*. That he was thoroughly familiar with the seventeenth-century polemicists in general and the parodists in
particular is proved by the scores of specific echoes of their
writings in the *Tale*.[3] But Swift's indebtedness is quite
balanced by the ways in which he differs from his predecessors. One difference, which we shall develop in the next section, is that in the *Tale* the pointing out of the error and
the development of the metaphor have been eliminated to-

3. See below, p. 236, Note A, on echoes of the polemical writers.

gether with the satirist, so that only the fiction remains. More important perhaps, the difference between the development of metaphor in Marvell and that which we shall trace in the *Tale* lies in the fact that Marvell's sounds more like the reiteration of a single point than the development of a theme. The metaphor that led up to Parker's rising to the ceiling and cracking his skull is carefully constructed; it says brilliantly that Parker is ambitious, proud and unaware of reality—but when this is said, we are left with nothing more than an ad hominem point scored. Thereafter, every time the metaphor is recovered a bell rings and Parker is reproached again; but no theme independent of the individual Parker is developed.

ii. The Voice of the Hack

A way to approach the difference between these earlier satirists and Swift is to examine the tone of a style which is common to both and to see how differently Swift has utilized it. An example of this tone in the *Tale* is the familiar sentence from the "Digression on Madness": "Last Week I saw a Woman *flay'd,* and you will hardly believe, how much it altered her Person for the worse" (173). If the first member shocks, we notice that the second implicates the reader, making an appeal to his imagination. By saying "you will hardly believe" the speaker avoids having to describe a scene but implies that it is too vivid to be expressed. Such a phrase, pointing with wonder at the flayed woman, has an odd effect upon the reader, which I shall try to trace.

This tone is one aspect of a style which became prevalent after the Restoration, called by some railery, by others banter.[1] If I prefer the term railery it is because I think of

1. See Hugh MacDonald, "Banter in English Controversial Prose after the Restoration," *Essays and Studies by Members of the English Association,* 32 (1946), 21–9. MacDonald cites a number of interesting examples, though he

it as implying monologue, while banter suggests dialogue
or witty intercourse. Another reason is that the kind of
argument found before the Restoration, in such writers as
Nashe, Harvey, and Milton, and that found after, in Marvell, Dryden, and Eachard, share the noun raillery; but the
verb of the first is *rail,* which is to utter abuse or invective,
while the verb of the second is *rally,* which is to utter "good
humored ridicule." [2] A distinction may be noted if we compare a passage from a Restoration railer, Richard Bentley,
on a long-dead monk, with one from Marvell's attack on
Parker:

> That Idiot of a Monk has given us a Book, which he
> calls the Life of Aesop, that, perhaps, cannot be match'd
> in any Language, for Ignorance and Nonsense.

---

does not attempt to define the style. Ian Watt has an altogether different
interpretation of "banter" in "The Ironic Tradition in Augustan Prose from
Swift to Johnson," *Restoration & Augustan Prose* (Los Angeles, William Andrews Clark Memorial Library, 1956), p. 23.

2. I am using "raillery" as I find it in the works discussed, not, for example,
as Swift himself defines it, although his definition does give an indication of
what I find. While he restricts "raillery" to slight subjects, referring to it
mainly in connection with conversation or with poems he addresses to his
friends, he defines it as "something that at first appeared a reproach or reflection; but, by some turn of wit unexpected and surprising, ended always
in a compliment . . ." ("Essay on Conversation," in *Prose Works,* ed. Scott,
11, 71).

Another possible source which may contribute to the tone of the Hack's
style should be noticed. This is the tone of the cheerfully meretricious hack
works like Dunton's *Voyage round the World,* which were doubtless the object of Swift's parody, but which tell us little about the operation of his satire.
It will be sufficient to compare the tone (the subject matter is, of course, being
parodied too) in passages like the Hack's claim that he is "confident to have
included and exhausted all that Human Imagination can *Rise* or *Fall* to"
(129) and Dunton's assurance that the reader will find in his work "the whole
Description of, I *scorn* to say one *Country,* one *Age,* or one *World;* but of all
the Habitable and Uninhabitable Creation" (*Voyage, 1,* 4); or note another
utterance of Dunton's that could have been the Hack's: "Could you know all
the good things in this Book, without my telling it you, and so buy it, and be
happy, I'd dye before I'd give it all this Commendation" (*1,* 6; cf. the Hack's
preface).

The whole *Posse Archidiaconatus* was raised to repress me, and great riding there was, and sending post every way to pick out the ablest ecclesiastical drolls to prepare an answer.[3]

Invective reveals too much emotion, too much personal commitment on the part of the speaker. If we are amused by the exaggeration it is at Bentley himself, the fussy pedant who uses words like "Ignorance and Nonsense," creating with them a self-portrait. The tone of Marvell's passage is set by the inversion "and great riding there was," which, while also a device of emphasis (the riding *was* prodigious), succeeds in giving the impression that this is not quite the real world. The words have an air of the superlative about them—they are the *most:* "whole Posse" and "ablest . . . drolls." Taking these adjectives with the almost gestural "every way," we have one characteristic of the style in question: there is always something about a passage of raillery that makes the reader almost *see* an expansive gesture being made by the speaker. And this suggests a special relationship between speaker and reader, which we shall examine in due course. But put briefly, Marvell has stopped short a moment in his argument and sketched in a world where ecclesiastics form posses and run around looking for the drollest of their brethren. Presupposing the truth (that the church authorities had looked for a wit to answer him), he creates an alternative truth, a *different* reality. In Bentley's passage only the "perhaps," a single qualification, suggests the beginning of a line of deviation from the real as Bentley saw it; Marvell has abandoned reality and has created a fiction about his problem. It is in this way that the Hack draws our attention to the picture of the dissection, setting it off from ordinary reality.

3. Richard Bentley, *A Dissertation upon the Epistles of Themistocles, Socrates, Euripides, etc. and the Fables of Aesop*, printed with William Wotton, *Reflections upon Ancient and Modern Learning* (London, 1705), p. 466; Marvell, *Rehearsal Transprosed, Pt.* II, *Works.* 2, 267.

The fiction is less a defining point of raillery than one of its characteristics. For the rhetorical implications of the method, Shaftesbury's account of raillery in his "Essay on the Freedom of Wit and Humour" has not been bettered. One point he makes is that raillery is a disguise. "If Men are forbid to speak their minds seriously on certain Subjects, they will do it ironically. If they are forbid to speak at all upon such Subjects, or if they find it really dangerous to do so; they will then redouble their Disguise, involve themselves in Mysteriousness, and talk so as hardly to be understood, or at least not plainly interpreted, by those who are dispos'd to do 'em mischief." [4] That is, the relationship between speaker and reader is an intimate, almost secret one; and this is why raillery is found in personal letters and in the little talk of lovers. When it is published, as a book for the public, the reader is given a flattering sense of being on the inside, one of the initiate.

Shaftesbury says further, speaking of the familiarity implicit in raillery, that it is "that sort of Freedom which is taken amongst *Gentlemen* and *Friends,* who know one another perfectly well" (p. 75). The important word, "Freedom," implies a conversational style, but more than that a style that is free, as one is in the company of friends, to blossom suddenly into fancy or fantasy: into the new world we saw Marvell or Eachard create. For example, Swift, in an early letter, tries to explain away a reported interest in a girl of Leicester:

> How all this suits with my behaviour to the woman in hand you may easily imagine, when you know that there is something in me which must be employed, and when I am alone turns all, for want of practice, into speculation and thought; insomuch that in these seven

4. Anthony Ashley Cooper, 3d Earl of Shaftesbury, *Characteristicks of Men, Manners, Opinions, Times* (London, 1727), *1*, 71–2. Cf. Watt's discussion of irony, especially pp. 20–7.

weeks I have been here, I have writ, and burnt and writ again, upon almost all manner of subjects, more perhaps than any man in England.[5]

Swift's case is that his advances to women are just symptoms of an overabundance of energy, other symptoms of which are writing and speculating. He gives the impression of energy through the contrast of extravagant universals with particulars. "The woman in hand," as related to his "behaviour," is contrasted to "all"—"all this," "something . . . which . . . turns all," "all manner of subjects." The sentence unfolds like a flower, ever moving outward in the direction of extravagance: from the specific woman to the generalization of his condition in terms of all England.

The line that separates Bentleyan abuse and raillery in Swift's letters can be seen in the following fragment, from the letter about the Leicester girl: "the obloquy of a parcel of very wretched fools, which I solemnly pronounce the inhabitants of Leicester to be" (1, 6). "Solemnly pronounce" does the trick: it puts the frame of the speaker's own idiosyncrasy around the utterance and makes him complicitous; it shifts the argument in the direction of drama.

One other characteristic of raillery which should be mentioned, because of its appropriateness to the Hack, is the preposterous gesture at ordering words and ideas. The more ordered the expression the further it moves from the representation of concrete reality. "I think you may henceforth reckon yourself easy, and have little [to] do besides serving God, your friends and yourself" (1, 23). The complex relations of life are reduced to one of service, and experience is radically simplified by the contrasting hyperboles of "easy" and the triad of services. Service itself is reduced to a triad of obligations.

In the *Tale* the tone we have examined colors almost

5. *The Correspondence of Jonathan Swift,* ed. F. Elrington Ball (London, Bell, 1910), *1,* 4.

every utterance of the Hack. "I confess to have for a long time born a part in this general Error; from which I should never have acquitted my self, but thro' the Assistance of our Noble *Moderns;* whose most edifying Volumes I turn indefatigably over Night and Day, for the Improvement of my Mind, and the good of my Country" (96). This can be considered as exaggeration piled on by Swift to crush the speaker; I prefer to think of it as the Hack creating a picture of himself turning the pages of books without pause all day and all night. "Confess" sets up the pose, or the imaginary scene; and the generalizing parallels attempt to equate the Hack's mind and his country.[6] Perhaps the most noticeable characteristic of sentences like this in the *Tale* is the curious rising action, which ends in an almost visible gesture of the speaker.

The reason for having quoted from Swift's letters of the same period as the *Tale* is that they represent the intimate relationship in which raillery operates best. Something very odd happens, accordingly, when the style is given to the enemy Swift is exposing. As the example quoted from Marvell may have suggested, it is important to remember that he and Eachard use the extravagance of this style to play with their opponent. But Marvell still keeps a steady line between himself and Bayes. It is Marvell who rallies and who makes the images grow larger and larger, not Bayes. The devices we have examined are used by Eachard and Marvell to set off the special world in which the reader judges the enemy.

6. An example of this sort of attempt to order can be seen in a small stylistic quirk like the Hack's use of doublets: "the Sharp with the Smooth, the Light and the Heavy, the Round and the Square" (167). In a single paragraph we find "Defects" divided into "Number and Bulk," "Art to sodder and patch," "Flaws and Imperfections of Nature," a science of "widening and exposing" flaws, man's "Fortunes and Dispositions," the *"Films* and *Images"* of the *"Superficies* of Things," "the Sower and the Dregs" of nature, "Philosophy and Reason," and "the sublime and refined Point of Felicity" (174). These will be seen in Ch. 3 to be reflections of the idea that everything can be ordered by being reduced to *two.*

If this style is given to the opponent to speak it has the odd effect, first, of making him a sort of friend or confidant; here, where we have all the apparatus of runaway metaphors and violated language, the Hack's function becomes one of exposing *himself*. Second, the placing of this style on the figure of the Hack tends to make him more of a fiction; it creates a figure who is trying to reorder reality and who at every step points to his handiwork. What succeeds in keeping him a comic figure are these gestures of showing, unaccompanied by self-awareness. He is forever finding something out of place—like a picture crooked on a wall—which he tries to set straight, in the process knocking over something else.

Third, like raillery, irony also involves two audiences, a "censor" and a friend; but the audience directly addressed is the "censor" who must be fooled, while in raillery the intimate friend is directly addressed. This is the reason for the odd effect of the irony in the *Tale,* where the reader is to some extent both audience and accomplice.

Finally, because the guiding hand of the satirist is not so evident as in the work of Marvell and Eachard and because the gesturing Hack is all that is in sight, the reader feels himself to be in a world in which reality, rather than the satirist, is the Hack's opponent.

For example, when the Hack, after using a number of images in which the moderns are the light and the ancients darkness, says that moderns have "eclipsed the weak and glimmering Lights of the *Ancients*" (124), the word itself seems to assert its true meaning in this context of light and dark.[7] By "eclipse" he means "hide or extinguish" the luster of the ancients, to cancel them out; but in the context of the metaphor he has set going, an eclipse is "the interposition of a dark celestial body between a luminous

---

7. Light is a typical image of the "elect," we shall see in Ch. 3; the Hack's speaking to an "elect" will be seen to be another reason for the intimate tone of his discourse.

one and the eye" (Webster). Thus the darkness of the
moderns conceals the light of the ancients. Then, a page or
so later, he speaks of the *"Save-all,"* "for want of which, if
the *Moderns* had not lent their Assistance, we might yet
have wandered *in the Dark"* (128). A "save-all," as the
footnote tells, holds candle ends so they may be burned to
the last drop. In the accepted sense of the term used, the
moderns are, accordingly, the butt ends of learning.

Such examples from the metaphor of light alone could
go on and on; but in these cases something more is hap-
pening than simply the Hack's committing himself to a
metaphor which becomes no longer relevant. The words
in these passages are not doing exactly what he wants them
to do. While he wants them to have a particular meaning
of his own at this moment, they stubbornly retain the
meaning they have always had. When meaning splits like
this and there are two levels of awareness apparent, that of
the speaker and that of the reader, language has reasserted
its right as sign over the Hack's employment of it as
symbol.

III. The Sovereignty of the Word

Such a reassertion of normal meaning as we saw in the
last section is inherent in language itself, and all Swift
needs to do with a word like "eclipse" is to use it in a
slightly wrong sense and the true sense will reassert itself.
In this section it will be our aim to examine the basis for
Swift's method of letting the word or object reassert its
own objectivity.

Probably the most self-conscious attempt at an employment of words which, like the Hack's, would convey one's
own idea of the moment to the exclusion of all the common meaning that has gathered about the words over the
years was made by the Royal Society. Sprat's ideal of "so

many things in almost as many words" would reduce words to a minimal function as sign—on the way to pure diagram. Sprat's attempt is to separate words from their commonly-accepted meanings or connotations. We shall see that what happens to the scientific style happens to the Hack's.

The Royal Society was extremely concerned about the problem of ambiguity and subjectivity, and one of its statutes of 1663 was: "In all Reports of Experiments to be brought into the Society, the matter of fact shall be barely stated, without any prefaces, apologies, or rhetorical flourishes. . . . And if any Fellow shall think fit to suggest any conjectures, concerning the causes of the phaenomena in such Experiments, the same shall be done apart." [1] Examples of practice lay ready to hand in the *Philosophical Transactions of the Royal Society,* at least parts of which we know Swift read.[2] Here, for example, Martin Lister, talking about some maggots he found, says, "I took up about a score of them, and put them into a Box, but they immediately offended me with an ungrateful and strong stink, which yet is not usual to the *Caterpillar* kind." [3] In this context the inexact "stink" comes as a shock. It is too emotional a word, carrying overtones of moral as well as physical corruption. The active verb "offended" (cf. "offensive") implies a malignant motivation on the part of the

1. Quoted by George Williamson, *The Senecan Amble* (Univ. of Chicago Press, 1951), pp. 282–3.

2. We know that Swift read at least parts of Vols. 13, 14, 15, and 16 (1683–86), since specific connections can be made between them and the *Tale.* See Robert C. Olson, "Swift's Use of the *Philosophical Transactions* in sec. v of *A Tale of a Tub,*" *Studies in Philology, 49* (1952), 459–67. See also Marjorie Nicolson, with Nora M. Mohler, "The Scientific Background of Swift's *Voyage to Laputa,*" *Science and Imagination* (Ithaca, Cornell Univ. Press, 1956), pp. 110–54. King aims some of his satire at the *Transactions* in the 9th dialogue in *Dialogues of the Dead relating to the present Controversy concerning the Epistles of Phalaris,* in *Original Works of William King* (London, 1776), *1,* 167–74.

3. *Philosophical Transactions of the Royal Society,* No. 160, *14* (1684), 596.

maggot: "sin against" happens to be one of the paraphrases in Bailey's dictionary. "Ungrateful" means to Dr. Lister unpleasant; but with "offended" its first meaning of "unthankful" (Bailey) comes out more clearly. The metaphor Dr. Lister has set working says that he feels he is being repaid for his kindness with this unkindness. Thus, we have what Dr. Lister says and what the metaphor he has unconsciously started says, which are at odds. This essential refusal of *res* and *verba* to separate, with the embarrassing consequences to the culprit, is what we have begun to observe as the effect of the Hack's attempt to reorder reality.

The Royal Scientists conducted relatively precise experiments, which have benefited mankind, and—being present at the birth of a glorious new enterprise—their enthusiasm was great; but, as this example makes obvious, they did not yet have a vocabulary with which to describe their experiments. That the trouble was perhaps deeper than vocabulary we can see from Dr. Lister, who goes on to say, "However I kept them [the maggots] 2 days, but by reason of some Apprehensions and fear the Ladies had of them, where I sojourned, and upon their intreaties I rid my self of them." Dr. Lister demonstrates the difficulties of the scientist who is not quite all scientist yet. At another point, examination of lepers proves too much for him: "his head was covered with such foul sores," Dr. Lister writes of one, "that I could not stay to view it, without loathing. . . . She offer'd to uncover her head, but I was satisfied without it; the more for being from home, and lodging at a Friends house" (No. 168, *15*, 1685, 893). The scientific and the moral reality had not yet been totally separated, and they continually jostle each other on these pages. A *body* dissected and a *body* with all the moral implications the word carries are two different things; and yet there is only one word to express them both. Carcass is no better; the moral connotations remain. In short, technique, or knowledge, had gone far beyond means of expression. The result is either horrible or laughable.

There are passages in the *Transactions* which could have been spoken by the Hack without alteration, so pervasive is the irony to a reader: "As to what was found in the Carkass, three or four Physicians of us having the fair occasion of a Body in private wholly at our own dispose . . ." (No. 157, *14*, 1684, 537–8). The words "fair occasion" are more appropriate for a picnic than a dissection. The same is true of one doctor's explanation of his working procedure, falling into the terms of an itinerary: "Having lately been imployed about the Eyes of Turky Cocks, I proceeded to examine the Brain" (No. 168, *15*, 883). Broadly speaking, these are funny because one field of reference (e.g., the scientific dissection of a body) is suddenly impinged upon by another ("fair occasion"). As Arthur Koestler explains, our understanding "does jump from the first field to the second, whereas our emotion, incapable of performing the sudden jump, is spilled." [4] When the intersection is less violent—less incongruous—the laughter, if it follows, is hysterical, and the effect is one of horror rather than of comedy. In the "fair occasion" example, if the pleasure of the dissectors were a little less gleeful the effect would not be funny. This is the case in the following experiment:

> I bespoke a *Bitch* of an ordinary size, to be delivered to me after she had been once lined [i.e. copulated with], which hapned to be the 30th of *December* last, upon the next day at 8 of the Clock in the morning, the Bitch was lined again, in my presence, and again at 2 a Clock in the afternoon, whereupon I caused her to be killed by running an Awl into the *Medulla Spinalis* near the head. As soon as she was dead, I bound her legs to a Table, and opened the *Vagina* [,]

4. *Insight and Outlook* (New York, Macmillan, 1949), p. 60.

where I found a white substance, which I took out &
viewed with my Microscope, discovering it to be nothing but Scales (of that sort which cover the inside of
the vagina) lying in a clear thin liquor [No. 174, *15*,
1121].

Of course the first thing to be noticed is that there is a contrast between what is said and the way it is said. But I believe that the effect comes from the contrast's not being great
enough; all emotion is *not* eliminated. If it were all made
Latin like *Medulla Spinalis*, the effect would be diminished
by its very remoteness. The specific dates and times are all
that place us in the world of a scientific experiment. "Be-
spoke" implies contact with another person for the procur-
ing of the dog; "lined" and "caused her to be killed" are
words denoting human, moral action. The lack of precision
intrudes the solidity of the human world: "of an ordinary
size," "which hapned to be." Finally, the personal pronoun
pervades the passage: "to me," "in my presence," "my
microscope," and the "I" who does all of these things.
These words set up a field of reference which summons up
our world, with its accompanying ideas of morality and
taboo.
     Insofar as these men are scientists, their mental attitude
is one of objectivity; they are interested in the operations
of the world about them. But objectivity implies superiority. In order to view the workings of nature properly, the
mind must dissociate itself from its individuality so that
it can look at the world from a superior vantage point. This
means dissociating it from its community with other people; sentiment, of course, must not stand in the way of an
objective reporting of the facts. But when sentiment remains in the betrayal of language, the scientist reveals himself as a self-appointed god.
     Even eliminating personal pronouns is not enough.

Words still have connotations. "A *Procidentia Ani* has been causd in a Dog, to the length of a foot. A Dog not much troubled at the pricking of the Meninges, was concernd when the spinal marrow was peirc't. Experiments have been tried by the Author, with Tallow injected into the veins of Dogs" (No. 169, *15*, 945). "Troubled" and "concernd" are human characteristics, and are, moreover, understatement. The absurd egotism of "by the Author," added after the impersonal "Experiments have been tried," produces the figure of the scientist. Two living personalities are communicated to us: the poor creature itself, and the conductor of the experiment, remaining aloof, cold and unfeeling. "A *Dog*, which had neither eaten, nor drank, in three daies, was suffered to lapp a quart of common water; an hour after which, he was open'd. . . . Another *Dog*, after three daies fasting, had a piece of fat Meat given him; an hour and half after which, he lapt (about) a Quart of common Water, and half an hour after this, was open'd . . ." (No. 165, *14*, 813). "Open'd" is the word: a word which refers to a jug or a bag of meal is here applied to a word which has the connotations of the living and the organic. "Suffered to" and "fasting" suggest the human, even the religious, nature of man, and the vivid "lapt" brings the dog to life. In all of these examples something which should be regarded as an inanimate object is brought to life by a word; or something that is alive is treated as if it were an inanimate object. In each case the reality of the object reasserts itself, to the undoing of the speaker's intention.

Ideally, the experiment would be "so many things in almost an equal number of words," i.e. the object itself, an algebraic equation, in which the human element has been completely removed. Even syntax would have to be eliminated, as a betrayer of emphasis and the subjective. Bishop Wilkins tried to substitute for live words and syntax "a cryptic system of 'integral' and 'particle' shorthand symbols that far exceed in degree of abstraction and generic orderliness all the living and dead languages which he rejected as models." [5] A Latin idiom, which comes closest to Wilkins' suggestion, was one solution to the problem of objectivity in communication. We noticed earlier that *Medulla Spinalis* carried fewer connotations than "Head," which followed it; and some of the *Transactions* are actually written in Latin.[6] But, more frequently, the *hard* words that are new coinages from Latin are used to reduce the irrelevant connotations, the smells and feelings of the words of English origin.[7] "Now, because all the parts of an undisturbed fluid are either of equal gravity, or gradually placed and storied according to the differences of it, any concretion that can be supposed to be naturally and mechanically made in such a fluid, must have a like structure of its several parts; that is, either be all over of a similar gravity, or have the more ponderous parts nearer its basis." [8] Even here "gravity" and "ponderous," as Swift was to show, have a number of very physical connotations.[9]

For a demonstration of how language asserts its rights in the *Tale* we can examine places where the usage is

5. See W. K. Wimsatt, Jr., *Philosophical Words* (New Haven, Yale Univ. Press, 1948), p. 11.

6. E.g., *Transactions*, No. 160, *14*, 601–8.

7. As Wimsatt, p. 11, points out, it also served an economic function, reducing the number of words needed (e.g., absorbent—that sucks in a liquid).

8. Sermon IV, preached June 6, 1692, in *Works of Richard Bentley*, ed. Alexander Dyce (London, 1838), *3*, 78–9.

9. See, e.g., G-S, p. 60, where "Bodies of much Weight and Gravity" leave "deep *Impressions*." The syntax in the Bentley passage, it should be noticed, is heavily Ciceronian, emphasizing causality. This sentence, from a sermon, is expressing a conclusion; the normal scientific syntax is, necessarily, anti-Ciceronian, for the *process* of discovery, not the discovery as *thing*, is analyzed; the most common form—as well as the most apparently objective—is the catalogue: "The distempers and symptoms, that afflicted him were," is the typical beginning, followed by the list. See, e.g., *Transactions*, No. 157, *14*, 538.

identical with the scientific style we have seen, and places
where it does not deal with the same kind of words but re-
tains the same principle of operation. An obvious example
of the former is at the beginning of the "Digression in the
Modern Kind":

> TO this End, I have some Time since, with a World of
> Pains and Art, dissected the Carcass of *Humane Na-
> ture,* and read many useful Lectures upon the several
> Parts, both *Containing* and *Contained;* till at last it
> *smelt* so strong, I could preserve it no longer. Upon
> which, I have been at a great Expence to fit up all the
> Bones with exact Contexture, and in due Symmetry;
> so that I am ready to shew a very compleat Anatomy
> thereof to all curious *Gentlemen and others* [123].[1]

A number of the characteristic touches we noticed in the
Philosophical Transactions are here: "smelt," "Carcass,"
the personal "I," "at a great Expence," and "curious"
(which almost comes to suggest prurience). Also present is
the familiar revolt of words that are too alive. In "with a
World of Pains and Art," for example, we have "Pains,"
which suggests (1) care taken, but also (2) physical pain (for
the dissector or for the dissected?). The syntax also plays a
part here. The casual, gentlemanly way of getting into the
subject, with the qualifying clauses, contrasts suitably with
the proud assertion of the dissection.

It will be useful to look again at the sentence, "Last
Week I saw a Woman *flay'd,* and you will hardly believe,
how much it altered her Person for the worse" (173). Much
of the force of this sentence would be lost if it said "A
woman was flay'd," and so, as one characteristic, we can
point to the personal pronoun. But this in itself would
carry little force if the wording had been "Last week I saw

---

1. This is specifically parodying Wotton's *Reflections,* p. 211; cited in
G-S, p. 123n.

a body dissected." "Flay'd" is another nonscientific word, which suggests skinning of animals or martyrdom of saints more than dissecting of bodies. When "flay'd" and "woman" are brought together, we see an attempt to reduce *woman* to *thing*, whereupon woman reasserts her humanness and the action appears monstrous.

The usual practice in the *Tale* is for a respectable context to be set up, and one word placed in it which, reasserting its normal meaning, completely alters the significance of the context: "not that he is curious to observe the Colour and Complexion of the Ordure, or take its Dimensions, much less to be padling in, or tasting it . . ." (93). Here the general noun, "Ordure," is used instead of the specifically denotative "excrement." [2] Balancing it are two scientific verbs, "observe" and "take . . . Dimensions." These verbs are too concrete, too impressionistic in effect, particularly when coupled with "Colour and Complexion." The latter is a technical term meaning the way in which the material is composed; but with "Colour" the sense of facial hue predominates (cf. 178), suggesting that this person—with "curiosity" attributed to him—is enamoured of the ordure. And so the step from "observe" and "take . . . Dimensions" to "padling in" and "tasting it" is a short one.

Swift can also use the reverse process, making the scientific context a distancing element: "The best Part of his Diet, is the Reversion of his own Ordure, which exspiring into Steams, whirls perpetually about, and at last reinfunds" (178). The Latin-derived hard words—"Reversion," "exspiring," and "reinfunds"—are more restrained than concrete English words that might have replaced them; and, surrounding the strong central word, "Ordure," they give an air of objectivity lacking in the feeling of the word itself. Applied to a madman eating his own excrement, they

2. Ordure is filth, which carries moral overtones and only secondarily means feces.

give us the impression that this is regarded by the partici-
pants as some sort of a rational, even scientific, procedure.
The distancing, of course, only brings out the central word
more strikingly.

The change of meaning is almost always toward the more
physical, the more sensory. A final example, which is as far
away as one gets in the *Tale* from the laboratory, is the
word "possession": "This is the sublime and refined Point
of Felicity, called, *the Possession of being well deceived;*
The Serene Peaceful State of being a Fool among Knaves"
(174). A few pages earlier we are told that happiness is *"a
perpetual Possession of being well Deceived"* (171), and
the point of the repetition lies in the appositive that follows and qualifies it: "The Serene Peaceful State of being
a Fool among Knaves." In both cases "possession" hovers
between two meanings: (1) "the holding or having something . . . as one's own," and (2) "the fact of being possessed" (*OED*), by demon, spirit or lover, or by madness.
The emphasis is placed on the second meaning by "Fool"
in the appositional member. "Possession" is actually parallel to "State" and makes the latter shift toward connotations of "state of mind" or even of "fit."

To summarize, we have seen that when the Hack sets up
a context like the one of dissecting and uses a word like
"pains" to mean care taken, the context causes the other
sense of physical pain to assert itself. That the reassertion
of meaning is more of Swift's doing than language's is beside the point; since Swift as satirist is absent, we are left
with the impression that natural laws are against the Hack,
and this is made particularly apparent because, as we have
seen, it is reality which the Hack is trying to reorder in
some way. At the same time, the activated word like
"pains" tends to bring out certain characteristics of the context, in this case the inhumanity of dissection: the result is
what we saw in some of the examples of scientific style, that

metaphors are set moving which the scientist never intended.

These metaphors then carry on with a life of their own. Significantly, one of the central metaphors of the *Tale,* which we shall examine in Chapter 3, is concerned with the relation between the human body and its organs, and partakes of the new scientific attitude toward the body. The satiric metaphor of body, in which defects are vice and folly and the barber-surgeon is the satirist, suffers some alteration when dissection becomes a commonplace and we actually see what the inside does look like when it is diseased.[3]

> The *Liver* upon deep Incisions appear'd bloodless [writes one Royal Scientist], stuft throughout like a bag of sand with a *yellow gritty substance,* the *Gallbladder* also was burnisht with the like, but of a darker hue. The *Spleen* was very large and of too soft and loose a texture, not much discolour'd. The *Omentum* rotten and *wasted.* The Membrane of the *Stomach* extremely flaccid and *very thin,* appearing black and *mortifi'd,* and upon taking it out within twenty four hours after death (tho ty'd at both ends very close) sent forth such an intollerable *sowr rancid sent,* that the strongest *double Aquafortis* (to which it might best

3. See Mary Claire Randolph, "The Medical Concept in English Renaissance Satiric Theory: Its Possible Relationships and Implications," *Studies in Philology, 38* (1941), 125–57. The two universal cures of the Renaissance were purging (Swift's "Purges and Pipes") and bloodletting, and so the satirist pictured his pen as "a searing, cauterizing scalpel which probes deep and cuts away dead or gangrenous flesh, leaving a clean wound to heal" (Randolph, p. 145). Dissecting, purporting to bring into the open the vices that lurk in shadows and escape the eye of the law, gave rise to titles like *Anatomie of Abuses* (1583) and *Follies Anatomie* (1619). The idea of whips used to scourge away the infected flesh or to beat the madman back to sanity is plain in popular titles of satires: *Scourge of Villainy* and *Virgidemiarum* (a "bundle of rods"), both of 1598.

be compar'd) could not prove so troublesome and
offensive to the Smell. The *Lungs* were distended to
the uttermost with a *purulent froth.*[4]

As the Hack noticed of the bodies he dissected, everything
is wrong inside: the gall bladder is too dark, the spleen
"too soft and loose," the omentum "rotten and *wasted.*" [5]
Since the dead seldom died of old age, when they were
dissected their insides invariably revealed some such picture of disorder. Now the question arises: when the passion
of the old satire is replaced by reasonableness and symbolism by "exactness," are the moral implications of words
sent underground and forgotten by the scientific mind? We
have already seen the answer. Whether aware or not, Dr.
Gould, who conducted the above dissection, sees the inside
of this body as an order disturbed by the intrusion of a
polyp in the heart, with chaos resulting:

> such hard shift did nature make to continue the vital
> stream and avoid the fatal stop, *each moment* threat-
> ned by the Polypus, that with *double* force she was
> oblig'd to maintain a Pulse, which (because it could
> not break or expel the unnatural load,) did by *little
> and little stretch* the sides of the ventricle, for the more
> easy passage of the blood, and by terrible palpitations
> for *a long time* protract a miserable life, till the mon-
> strous body growing too big, the weakened Fibres
> could stretch no more, nor yet regularly contract them-
> selves any longer; so that the Heart at last just ready
> to sink under the burden, is forced to collect its little
> remaining strength into one brisk effort, and assisted
> by *all the spirits* of the Body caus'd the poor wretch to
> expire in an universal Convulsion [p. 545].

4. *Transactions*, No. 157, *14*, 538–9. Notice the effect of "sent" (scent) in
this context.

5. Cf. G-S, pp. 173–4.

Dr. Gould's metaphor, because to him it is not a metaphor, shows that, far from reducing the significance of the body metaphor, the new science has made it richer in connotation. It has removed the last bit of abstraction from it without taking away its meaning.

Much the same applies to the scientific interest shown in the various bodily excretions, particularly urine, in which the virtuosi seemed to find an extraordinary number of kidney stones. Nehemiah Grew gives sweat a close examination, finding that the pores in the hands and feet "are a very convenient and open passage for the discharge of the more noxious and perspirable parts of the Blood"; Anthony Leeuwenhoek conducts experiments with human spittle, and the pox is described as a vapor.[6] In all of these the healthy discharge of the excretion is contrasted with the disastrous results of nondischarge, which results in some sort of corruption within the body. The moral, or symbolic, quality in such investigation of the human body is just beneath the surface, waiting for the smallest slip to reassert itself.[7]

What we have said about the scientific style and method can be said as well about other modern trends, from literary criticism to sermons.[8] Life and language, though seeking a new discipline in the new age, were still a patchwork of the tatters and ends of the older customs and rhetoric; a careless writer filled his pages with expressions that meant one thing now in the age of enlightenment but had not entirely cast off their old connotations. The reason I have emphasized the scientific style as perhaps the most important for an understanding of the *Tale* is that it seeks com-

6. *Transactions,* No. 157, *14,* 523–31; No. 159, *14,* 567, 568; No. 160, *14,* 620.

7. When we read today of the emetic administered by Alexander Pope to Edmund Curll, we tend to take Pope's action as altogether childish; whereas, it actually shows that the contact with the old symbolism of satire was still meaningful to Pope and his practical joke was a reassertion of the moral in the only terms Curll, being a modern, could understand.

8. See Note B, below, p. 246.

plete secularization while revealing the strongest moral quality in its every action. The scientist is a particularly vulnerable person in this world because of the discrepancy between his claims and the sensory fact. He claims to be "performing an experiment" ("for the Universal Benefit of Mankind"); the reader sees him butchering.

iv. Order in Seventeenth-Century Form

We have seen the extent, and the limits, of Swift's debt to the satirists like Eachard and Marvell, whose imitations of eccentricity operate essentially on the level of polemic. The differences have proved to be as striking as the similarities. Whatever the qualities of the fiction or of the symbolism, they are strictly subordinated in the works of Eachard and Marvell to the end of convincing an audience by hook or crook that Bramhall or Parker is wrong, that the clergy should be better educated, or that toleration of religious belief is necessary. Thus the larger theme of the relation between language and reality or between ceremonies and religion is merely ammunition to carry the tactical situation. The theme is used to support the attack, as Bayes is brought in from the outside to characterize Parker. In the *Tale* the seventeenth-century forms and poses, as well as the specific details concerning contemporaries like Bentley and Wotton, to say nothing of the Hack himself, are used to support a theme, which is the important consideration. In short, the tactical situation is employed to support the strategic situation.

Therefore, to find the models which contribute most to the *Tale* we must turn back to the seventeenth-century forms, whose failings we observed in Chapter 1, and see what the method of Eachard and Marvell may have taught us about them. In this section we shall see how the anti-Ciceronian form carries within itself the seeds of reordering, and in the final section we shall examine specific works to see what theme the procedure we have been tracing may express.

The reordering of Eachard and Marvell is only an extension of the principles used by the more skillful writers of the mode they attacked, such men as Donne or Andrewes.[1] The idea of the digression which advances the theme while pretending to be sheer amusement is as old as Homer and a common device of the medieval sermon, though it draws more attention to itself in the self-conscious seventeenth century. The subplot of the Elizabethan and Jacobean play is an example of this, and the interaction of the two plots in plays like *King Lear* and *The Changeling* shows a pattern for Swift's employment of digressions running in counterpoint to his allegorical narrative. In fact, Donne's expressed intention is not far from that of the parodists: to arrange his rhetorical effects in such a way as "to trouble the understanding, to displace, and discompose and disorder the judgment . . . or to empty it of former apprehensions, and to shake beliefs, with which it had possessed it self before, and then, when it is thus melted to poure it into new molds, when it is thus mollified, to stamp and imprint new formes, new images, new opinions in it." [2] This is an explanation of the anti-Ciceronian method we have not entertained before: a conscious disordering for the

1. An indication of Swift's attraction to the seventeenth-century forms may be sensed in his early poetry, which was in the typically seventeenth-century mode of the Pindaric ode. This form offered license to those poets who felt prosody settling toward the couplet (in which Swift more characteristically expressed himself): in an ode, as George Saintsbury remarked, "you were allowed to be mad" (*A History of English Prosody*, London, 1908, 2, 338). To a poet wishing to express himself or a great thought, the irregular stanzas of the ode, lengthened or shortened at the pleasure and judgment of the poet, gave an excellent form for the eddies of his thought. Thus the ode could be adjusted to almost any length, and invited Metaphysical excitement, digression, parenthesis, and all the Longinian figures.

2. Sermon LXXI, "Dec. 19th, 1619," in *LXXX Sermons,* p. 723 (E).

purpose of deriving a new and compelling restatement of order. As Bacon puts it, "Aphorisms, representing a knowledge broken, do invite men to inquire farther; whereas Methods, carrying the show of a total [i.e. the Ciceronian form], do secure men, as if they were at farthest." [3] The anti-Ciceronian sentence indeed goes far toward explaining how the development of theme is carried out on the larger scale of the digressive form.

The important thing to remember about the loose period is that the organic unity which we observed in Hooker's periods is here dispersed. As Croll writes,

> The successive processes of revision to which [the Ciceronian] periods had been submitted had removed them from reality by just so many steps. For themselves, [the anti-Ciceronians] preferred to present the truth of experience in a less concocted form, and deliberately chose as the moment of expression that in which the idea first clearly objectifies itself in the mind, in which, therefore, each of its parts still preserves its own peculiar emphasis and an independent vigor of its own. . . . [4]

The art of the anti-Ciceronian sentence, then, is one more of juxtaposition than of unified organization, and is typical of the literary movement we have discussed. Whether the connection is asyndetic or is accomplished by weakened subordinating conjunctions, a purer reality (of a kind) is expressed in the failure to relate meanings. But the anti-Ciceronians, in seeking the reality, have consciously destroyed the ways to emphasis and order which depend upon subordination.

In an unemphatic syntax, emphasis, as well as order,

---

3. *The Advancement of Learning,* ed. G. W. Kitchin, Everyman Library (London, J. M. Dent, n.d.), p. 142.
4. Croll, "The Baroque Style in Prose," p. 430.

must come in at the back door, and the lack of emphasis, which imitates unfiltered reality, must be only an appearance; the syntax must actually say something different. An extreme example of the breakdown of thoughts into their components is demonstrated in Swift's parody of the chapbook fairy tale, beginning with "Once upon a Time" and concerning dragons and giants. Describing the brothers' history following the death of their father, the Hack tells us "that they carefully observed their Father's Will, and kept their Coats in very good Order; That they travelled thro' several Countries, encountred a reasonable Quantity of Gyants, and slew certain Dragons" (74). The first thing to notice is that by keeping their coats in good order they *were* obeying their father's will (or a part of it), and yet the two are not related in any other way syntactically than by coordination. The breakdown into series tends to make two distinct actions of it, minimizing causality and, consequently, rendering one act no more important than the other, when in Christian terms the obedience is crucial. They may have kept their coats in good order for very different reasons (as they do later). In the same way, *while* they traveled they encountered and slew their giants and dragons; but here they are listed, like places on an itinerary, with the perfunctory quality of the reciting of a lesson.[5]

Given the "process of revision," the ideal form of this passage would be the hypotactical sentence, where subordination would give the exact relationship of part to part. By breaking this down into parataxis, Swift is able to suggest by juxtaposition that the seeds of the brothers' future difficulties are in the attitude which accompanies their commendable actions, while the subject level of his words merely recounts their deeds. The Hack's unconnected thoughts and detached metaphors serve the same function

5. The words "several," "a reasonable Quantity," and "certain" also contribute by their suggestion of the perfunctory.

as the anti-Ciceronian syntax on the smaller scale. By breaking down the *Tale* as a whole into parataxis, Swift has imitated the aimless wandering, the digressions, and the copia of the seventeenth-century writers, and he has also shown the disorder of the Hack's mind and of the modern world; [6] but he has also produced a new meaning by the juxtaposition of the parts. This arrangement will, in the later chapters of this study, help us to find the causes of the surface disorder.

We can now answer part of the charge that the *Tale's* juxtapositions are merely playful. Much of the humor of the book is, of course, based on these juxtapositions; but the critics who accuse these of lacking significance are looking for a Ciceronian periodicity which, because of Swift's basic assumptions about the Hack, is absent. The difference between the *Tale's* syntax and Ciceronian periodicity is that the climax is made of peripheral material, while the Ciceronian sentence, having subordinated all but its main point from the beginning, moves in a relatively straight line. The difference is between a cumulative and a culminative effect. The peripheral matter is all piled up toward the making of a single unified idea in the Ciceronian sentence. In a loose syntax the climax may follow a minor, even a tangential, element of the subject level; this minor element of the subject—perhaps a metaphor begun by the Hack, or a fact he lets drop—is thus shown to be symbolically important, to represent perhaps the one significant feature of the whole, as the tiny, plunging figure of

6. The list that follows the passage we read about the brothers—beginning "They Writ, and Raillyed, and Rhymed, and Sung, and Said, and said Nothing . . ."—is made up of actions which have as little effect on anything as the first series. The series is wholly alliterative, the implication being that all the meaning there is to the series is that some of them begin with the same letters; and this is the only principle of order in the lives of fops. On the larger scale of the book, the same effect is achieved by the aimless progression of the Hack's talk.

Icarus, when found, illuminates the ploughman, the ship, and the rest of Breughel's canvas.[7]

The metaphorical structure, which we have spoken of as sometimes replacing a logical structure, works in the same way. If it is used merely to underline the speaker's theme it often carries him afield, or can be interpreted so as to do so by an Eachard or a Marvell. But, employed by a conscious artist like Donne, the metaphor has as much independence as the logical structure, and the theme has to be drawn from the interaction of the two levels of thought.

What remains is to show how this new appraisal of the seventeenth-century works we discussed in Chapter 1 is based, ultimately, on a distinction between two ways of reading and interpreting texts—a distinction which can best be seen at work in Metaphysical and Puritan sermons, both concerned primarily with reading Biblical texts. Following the grammatical, or exegetical, tradition of the Church Fathers, Anglican divines like Andrewes and Donne regarded imagery, figures of speech, syntax, all as intrinsic to the meaning of the passage. For example, taking the text "For Thine arrows stick fast in me, and Thy hand presseth me sore" (Psalms 38:2), Donne would find it important that the metaphor of "arrows" is used: that "arrows" is plural, because "The victory lies not in scaping one or two"; that they "stick fast," because they do not find their target so perfect "as to rebound back again, and imprint no sense"; "me" is important because it implies the whole man, body, soul, sins as well as good works.[8] A total meaning is gradually constructed as the preacher examines "literal," "moral," "allegorical," and "anagogical" meanings, all of which are equally true and mutually supporting.

7. See W. H. Auden, "Musée des Beaux Arts," in *The Collected Poetry of W. H. Auden* (New York, Random House, 1945), p. 3.

8. "Sermon Preached at Lincoln's Inn, Spring, 1618," in *The Sermons of John Donne*, ed. Theodore A. Gill (New York, Meridian, 1958), p. 37.

The Puritans saw all that as decoration. Like the rationalists who followed, they based their interpretation on the logical revolution of Peter Ramus, who had split off the cognitive parts of rhetoric (invention and disposition or arrangement) and called them dialectic; the Ramist accordingly thought he could strip away the images, figures, and the rest, "plane off the colors of speech from Scriptural utterances, leaving the smooth white surface of 'that one entire and naturall sense.'" [9] This then was the single meaning; all the rest consisted of devices of persuasion. Sir Philip Sidney expresses this view of rhetoric in his *Apologie for Poetrie* when he remarks that "even our Saviour Christ could as well have given, the morall common places of uncharitablenes and humblenes, as the divine narration of *Dives* and *Lazarus* . . . but that hys throughsearching wisdom, knewe the estate of *Dives* burning in hell, and of *Lazarus* being in *Abrahams* bosome, would more constantly (as it were) inhabit both the memory and judgment." [1] Regarding the text from Psalms, the Ramist would say the image of an arrow shot into man is there to dramatize the argument "Man must obey God."

The distinction we have made applies equally to interpretation of texts and to the rhetoric of sermons. To the Puritan tropes were merely persuasive devices which did not affect the meaning of the sermon's "plain sense." Ordinarily they should be eschewed but, when used (and, to gain attention, they were constantly used), they would not hurt anything. While held back when the Puritan preacher opened his text and stated his doctrine, they came into play in his reasons and were given full swing in the applications, which were to persuade men to right conduct. [2] Now it

9. Perry Miller, *The New England Mind: The Seventeenth Century* (New York, Macmillan, 1939), p. 343.
1. Smith and Parks, eds., *The Great Critics*, p. 202.
2. Miller, p. 347.

should be obvious why, on the one hand, Swift would regard excesses in the language of Metaphysical sermons as heinous, since he saw this as part of the cognitive structure of the sermon, distorting sense; and, on the other, it should suggest why the Puritan sermon, which simply disregards the problem, wishing only to persuade, would be even more open to his attack. If handled correctly, the Metaphysical sermon was a positive good; as we have seen in the present section, the syntax and tropes, however eccentric, might contain an order and meaning of their own. The Puritan sermon represented a basic disagreement as to the nature of reading and interpreting Scripture.

Now with all of this in mind, let us look back at the Grub Street Hack. The metaphors and examples we saw him employ with such abandoned casuistry may be regarded as simply a parody of the excesses of Ramist rhetorical persuasion (we shall see in the next chapter that he is connected with Puritanism). Whatever persuades at any one moment will be used, since the device has no intrinsic meaning anyway. But read by men like Swift in the older tradition—or, in fact, by most men—an image becomes part of the meaning of the passage, altering the "plain sense" accordingly. In terms of an ironic structure, the "censor" is the Puritan who would regard the images as mere decoration, and the true audience is the Anglican who would read them as part of the cognitive structure. The extent to which the *Tale* has been misread and misunderstood is perhaps indicative of the success enjoyed in the last two hundred and fifty years by Puritan assumptions, including the Ramist definition of rhetoric.

With this in mind, the fact that the list of authors Swift parodied and the list of authors who were his favorite reading coincide at certain points is easily explicable. The functioning of style in *Gargantua and Pantagruel* and the *Tale* is ultimately not very different. The chaos of Rabelais' world serves the same function Donne's dislocation of syntax did: it destroys the familiar pattern in order to jolt the reader into a reappraisal. Rabelais' method is to trip up the system maker (specifically the schoolman) by releasing him in a world of contradictory particulars, a complex reality which will never fit into his oversimplified scheme. The result is a world where one can proceed only by analogy, not by a reliance on mind alone. As Auerbach has pointed out about Rabelais, what he attacks is "Thickheadedness, inability to adjust, one-track arrogance which blinds a man to the complexity of the real situation." [3] The Rabelaisian epic is not just a story of Gargantua, Pantagruel, and Panurge, but an encyclopedia of attitudes toward life which are tested and judged in various ways. Rabelais not only contrasts all through his book the two ways of reading we have discussed, attacking the reliance on dialectic, but also assumes that his own work will be read in the grammatical manner.[4] Swift is echoing, if not invoking, Rabelais when he has the Hack in his introduction advise the reader to look below the surface for the meaning in his book: Socrates is a specific recollection, and the nut, sackposset, and the rest (66) more general ones, of Rabelais' prologue to Book I of *Gargantua and Pantagruel*. While the Hack tries to prove his point of the moment, that the Grub Street productions contain nourishment if one looks

3. *Mimesis*, p. 275. That Rabelais' intention was orthodox so far as the Church of England is concerned is evident if we notice that the centers of attack on his work were Geneva and Paris, the centers of Calvinism and Scholasticism, and that he was defended by the humanist party within the Church. It is also true, however, as Auerbach concludes, that in spite of Rabelais' undoubtedly orthodox intention the final effect of his work is disintegrative (the effect I referred to in Ch. 1, sec. II). Only a thin line separates Pantagruelism as a humanist image of the well-rounded man from mere individualism and self-indulgence.

4. See *The Works of Rabelais* (The Bibliophilist Society, n.d.), e.g., Bk. I, chs. 9 and 10, pp. 22–6, where the colors blue and white are first analyzed dialectically and then grammatically.

for it, the major premise he is forced to use is offered to the
reader: this book must be looked into.

Rabelais, Montaigne, Pascal, Browne, and Burton were
all writers in the old exegetical tradition (all attacking the
schoolmen), writers in whose work Swift could find the solution to the problem of how to parody the soaring disordered
thought of the religious enthusiasts or the eccentric projector, and at the same time produce a work of art that was
not merely an imitation of chaos but a criticism, commentary, and reordering.

In the final section of this chapter we shall examine some
of the works of these writers which either contain seeds of
the *Tale* or demonstrate the same sort of absorption and
utilization of the eccentric which we see in the *Tale;* and
while they are most self-consciously present in the sixteenth
and seventeenth centuries, they range back as far as the
second century A.D.

v. Some Tales of Tubs

The Hack has long roots. This section will take a look
at some of the works from which Swift constructed his
symbolic fulcrum.

We should at least take note of the probable influence of
Rabelais' method on Swift's creation of the Hack.[1] *Gargantua and Pantagruel* offers all the obscure learning and
information that Browne's *Pseudodoxia Epidemica* did,
but with the added advantage for Swift's purpose of employing a narrative form and a speaker more clearly charac-

---

1. The connection between Swift and Rabelais has often been noted.
Pope referred to Swift as sitting in "Rab'lais' easy Chair" (*Dunciad,* London,
1729, Bk. I, l. 20), Lord Bathurst accused Swift of "improvements" upon
humor "stolen from Miguel de Cervantes and Rabelais," and Voltaire
called Swift "Rabelais perfectionné." And Swift had "well-handled" copies
of Rabelais in his library at the time of his death; see Harold Williams,
Dean Swift's Library (Cambridge Univ. Press, 1932), p. 50.

terized than Browne's curious searcher after truth. In Rabelais we have a prototype of the story interrupted by digressions which develop into philosophical discussions, carrying along the theme at the same time. Another example of the Rabelaisian combination of narrative and discussion would be hard to find. In *Don Quixote* there are digressions, but they appear as part of the plot itself, spoken by the people Don Quixote and Sancho Panza happen to meet. These people tell their stories, which often have some ironic relationship to the occasion for their telling. While in Cervantes the plot is always in the foreground, in Rabelais the narrator is himself in the foreground. In both works the narrator is an author, a historian, but in Rabelais he becomes one of the characters of the work. The main factor which effects this emergence is the commitment of his style. He is as much a Pantagruelist as Pantagruel, and his savoring of every object separates him from an altogether mechanical function of telling a story. He is a more particular person, who keeps inserting bits of his learning and referring to his other works, such as *The Dignity of Codpieces.*

Rabelais' speaker is, therefore, more than merely an attitude or more than James' slightly implicated observer. He is a symbol himself, because the world he describes is in his mind and he accepts and praises its standards. Still he is a minor character, complementary to Pantagruel and Panurge, or rather a reflection of them. All three maintain separate existences. Pantagruel and Panurge exist outside the narrator's mind: they *are* the story. But in the *Tale* the Hack is himself the story: even the story of the brothers is to some extent a reflection of his mind. A second important difference is that Swift could not afford the breadth —the duration—that Rabelais allows himself. The one element of duration in the *Tale* is the temporal development in the scattered fragments of the brothers' story. Taken all in all, the *Tale* is more like a fragment of the Rabelaisian epic, with representative narrative and representative digressions: a fragment that implies the rest. The texture is thus closer, the style more allusive, and it is more like a poem.[2]

Other, very different anatomies which bear affinities with the *Tale of a Tub* are those compendia of errors the early Church Fathers, as well as some seventeenth-century writers, loved to construct. Irenaeus' great catalogue of heresies in his *Adversus Haereses* or Tertullian's *Praescriptio Adversus Haereticos* are two examples. General parallels to the *Tale* could be found in Tertullian as well as in Irenaeus (though, of course, Irenaeus was an important source for Tertullian's attack on heresies), but their methods are so different that there is little doubt which Swift followed in the developing of his own method. Tertullian will countenance no other view than his own, and his attack is direct and unyielding. "Let us leave the Holy Spirit out of the discussion," he says, "because after all he is a witness on our side." [3] Al-

---

2. There are frequent echoes of Rabelais in the *Tale*, such as Swift's genealogy of the critic (93–4) which is reminiscent of Rabelais' genealogies (e.g., *Works of Rabelais*, p. 123). Rabelais' linking of ears and genitals (pp. 170–1) may have given Swift a hint for his similar equation (201ff.), as his reference to Hippocrates' opinion that the severing of the parotid artery makes a eunuch may have been Swift's source (Rabelais, pp. 326–7; G-S, 202). Panurge sounds rather like Jack, particularly in Bk. II, ch. 16, where his carryings-on around Paris are described in much the way Jack's are described in section 11 of the *Tale*. Like Swift, Rabelais uses the printer as an excuse for any seditious material that may have appeared in his book: e.g., the printer is supposed to have replaced an *m* with an *n*, making *asme* become *asne* (p. 397). Finally, there are a number of stylistic echoes, such as the use of preposterously precise numbers: e.g., "to the number of eighteen hundred and fifty six thousand and eleven, besides women and little children" (p. 211); in the *Tale* there are "one hundred thirty six" poets of the first rate, "nine thousand seven hundred forty and three" wits, etc. (33, 41). For other parallels see Huntington Brown, *Rabelais in English Literature* (Cambridge, Harvard Univ. Press, 1933), pp. 154–61.

3. *De Monogamia*, iv; cited in R. A. Knox, *Enthusiasm, A Chapter in the History of Religion with special reference to the* XVII *and* XVIII *centuries* (New York, Oxford Univ. Press, 1950), p. 46.

though Irenaeus is as dogmatic as Tertullian in his beliefs, his approach is that of the seeker of truth, a rhetorical pose which is more effective in argument than Tertullian's. The doctrine must be tested, often by his wit, and its error made self-evident. While to Tertullian heresies are the offspring of a perverse will and idle curiosity, to Irenaeus they are (even when instigated by an evil person) diseases of the human mind which must be described and classified to be avoided.

Irenaeus' technique as he describes the customs of the Gnostics is to let them speak for themselves. In explanation he writes, "I have deemed it my duty (after reading some of the *Commentaries*, as they call them, of the disciples of Valentinus, and after making myself acquainted with their tenets through personal intercourse with some of them) to unfold to thee, my friend, these portentous and profound mysteries, which do not fall within the range of every intellect, because all have not sufficiently purged their brains." [4] The last half of the sentence (after the parenthesis) has slipped into the Gnostic jargon. To this assumed voice, purging the brain means clearing it of the impurities *we* carry with us; to us, it means draining *his* brain empty, when of course his thoughts would indeed be outside "the range of every intellect."

Thus Irenaeus' method is to employ the jargon which was common among the heretics themselves, so that he "may come down to the level of their impiety," as he puts it, "and by descending to their argument, may often refute them by their own doctrines" (p. 403). Presentation and criticism are the two techniques he uses: the reasonable tone of the criticism is meant to be in sharp contrast to the

4. Irenaeus, *A Refutation and Subversion of Knowledge Falsely so Called*, in *The Ante-Nicene Fathers*, ed. Alexander Roberts, James Donaldson, and A. Cleveland Coxe (Buffalo, 1885), *1*, 315. Compare the concluding phrases with the Hack's reference to the "*Modern Saints in Great Britain*" (the Puritans), who "have spiritualized and refined [their writings] from the Dross and Grossness of *Sense* and *Human Reason*" (61–2).

fanatical sound of the Gnostic jargon. It is because of this shift of emphasis to the jargon of the opponent, who is allowed to damn himself, that the technique differs from the fiction set up by Marvell.

One difference between this method and Swift's, however, presents itself at first glance: like Marvell, Irenaeus is always careful to insert a "they [the heretics] affirm" or "as they believe" between himself and the heretics, a precaution Swift does not take, thus presupposing a greater, and often misplaced, confidence in his reader.[5] While Irenaeus is posing as the truthful reporter, in the *Tale of a Tub* the heretic is describing, with reverence, the customs of his friends. There is no shift in tone from the straightforward attack to the oblique attack of ironic reverence. Swift's whole work is the speech of the heretic.

There were a number of seventeenth-century compendia of heresies with a scope not unlike that of Irenaeus. In 1645 the Presbyterian Thomas Edwards' *Gangraena* appeared, attacking the proliferation of sects.[6] Though a crude performance compared to the *Adversus Haereses*, *Gangraena* is composed along similar lines. Making no attempt at argument to controvert the "heresies," Edwards simply reports "what they said and did."[7] "Such discoveries,"

5. The obscurity of style in the *Adversus Haereses* has, even so, been blamed on Irenaeus, whereas in the critical sections it is quite clear; see introductory note to Irenaeus, p. 312.

6. Full title: *Gangraena: or a Catalogue and Discovery of Many of the Errors, Heresies, Blasphemies and Pernicious Practices of the Sectaries of this Time*, London, 1646. A copy appears in the catalogue of Swift's library, No. 515, p. (13). See also Ephraim Paget's *Heresiography: or, a Description of the Hereticks and Sectaries of these Latter Times*, 1645; Paget's *A Catalogue of the severall Sects and Opinions in England*, 1647; Robert Baillie, *A Dissuasive from the Errours of the Time*, 1646; Roger L'Estrange, *The Dissenter's Sayings, In Requital for L'Estrange's Sayings Published in Their Own Words, For the Information of the People*, London, 1681.

7. See Edwards, *Gangraena*, Pt. I, p. 3: "the naming of them will be a sufficient confutation." Edwards says he will recount the ideas of the heretics "in their own words and phrases syllabically, as neer as possible can

he claims, "are a more sensible practicall way of confutation . . . than so many syllogismes and arguments." [8] In
1646 Browne's *Pseudodoxia Epidemica* appeared, in which
heresy has become error, and the object designated for attack is, if anything, the mind of the people, with whom
"all Heresies, how gross soever, have found a welcome." [9]

Another chronicle of errors which has closer associations
with the *Tale of a Tub* is that recited by Erasmus' Folly,
who, like so many of the *Tale's* characters, wears a cap
which covers asses' ears. Like the *Tale*, *The Praise of Folly*
is the eulogy of folly spoken by Folly. Basically, this appears
to be the situation of Irenaeus' and Edwards' work: the
enemy exposing himself. But, as we read on into *The Praise
of Folly*, we see that the central image is radically ambiguous. She extends from the Christian quality of simplicity
(as goodness) to stupidity and shortsightedness; and, accordingly, "wisdom" goes from true wisdom (which becomes
synonymous with the Christian simplicity of folly) to the
deluded wisdom of analysis, reason, and theological controversy. As he builds to a climax, Erasmus puts his emphasis increasingly on Folly's goodness, until by the end
she has become apotheosized into true Christianity as
against the complex theologizing of Scholasticism.

The Grub Street Hack should be seen as an imitation
of Folly, with some of her ambiguity.[1] The intimate tone
of raillery which we have discerned in the *Tale*—the joy
that shows through when the Hack is busy putting things

---

be, or I can remember them" (p. 4). Many of the lampoons collected in the
Rump (London, 1662) are composed along this same line.

8. *The Second Part of Gangraena: or a Fresh and Further Discovery of the
Errors, Heresies, Blasphemies, and Dangerous Proceedings of the Sectaries
of this Time*, London, 1646, "To the Christian Reader," page unnumbered.

9. *Works of Browne*, ed. Sayle, *1*, 138. We might list many more works
in the "error" tradition, such as Bacon's *Advancement of Learning*.

1. As opposed to the fairly simple blackening of the Puritan fool in, for
example, Butlers' *Hudibras*. Hudibras, like the Hack, is "a tool /That
knaves do work with, call'd a Fool" (Bk. 1, Canto 1, ll. 35–6).

in "order"—brings Folly to mind at times. Moreover, image after image from *The Praise of Folly* is repeated in the *Tale*. For example, Folly points out that "If a person were to try stripping the disguises from actors while they play a scene upon the stage, showing to the audience their real looks and the faces they were born with, would not such a one spoil the whole play?" [2] And the Hack finds the "Art of exposing weak Sides, and publishing Infirmities . . . neither better nor worse than that of *Unmasking*, which I think, has never been allowed fair Usage, either in the *World* or the *Play-House*" (172–3). Folly's statement puts the reader's sympathy—while leaving him aware of the other side—on the side of the gratifying, easy illusion. This comes down to a conflict between reason and imagination, reality and appearance, in which reason and reality seem to be less important than the pleasing appearances created by our imaginations, which make living bearable. We shall see that so easy an answer is not enough for Swift, who, one can suspect, makes his speaker another Folly as an answer to Erasmus. While Erasmus' Folly, though expressing the inherent ambiguity of the question, presented her light side to view, Swift's Folly turns toward us his dark side. [3]

We should dwell a moment, however, on the ambiguity of Folly, because it will lead us back to her origins and will tell us something more about the Hack's role. Shakespeare's Touchstone can be imagined as clothed in two colors, split down the middle, half for city, half for country, half for folly, half for wisdom. The concept of the fool whose folly is a kind of superior wisdom is the one Erasmus is playing on: this seems to him the symbol of primitive (or true) Christianity. But viewed from a slightly different angle, the wisdom becomes perceptiveness, as in Shakespeare's fools, a prophetic pose.

2. Desiderius Erasmus, *The Praise of Folly* (1509), tr. Hoyt H. Hudson (Princeton Univ. Press, 1941), p. 37.

3. For a fuller discussion, see Note C, p. 249 below.

The medieval concept of fool reached the seventeenth century in a curious dichotomy which corresponds to Swift's dichotomy of fool and knave. The fool as knave is best illustrated in the writings of the moralists, particularly in Sebastian Brant's *Narrenschiff* (1594).[4] Here there is nothing comic about the fool, who, as Enid Welsford has pointed out, is simply the wicked man, "stupid and short-sighted enough to be blind to his own eternal interests." [5] An example of this sort of fool—the knave—is to be found in the self-interest of the lawyer, doctor, and preacher revealed by the description of madmen in Bedlam in those terms. This fool is a man without perception of any sort. On the other hand, the fool qua fool was thought of as "a being apart who gossiped and meddled but had no real concern in the affairs of the world around him." When he appears in the medieval drama he voices the mundane, unheroic point of view; he converses with minor characters in the play, the servants, beggars, and soldiers, but only talks *about* the important persons, who seem to be unaware of his existence. He becomes, in effect, "an invisible as well as a detached commentator on the action" (Welsford, p. 231). Like the Grub Street Hack, he is generally ignored by the contemporaries he tries to flatter and emulate. The concept of fool implied here is that of the " 'sage-fool' who could see and speak the truth with impunity. From this point of view, the fool was the truth-teller whose real insight was thinly disguised as a form of insanity" (p. 237).

4. It contains, incidentally, a woodcut of two ships—one full of the worldly (the fools), floundering; the other (St. Peter's ship) full of the spiritually inclined, being pulled to shore by St. Peter's key. The former looks suspiciously like a tub.

5. *The Fool, His Social and Literary History* (London, Faber and Faber, 1935), pp. 235–6. Erasmus employs this aspect of the fool too (*Praise of Folly*, pp. 71ff.); Folly scrutinizes those who pretend to wisdom, the learned, poets, lawyers, scientists, theologians: "the actually worthless character that lurked beneath the veneer of wealth, learning, and respectability" (Welsford, p. 237).

The Hack, by his own equation, is a "Fool among Knaves." In terms of the fool convention, then, his function is to reveal the knaves, without being altogether conscious of it. We must, however, distinguish between the Hack as fool and the dissenters, pedants, critics, and moderns as fools. The latter are essentially knaves, since they are blind to their resolutely wrong paths; the Hack is a knave to the extent that he becomes one of these. His singularity lies in his ability to be one of these in all outward manifestations, but to be sufficiently unchanged underneath (where he is presumably all fool) to carry their policies to their maddest conclusions; the result is that his prophetic side reveals his scoundrelly side, or, as we have seen, his gestures point out the shoddy material of his argument.[6] This is only a provisional indication of the Hack's meaning; but it does give a useful idea of his function as a fool, much of which, though obscured, is somehow felt to be operative.

Finally, it must not be forgotten that the general theme of the sottie, as opposed to the moralists' writings, was the universal sway of Mother Folly. The dramatic form of the sottie is the roll call of the apparently divergent classes of humanity into one simple type: the fool. Thus, the farther we read the *Tale*, the more implicated we all become, as the at first specific aspects of foolishness are generalized.[7]

The central act of any fool comedy is his collision with reality, from which either laughter or illumination can result and the real world or the ideal (that of his madness)

6. We might think of him, therefore, as a reversed Shakespearean fool: a fool who reveals *himself*. The important point is that, as with the traditional fool, it seems to be something beyond him that does the revealing—a mystic force. A mere dolt sounds stupid; but his stupidity does not make sense, as the Hack's does.

7. Cf., e.g., Feste in *Twelfth Night* or Thersites in *Troilus and Cressida*. But the reader of the *Tale* is implicated only up to a certain point; we shall see that a distinction is made between the mad and the sane in the "Digression on Madness" (Ch. 4, sec. iv).

will be shown to be the better. In *King Lear* the ideal world of the Fool's mind turns out to be the real, and when the two have coincided he disappears; in Erasmus' Folly the ideal world of madness is seen to be the only way to survive in the real world; in the romantic madmen of Pirandello the ideal world is shown to be preferable to the real. The great model for a juxtaposition of the ideal and the real, the imaginary and the physical, is, of course, Don Quixote.

Swift had a copy of Shelton's translation in his library at the time of his death, and the *Tale* contains occasional references to the Don, a notable one being in the Aeolist section: "The other was a huge terrible Monster, called *Moulinavent,* who with four strong Arms, waged eternal Battel with all their Divinities, dextrously turning to avoid their Blows, and repay them with Interest" (160).[8] Here the Aeolists are shown, like Don Quixote, tilting at windmills, which their imaginations have created out of a commonplace physical object.[9] The Hack himself bears a certain resemblance to the Don. Don Quixote was a squire who abandoned his town one morning impelled by some disease of the brain, and, thinking himself a knight, went on his way to fight monsters of the imagination. The Hack is not notable for his excursions beyond his garret,[1] but if Don Quixote were confined to his room his meditations would have been as lively as the Hack's.

The Hack's brain is cracked, and presumably after his stay at Bedlam he undertakes the project of tilting with imaginary monsters like the sharp-toothed Time and the penetrating wits. Having spent his life as a Grub Street

8. See also, e.g., G-S, p. 194, "*the Giant* Laurcalco, *who was Lord of the* Silver Bridge."

9. In the over-all picture, however, the Aeolists have more in common with the windmill which tilts at the wind.

1. He does, however, go out to post the works of moderns (34), and he has "just come from" being initiated into Grub Street (63).

Hack, he has suddenly decided that he has a mission to reveal the gospel of modernism. He is given to seeing in the natural process of mutability a crafty enemy with "Nails and Teeth" and a "baneful, abominable Breath," and in the London wits enemies who "pick holes in the weak sides of Religion and Government."

Like Quixote, who "encountering every day phenomena, spontaneously saw and transformed them in terms of the romances of chivalry," [2] the Hack transforms all he encounters into the false reality he desires. Both of them are filled with missions they regard as man's highest duty— Quixote's to champion, and later save from a sorcerer's spell, Dulcinea, and the Hack's to champion the moderns. Although Quixote has become something of an ideal with the rise of romanticism, in terms of Cervantes' novel and in Swift's time he was nothing so simple. Whenever Quixote attempts one of his rescues, in fact whenever he appears, dissension follows, people in their right senses are annoyed, often coming to blows with him or with each other. As Auerbach has commented, "In the resulting clashes between Don Quijote and reality no situation ever results which puts in question that reality's right to be what it is. It is always right and he wrong; and after a bit of amusing confusion it flows calmly on, untouched" (p. 345). "The whole book," Auerbach concludes, "is a comedy in which well-founded reality holds madness up to ridicule" (p. 347). This is not the whole story about *Don Quixote*, but it is very largely the story about the *Tale of a Tub*. The main difference between the Hack and Quixote is between the Hack's self-confidence and Quixote's dignity. The latter shines through Quixote's madness, while the Hack's materialistic background shines through his. In the *Tale* madness has reached the level of language, the rational clarity of which conveyed the dignity of intention behind Quixote's abortive quests. Since the *Tale* has no

2. Auerbach, *Mimesis*, p. 339.

Sancho Panza to point out the real, the language itself has to reassert reality; [3] it does, in fact, reveal the pettiness and ugliness that are mixed with the Hack's noble ("universal Benefit of Mankind") intentions.

To understand the effect of *Don Quixote* "for aesthetic purposes," as Ortega y Gasset has said, "it is essential to see the work of Cervantes as a polemic against books of chivalry." [4] Until the appearance of this book, he says, we had reached poetry "by transcending and abandoning the circumstantial, the actual." This was a timeless world of imagination, and "actual reality" was the equivalent of "non-poetic." Ortega uses the image of a mirage. The imaginary world, the chivalric romance, the epic are the water we see in the mirage. The realistic novel, which was born in *Don Quixote,* is the observation of the dry earth through the cool water of the mirage (p. 27). The result thus bears the world of imagination *within* it, absorbed.

> This offers an explanation of what may seem inexplicable: how reality, the actual, can be changed into poetic substance. By itself, seen in a direct way, it would never be poetic: this is the privilege of the mythical. But we can consider it obliquely as destruction of the myth, as criticism of the myth. In this form reality, which is of an inert and insignificant nature, quiet and mute, acquires movement, is changed into an active power of aggression against the crystalline orb of the ideal [p. 28].

The ideal is reabsorbed into the real. I believe that the nature of the *Tale of a Tub* is illuminated by the distinction Ortega makes here. It is a comparison that should not be carried too far, but which shows the basic structure of

3. We shall see, however, that there are other standards of reality, and that they, in effect, draw our attention to the standard of language (see below, Ch. 4).

4. "The Nature of the Novel," *Hudson Review, 10* (1957), 25.

the *Tale* to be the juxtaposition of the real and the ideal, the world of men and the world of the imagination.[5] Swift contrasts the imaginary world of the Hack with the real world of objects and sensations, where even words work to trip up the proud and unwary. All the real world is hostile to the imagination of the Hack. But the result is an intensification of the poetic.

The purpose of these two chapters has been to discuss a few of the works one automatically associates with the *Tale of a Tub,* either because of their similarity or their influence. There is little doubt that Swift read all of the works I have discussed.[6] But it is not strictly important that he should have read these books; whether he did or not, they stand as a context of thought, pertaining to religion, literature, and style, within which the *Tale* lives its life. For the *Tale* stands as a monument, or a gravestone, to the seventeenth century; its important themes are here, its prose styles, its religious controversies, its literature, and its science. In the light of these, we have seen some of the more obvious things about the *Tale's* form and appearance. Looking back over the works we have discussed in this chapter, it may be noted that they all deal with the problem of the Quixote who collides with reality, whether from the point of view of the madman or of reality. We can conclude that the general theme of the *Tale* is the conflict of illusion and reality; it remains for us to attach this to a specific subject, which will be the aim of Chapter 3.

5. It also offers a preliminary approach to the question of revelation; we can take the ideal as one kind of revelation, and the real as another. See below, Ch. 3, secs. 11ff.

6. For the years when Sir William Temple's library was his main source of books, we have the record of the years 1696–97 in a list Swift drew up of the books he read; from secondary sources or from knowledge of Temple's reading we can infer the rest. We have also Deane Swift's account of his uncle's commonplace books, and the catalogues for Swift's own Dublin library, to which we have referred and shall refer from time to time.

CHAPTER THREE

THE GNOSTIC VIEW OF MAN

> "Why do all the painters have to sit in front of what they paint?" you inquire, irritably.
>
> "Quién sabe," I reply.
>
> "It's because," you continue, "they feel nothing inside them, so they must have it before their eyes. It's all wrong and stupid: it should all be brought from inside oneself." And you spit neatly past the picture onto the grass.
>
> —Dorothy Brett, *Lawrence and Brett: a Friendship* (Philadelphia, Lippincott, 1933), p. 241.

1. The Ancient-Modern Conflict

The *Tale of a Tub* has been accused of topicality and disunity, of having a dated subject or no subject at all. In the "Author's Apology" prefixed to the *Tale* the author himself offers as his subject "the numerous and gross Corruptions in Religion and Learning" (4). While this does not appear to support a case for universality and unity, it does suggest that our first step should be to make a distinction between subject and occasion. "Rarely has so great a book been written in a lost cause," Miriam K. Starkman writes, thinking of the advances made in science and philosophy since Swift's day which render the ancients' position no longer tenable. The *Tale*, she goes on to say,

87

is "one of the greatest satires on progress ever written." [1]
It is true that Sir William Temple had the worst of the
Phalaris dispute and was less than just to Harvey's theory
of circulation; if Swift were equally wrong, it might be
argued, there would be little reason for reading this "dated"
book except as a piece of cleverness.

By looking at the ostensible occasion for the *Tale*, which
is admittedly topical, and comparing its constituents with
those found in the *Tale*, I believe we can see a way through
both of these problems. To review briefly the history of this
segment of the battle of ancients and moderns, Sir William
Temple revived the controversy in 1690 with his *Essay upon
the Ancient and Modern Learning*. This was answered in
general four years later (1694) by William Wotton's *Reflections upon Ancient and Modern Learning*, and more
specifically three years after that (1697) by Richard Bentley
in his proof of the spuriousness of the Phalaris letters which
was appended to the second edition of Wotton's *Reflections*.
Temple's reply, "Some Thoughts upon Reviewing the
Essay of Ancient and Modern Learning" was published
posthumously by Swift in 1701. The argument between
Temple and Wotton has two essential points of contention:
(1) whether the ancients or moderns actually are greater,
and (2) whether tradition helps or hinders the advancement
of knowledge. Temple's importance in the controversy
rests primarily on his emphasis of the second point.

The source of the argument, however, was largely a
matter of individual evaluation; the category of literature
is glossed over by Temple and conceded by Wotton, and so
the primary contention, centered in science and philosophy,
comes down to a question of whether the compass will stand
against the pyramids, whether "the productions of Gresham
college, or the late academies of Paris, outshined or eclipsed

1. *Swift's Satire on Learning in* A Tale of a Tub (Princeton Univ. Press,
1950), pp. 3, 4.

the Lyceum of Plato, the academy of Aristotle, the Stoa of Zeno, the garden of Epicurus." [2] Temple's attachment to the past is a sentimental one, perhaps most tellingly characterized by the quotation with which he ends the *Essay:* "That among so many things as are by men possessed or pursued, in the course of their lives, all the rest are baubles, besides old wood to burn, old wine to drink, old friends to converse with, and old books to read" (p. 470). But accompanying this love of a comfortable past and underlying the vainness of historical knowledge which tends to direct Temple's argument, there are evidences of more significant assumptions.

The second point of contention, perhaps originally deriving from a belief in the ancients' superiority in moral philosophy, claims that by cutting themselves off from the influence of the ancients the moderns have allowed their discoveries in the sciences to divert them from moral progress. In his first paragraph Temple makes a casual distinction that informs the rest of his essay: between "substance" and "form," between "relations of matter of fact" such as scientific discoveries, and the employment of these (p. 430); later, his definitions of learning and knowledge are based on the same distinction (p. 435). Writings by moderns, he says, are only pale copies of ancients' writings, "unless upon subjects never touched by them" (p. 431); thus, it is particularly in form that the ancients excel. Wotton, in his reply, recognizes the area of attack, for he asserts that the ancients were more eloquent than moderns because they cultivated such trifles as eloquence over content: "when Men have spoken to the Point, in as few Words as the Matter will bear, it is expected they should hold their Tongues." [3] The distinction here is the same we saw in the last chapter between a definition of rhetoric that includes both fact and

2. Temple, *Essay*, in *Works*, *3*, 460–1.
3. Wotton, *Reflections* (3d ed., 1705), p. 35.

expression and one that finds expression a veritable hindrance to the truth of fact. Temple's point is that content or discovery for its own sake or for some ignoble end is wrong, and by eloquence or form he means the direction of the discovery to a useful, moral end.

Although the choice of Phalaris as an example was to be interpreted as damaging evidence to the contrary, Temple makes no claim for an inherently greater genius in that which is old, but rather admits that a great man can appear at any time. If he does not believe in the idea of decline he sees no reason to believe in the idea of progress either: there have been regressions and disasters, like the Dark Ages after the fall of Rome, which prove that "knowledge and ignorance, as well as civility and barbarism, may succeed each other" (pp. 433–4). He admits that in the last hundred years there has been a renewal of learning and advances have been made in many fields; but this mechanical progress, he believes, has been paralleled by a moral regression. The object of ancient knowledge was always how to live well (how to produce strong, intelligent children, how to endure pain with fortitude, how to administer justice). But much of the modern renewal of learning has been wasted in theological disputes or abstract speculations, and the important inventions like the compass have been used for commercial exploitation—for "great increases of wealth and luxury, but none of knowledge" (p. 456). Accordingly, the most important fault of the new learning, Temple insists, is its conscious break with the ancient cultures, with a consequent assumption of its own superiority and self-sufficiency. Here we reach the center of Temple's assumptions, and the most important point for an understanding of the *Tale of a Tub:* Temple regards the ancients as being superior to moderns primarily because they built within a context of the wisdom of their predecessors, which guided them toward greatness. The Egyptians, Chinese, and Indians were "mighty reservoirs or lakes of knowledge, into which some streams entered perhaps every age, from the observations or inventions of any great spirits, or transcendent genius's, that happened to rise among them; and nothing was lost out of these stores" (p. 434). Time to Temple is acceptance and absorption into meaningfulness, and this is the advantage that the old, which has survived, has over the most brilliant of modern works.

The moderns oppose to this their theory of cumulative knowledge, "illustrated by the similitude of a dwarf's standing upon a giant's shoulders, and seeing more or farther than he" (p. 432). But the important consideration, as far as Temple is concerned, is how to use the past, whether as an accumulation upon which modern man stands as upon a giant's shoulder, and from which he is largely independent, or as a tradition which guides, counsels, and restrains him. The difference can be inferred from Temple's metaphors. Cumulative knowledge is a heap of sticks which, unless judiciously handled, "suppresses, and sometimes quite extinguishes, a little spark that would otherwise have grown up to a noble flame" (p. 447); but tradition, we have seen, is a reservoir. In Temple's essay "Of Poetry" tradition is the garden in which bees range, choosing "such flowers as they please, and by proprieties and scents they only know and distinguish" [4]—an image which suggests freedom as well as limitation. But the modern, saying that to discover the theory of the circulation of blood one must disregard, not follow, the ancients, may next say that the individual is equally autonomous in his search for morals and law. His pride in himself as discoverer overshadows the discovery, and, as Temple says, "When he has looked about him as

4. "Of Poetry," in *Works*, *3*, 405. He probably gets the bee from Plato's *Ion*, where it is used in the same way: poets are seen, "like the bees, winging their way from flower to flower": *The Dialogues of Plato*, tr. B. Jowett (New York, Random House, 1937), *1*, 289.

far as he can, he concludes there is no more to be seen . . ."
(p. 460). What started Temple off on his essay, he claims,
was the modern's praise of himself and disparagement of
the ancients: this, he says, is "sufficiency, the worst composition out of the pride and ignorance of mankind" (p. 431).
And it is the stigma of "sufficiency" (which Temple only
repeats twice, pp. 460 and 470) that Wotton finds most gal-
ling, and his references to it becomes obsessive.[5]

As everyone knows, the immediate reason for *A Tale of
a Tub*—or at any rate for *The Battle of the Books*—was a
defense of Temple, who appears there rather embarrass-
ingly as informer on the moderns and the "greatest Favorite"
and the "greatest Champion" of the ancients (228). Swift
pays lip service to the greatness of Phalaris and the other
points upon which Temple was incontrovertibly proved
wrong.[6] But minimizing individual evaluation, he puts all
of his emphasis on the theme of prideful self-sufficiency.
In the *Tale* proper this is accomplished by the simple device
of making the speaker—the first-person singular—a modern.
By letting a modern talk, Swift absolves himself of the burden of proving the ancients' superiority, and shifts the
ground of the argument from the general question of who
is greater to the fact—demonstrated by the picture of a
modern arguing for moderns—that such a boast is an ex-

5. Wotton, e.g., pp. 5, 10, 42, 44, and 6–7, where he summarizes his ob-
jections to it.

6. In the battle Phalaris dreams "how a most vile *Poetaster* had lam-
poon'd him, and how he had got him roaring in his *Bull*." Another bone
of contention, Aesop, dreams "that as he and the *Antient Chiefs* were
lying on the Ground, a *Wild Ass* broke loose, ran about trampling and
kicking, and dunging in their Faces" (254). This, the level of Swift's defense
of specific cases, seems to me perfunctory at best. On the other hand, it is
the sort of defense that carries echoes of Temple himself: for example, his
reference to "some young barbarous Goths or Vandals breaking or defacing
the admirable statues of those ancient heroes of Greece or Rome, which
had so long preserved their memories honoured, and almost adored, for
so many generations" ("Some Thoughts upon Reviewing the Essay," *Works*,
3, 571–2).

ample of absurd pride. The reader can assume what he likes
about the ancients: what is made obvious is that the moderns
are trying to pull them down for their own self-aggrandizement. What Swift dramatizes is man's refusal to rely on
anything but himself, which is the inference Temple drew
from the modern position. This then is what Swift abstracts
from the "battle" rather than questions of whether "agricul-
ture, physic, and legislature, or political orders and institu-
tions" were better handled by ancients or by moderns.[7] He
attacks not merely the idea of progress but man's pride
in the idea of progress, not the dwarf on the giant's shoulder
but his steadfast refusal to look away from himself—not
his weak eyes, but his "Eyes turned inward" (240).[8]

The basic assumption which underlies Temple's position
is one of man's helplessness and lack of perception. "The
abilities of man must fall short on one side or other," he
warns, "like too scanty a blanket when you are a-bed, if
you pull it upon your shoulders you leave your feet bare;
if you thrust it down upon your feet, your shoulders are
uncovered"; and he concludes his critique of sufficiency:
"We are born to grovel upon the earth, and we would fain
soar up to the skies" (p. 459). Although Temple's expression of this assumption was probably the important one for
Swift, the secretary, protégé, and friend who copied his
essays, conversed with him daily, and read the books of his
library during ten formative years, it was nevertheless a
view of man which was hardly unique in his time. The idea
of man's helplessness was a part of the conservative complex
of ideas, along with a belief in man's proper concern with
moral philosophy, a distrust of the thinker who aspires too

7. Ibid., p. 498.
8. Cf. Temple's version of the giant-dwarf metaphor: even placed on the
giant's shoulder, "yet we see less than he, if we are naturally shorter
sighted, or if we do not look as much about us, or if we are dazzled with
the height, which often happens from weakness of heart or brain" (*Essay*,
p. 447).

high, and the conclusion that because our reason is limited
and capricious we had better accept the status quo than
change, when the change will inevitably be for the worse.[9]
While these beliefs have much in common with the Christian view of man, they constitute an essentially secular
philosophy, skeptical and antipathetic to Christianity in
that they lead, as in the case of Temple, to a withdrawal and
a refusal to commit oneself—in short, to Montaigne's "pillow." [1]

The philosophical exemplar of this view of man in the
last years of the seventeenth century was John Locke (a
possible acquaintance of Temple's),[2] who more than once
informs his reader that it was the success of the charlatans
of learning in the world that made him undertake his
philosophical examination of the limits of reason. The
Descartes-Locke conflict represents the main issues at stake
in the battle of which Temple's skirmish was a part.[3] To

9. See Clara Marburg, *Sir William Temple, A Seventeenth Century
"Libertin"* (New Haven, Yale Univ. Press, 1932), pp. 1–14, where we are given
accounts of these converging traditions, humanist, *honnête homme*, and
skeptical.

1. I refer to Temple's retirement and refusal to have any more to do
with political life after his disillusionments at the hands of Charles II.

2. Temple is quoted in *An Essay Concerning Human Understanding* and
referred to as an "author of great note" (*Works of Locke*, Bk. II, ch. 27,
sec. 8). It is even possible that Locke and Swift may have been acquainted.
See Kenneth MacLean, *John Locke and English Literature of the Eighteenth
Century* (New Haven, Yale Univ. Press, 1936), p. 9. Locke is not mentioned
by name in the *Tale*, nor is he included in the ranks of the moderns in the
Battle of the Books.

3. Again, as with the interpretation of seventeenth-century literature in
Ch. 1, this polarizing of Locke and Descartes is intended more to illuminate
the world of Swift's *Tale* than the Lockean and Cartesian philosophies. In
the seventeenth and eighteenth centuries Locke and Descartes meant all
things to all men; there was also the Descartes who could lead toward
mechanistic materialism and the Locke whose distinction between primary
and secondary qualities could lead to Berkeley and Hume.

Descartes appears in the *Tale* in connection with his quasi-mechanistic
theory of vortices, which Swift considers a system of the same sort as
Aeolism or any of the others alluded to in the *Tale*. It is a *"Romantick*

the seventeenth century Descartes represented an epistemological view which puts reality inside the individual's head
and sees universals as the only reality; and Locke represented a view which puts reality in the physical world
around us and largely limits the mind to the perception of
particulars. "Reason" for Descartes is the infallible intuition
of the individual mind, and he is highly optimistic about
the ability of other minds to reach the same conclusion:
"Good sense is of all things in the world the most equally
distributed," he writes hopefully in his *Discourse on
Method.*[4] A basic difference between Descartes and Locke
lies in the former's intense desire for certainty and belief
that the mind unaided is all that can find it. "Most of all,"
he writes, "was I delighted with Mathematics because of
the certainty of its demonstrations and the evidence of its
reasoning" (p. 85). And accordingly mathematics became
for Descartes, as other "keys" did for the charlatans of
learning, the basis for a great metaphysical structure which
included a system of values and a god.

Locke, on the other hand, maintains the skeptical belief
that man's mind is radically limited: "The dominion of
man, in this little world of his own understanding, being
much-what the same as it is in the great world of visible
things; wherein his power, however managed by art and
skill, reaches no farther than to compound and divide
the materials that are made to his hand; but can do nothing
towards the making the least particle of new matter, or

System" (167), and when Descartes is killed in the *Battle* he is "whirled . . .
round, till Death, like a Star of superior Influence, drew him into his own
Vortex" (244). He is a symbol of the mind run wild. See also Temple, who
remarked that neither the philosophy of Descartes, who "among his friends,
always called his philosophy his romance," Amadis, nor the prophesies of
Nostradamus were intended for "true stories" ("Some Thoughts," *Works, 3,*
472).

4. *The Philosophical Works of René Descartes,* tr. E. S. Haldane and
G. R. T. Ross (Cambridge Univ. Press, 1931), *1,* 81.

destroying one atom of what is already in being." [5] Consequently, Locke saw no possibility for certainty. Reality being in the physical object, our perception lies only in our senses, and experience—reliance on the senses—is the origin of *all* ideas, including those that were supposed to be innate.[6] Moreover, the understanding remains passive and has very little choice as to whether or not it will accept these materials; it can create no new simple ideas at will. And finally, the mind is limited in the amount of knowledge it can attain, even by these means.

This is the more general position that stands behind Temple's rather querulous one. If Swift received his impetus from Temple's "battle," he saw it, with perhaps greater clarity than did Temple, in the larger context of a conflict between two irreconcilable views of man; at any rate, in the *Tale* we have lost the bickering and the elaborate theorizing on history, and gained the focus which is so conspicuously absent in Temple's *Essay*. Further, Swift found ready to hand in the Descartes-Locke conflict two contradictory epistemologies which offered large possibilities for the satirist who wrote in the tradition of Eachard and Marvell.

II. The Gnostic Heresy

Having seen an indication of the theme Swift draws from the battle of ancients and moderns, we can move into the second half of the subject he claimed for the *Tale of a Tub* in his "Author's Apology," the abuses of religion.

5. *An Essay*, Bk. II, ch. 2, sec. 1, in *Works, 1,* 94–5.
6. In a letter to the Royal Society from Ireland, William Molyneux (who introduced Locke's works to Trinity College, Dublin), reveals himself as a man of real Lockean sensibility: "I here send you inclosed the figures of our Connough-worm, which is reported to be the only poysonous Animal in our Kingdome; but whether it be really so, or not, I cannot assert on my owne experience" (*Philosophical Transactions, 14,* 876).

While Swift's immediate reason for writing against the abuses of learning was the attack on Temple and the ensuing battle, there is no such immediate cause for the religious theme, unless it is Swift's settling, in 1695, in the parish of Kilroot, an Anglican priest in a stronghold of dissenters.[1] However, there may have been more general reasons such as the new threat posed by dissenters under William III's toleration, and the power wielded by Latitudinarians in the Church of England.[2] The tub in the *Tale's* title would at once have suggested to a contemporary the dissenter's pulpit and the direction of attack the work was going to take.

That Swift's intention was, as with learning, to isolate one characteristic which was central to all abuses of religion, is suggested by the epigraph he placed on his title page from Irenaeus' *Adversus Haereses*. The line, which caused Wotton some trouble, is a bit of Gnostic jargon about body and spirit (or so the Gnostics claimed):

> Basima eacabasa eanaa irraurista, diarba da caeotaba fobor camelanthi.

It appears in a chapter on the Gnostics' views of redemption, a difficult doctrine, says Irenaeus, "for every one of them hands it down just as his own inclination prompts. Thus there are as many schemes of 'redemption' as there are

1. See Louis A. Landa, *Swift and the Church of Ireland* (Oxford, Clarendon Press, 1954), p. 21.

2. The Puritans had been willing to accept comprehension with the Church before the Glorious Revolution, when the alternative was an indulgence shared with Roman Catholics from a Roman Catholic king. But now with a Calvinist on the throne and sure of toleration, their prospects were so bright that their thoughts turned from compromise toward power. The situation was bad enough in England and worse in Scotland, but in Ireland, where the Anglican minority was caught between Roman Catholics and Presbyterians, it was desperate. We shall discuss the religious situation in England in more detail in Ch. 4, sec. II.

teachers of these mystical opinions." [3] This is one version
of the initiation ritual leading to redemption: "Some of
them, moreover, say Hebrew words in order to stupefy or
terrify those who are being consecrated, thus: *Basyma
eacabasa eanaa, irraumista diarbada, caeota bafobor camelanthi.* The interpretation of these terms runs thus: 'I in-
voke this which is above every power of the Father, which
is called light, and spirit and life, because Thou hast reigned
in the body.' " [4] There is, of course, no linguistic connection
between the "Hebrew" words and the translation the
Gnostics offer.[5] Thus, Swift's epigraph is a series of unintelligible words with no discoverable meaning behind them,

3. Irenaeus, *Ante-Nicene Fathers, 1*, 345.

4. My own translation from the Latin text of Johann Ernst Grabe (1702),
reprinted in *Sancti Irenaei Episcopi Lugdunensis, Detectionis et Eversionis
Falso Cognominatae Agnitionis seu Contra Omnes Haereses Libri Quinque
. . .* , ed. Adolph Stieren (Leipzig, 1853), pp. 227, 229: "Alii autem et He-
braica nomina superfantur, ut stupori sint, vel deterreant eos qui sacrantur,
sic: *Basyma eacabasa eanaa, irraumista diarbada, caeota bafobor camelanthi.*
Horum autem interpretatio est talis. *Hoc quod est super omnem virtutem
Patris invovo, quod vocatur lumen et spiritus et vita: quoniam in corpore
regnasti.*"

Elsewhere I use the Roberts-Donaldson-Coxe translation from the Greek
text (which goes back to Hyppolytus and Epiphanius, who quoted large
pieces of Irenaeus); Swift, however, used the Latin text, first edited by
Erasmus in 1526. We know that the citation on the title page is from "the
very Learned Mr. Grabe's Edition of Irenaeus" (Wotton, *Observations*, in
G-S, p. 323), because Swift's and Wotton's citations agree with his chapter
division (Bk. 1, ch. 18) as opposed to the more common division (Bk. 1,
ch. 21). Although Grabe's edition did not appear until 1702, we know
from the entry Deane Swift claims to have seen in Swift's commonplace
book that he had read Irenaeus by "*Dec.* 12, 1697" (*Essay upon Swift*, London, 1755, p. 276; cited in G-S, p. lviin.). Thus we must assume that Swift
made his citation from Grabe (the chapter number, if not the actual
words), but that he was already quite familiar with Irenaeus.

5. The words in the Greek text are even more obviously gibberish than
these, which have been doctored by Grabe (see Wotton, *Observations*, in
G-S, p. 323): "Basema, Chamosse, Baoenaora, Mistadia, Ruada, Kousta,
Babaphor, Kalachthei" (Irenaeus, p. 346). A footnote to this edition remarks
that "a very different list, but equally unmeaning, is found in the Latin"
(p. 346n.).

but with an impressive, if arbitrary, meaning attached to them by the Gnostics. On the threshold of the *Tale* it is a symbol of the sufficiency which goes so far as to create its own religion and language.

If the epigraph from Irenaeus is ostensibly an initiation of the reader into the religious mysteries of the book, the second epigraph, from Lucretius' *De Rerum Natura,* extends the theme to literature. It is an invocation of the muses, but one which asks them to keep their distance: the poet wants to find something altogether new.

> ————Juvatque novos decerpere flores,
> Insignemque meo capiti petere inde coronam,
> Unde prius nulli velarunt tempora Musae.[6]

Although the reference to the muses brings out the literary claims of the work, the poet's emphasis is wholly on himself, cut off from tradition, doing something that has not been done before. Even the verb, *velo,* has the primary meaning of "cover up, wrap up . . . conceal." [7] From the context of the quotation it is evident that religion is still present and closely connected with literature.

> Not that I am unaware how obscure these matters are; but the high hope of renown has struck my mind sharply with holy wand, and at the same time has struck into my heart sweet love of the Muses, thrilled by which now in lively thought I traverse pathless tracts of the Pierides never yet trodden by any foot. I love to approach virgin springs and there to drink; *I love to pluck fresh flowers, and to seek an illustrious chaplet*

6. Lucretius, *De Rerum Natura,* Bk. 1, ll. 928–30; bilingual text, tr. W. H. D. Rouse (London, Heinemann, 1937), pp. 68–70. Swift claimed to have read Lucretius three times before or during 1696–7 (see the list in G-S, p. lvi).

7. *Andrews' Latin Lexicon.* The only deviation in Swift's quotation is the substitution of *velarunt* for *velarint,* the perfect tense for the future perfect.

for my head from fields whence ere this the Muses have
crowned the brows of none: first because my teaching is of high matters, and I proceed to unloose the
mind from the close knots of religion; next because
the subject is so dark and the lines I write so clear,
as I touch all with the Muses' grace.[8]

But religion, as the quotation makes clear, has no place in
Lucretius' reasonable world. The exact opposite of the
Gnostics, Lucretius' theme is dark (*obscura*), but his method
is to be lucid. This clarity—and he continually refers to
himself as illuminating dark areas—is opposed to the "close
knots of religion" (*religionum . . . nodis*), the darkness
of the minds which are governed by fear. The light of intelligence, he is saying, needs no religion to guide it.[9]

Both epigraphs present a world in which religion is a
matter for consideration, but is either corrupted or absent.
Thus, we have an indication at the outset of the importance
Swift attaches to religion, and a statement in religious terms
of the view of man Temple has been seen to present in a
secular context. The reference to Irenaeus implicitly connects Swift with orthodoxy and those he attacks with heresy.
Moreover, it is not strange that an Anglican divine should
have made a reference to Irenaeus, who represented both
a source of the primitive church to which the Church of
England attributed its roots and a defender of this institution against the chief enemy of institutionalism, the Gnostic
heresy.[1] The view expressed by Irenaeus was that the few

8. Lucretius, I, ll. 922–34; pp. 68–70. I have italicized the passage used
in the epigraph. Cf. G-S: "certain Discoveries that are wholly untoucht
by others" (129).

9. In *De Rerum Natura* Lucretius presents a world made up of atoms
moving in a void, where religion or a god is sheer illusion. His use of light
imagery may have been a source for the secular aspect of the light imagery
in the *Tale*.

1. On the authority of Deane Swift and John Lyon, we know that Swift

truths necessary for salvation are contained in the message
of Christ to his apostles, which in Irenaeus' own words
closely anticipates the "Apostles' Creed"; any necessary
interpretation, he believed, should be agreed upon by a
council of the bishops who are in the direct apostolic suc-
cession. Accepting this view, the Church of England eliminated all doctrines subsequent to the rise of papal authority,
but kept the episcopate to be a barrier against the individualism of splinter sects.

Implicit in Irenaeus' position is a view of man as reliant
upon guides to the truth and upon a mediating agency between himself and God. One cannot interpret Scripture
or rule a kingdom, he felt, without the aid of the experience
and wisdom of others, without the knowledge of the past.
This is the expression of an epistemological view which,
minimizing the correlation between the independent mind
and external reality, makes it necessary for men to verify
their perceptions by checking them with the perceptions
of others. The Gnostic movement was an attempt to phi-
losophize the Christian religion, minimizing the institutional
aspect in favor of the individual inquiring mind, which
it regarded as the ultimate gauge of truth in the world,
able, for example, to interpret Scripture for itself. What
this heresy stimulated in man was a natural inclination to
separate himself from his neighbors, surroundings and
responsibilities—in short to secede from the human state.

---

kept commonplace books in the days of his service with Sir William Temple
which he filled with extracts from Irenaeus, Tertullian, Epiphanius, and
other Church Fathers (G-S, p. lv). The common heresy attacked by all three
of these fathers was Gnosticism. For an indication of the seventeenth-
century view of Irenaeus, see the anonymous tract, *A Compendious Discourse, Proving Episcopacy To Be of Apostolicall, and Consequently of
Divine Institution*, 1641, and Milton's *Of Prelatical Episcopacy*, 1641, both
of which use Irenaeus as the symbol of episcopal organization; Milton calls
him the "Patron of *Episcopacy*" (*Prose Works of John Milton*, ed. Wolfe, *1*,
642).

It is possible, as some of Swift's contemporaries saw, to place any sect which claims to be an inner, higher form of a religion, or more spiritual than the mass, in the Gnostic line of descent.[2] Indeed, the term "Gnostic," which was alive in the patristic writings, also found currency in seventeenth-century polemical tracts. The Anglicans of Swift's day were particularly aware of the parallel between Gnosticism and Puritanism. Parker, in his *Reproof to the Rehearsal Transprosed,* claims that the dissenters derived from "the Gnostick Fanaticks of old, and the *German* Anabaptists of late" (p. 44), and speaks of their interpretation of Scriptures in terms of "the perfidiousness of the Gnosticks" and "the contentiousness of the Gnosticks."[3] But that "Gnostick" was not used solely in reference to the dissenters may perhaps be indicated by Marvell, who, answering Parker, accuses him in turn of the same Gnostic tendencies, claiming that he has "mis-interpreted . . . only out of love to [his] notion."[4] Parker emphasizes the dissident effects of Gnosticism, while both men seem to associate the label with a misinterpretation of reality. Parker accuses the dissenters of believing in "the old Grace of the *secret ones,* a Grace that is invisible to all the world beside your selves" (p. 47). Parker goes on to extend his accusation to language itself: they "tell fine Romances," he says, "of the secret amours between the Believing Soul and the *Lord Christ,*" and often talk mere "gibberish; they are perfect *Barbarians* to the People, & prophesie in an unknown Tongue; they gaze at the Mystery, and perhaps lay up the Phrase, but yet

2. See M. C. D'Arcy's discussion of Gnosticism in *The Mind and Heart of Love* (New York, Meridian, 1956), pp. 55–62. And, for a reading of the Gnostic heresy into our own age not too different from Swift's reading of it into his, see Eric Voegelin, *Order and History,* Louisiana State Univ. Press, 1956–7, three volumes of which have appeared: volumes 5 and 6 are to treat modern Gnosticism (see *1,* x, xii–xiii).

3. P. 121; cited by Marvell, *Works,* ed. Thompson, *2,* 420.

4. Marvell, *2,* 421. Marvell refers to Parker's accusation on pp. 408, 420ff.

understand its meaning no more than if they had discoursed to them in Chinese or High-Dutch" (p. 56).

Whether Swift himself had Gnosticism in mind is not so important as that some such category appeared to him to catch all the various sects and societies, religious fanatics and scientists, in one very basic error. But, as presented by Irenaeus, the Gnostic heresy was particularly appropriate for Swift's purpose, because it not only expressed a philosophical, or at least mythical, basis for sufficiency, but at the same time manifested the wildest examples of what sufficiency can lead to in practice.

We can see now what the general arrangement of Swift's scheme will be: the free imagination and the chaotic form of the seventeenth-century writings we studied in Chapter 1 are used to represent the illusion that one's own mind is the only worth-while standard of reality; the real then becomes, first, the world of external objects and, second, knowledge as seen in a context of other minds. In the following sections we shall see what assumptions the agents of illusion work under and what form their illusion takes. To do this we shall examine the Gnostic myth, showing that as an archetype of the sufficiency Temple attacked, as well as of the abuses in religion, it offered Swift images which were, in effect, the sources of the moderns' clichés of his own day, as well as their reductio ad absurdum.

III. Sufficiency as a Body

To begin with theory, as opposed to practice, the elaborate and poetic hierarchy of the invisible world which the Gnostic Valentinus expounds in Book 1 of the *Adversus Haereses* is both an explanation of the Gnostic view of man and an example of the Gnostic imagination. We shall examine this peculiar view of man in the present section, and the imagination which produced it in section IV.

Valentinus' story of the creation is far too complicated to recount in detail. Greatly simplified, it claims that man was created by a demiurge who was wholly outside the Pleroma (the world of spirit), "incapable of recognizing any spiritual essences," and who imagined "himself to be God alone." But the demiurge's mother Acamoth, an outcast from the Pleroma (but still of its spiritual essence), had brought forth an offspring "as a consequence of her contemplation of those angels who waited on the Saviour, and which was, like herself, of a spiritual nature." [1] Taking advantage of the demiurge's ignorance, she deposited her offspring in the material body of man which he created. In short, we have the common factor of all Gnostically inclined sects, a spiritual essence which is of God imprisoned in matter.

If the transcendent God does not dirty his hands creating and the demiurge who does is a bungler, it is reasonable to regard creation as worthless if not evil, and to see man's one contact with reality as the bit of spirit he shares with the transcendent God. Thus, a few centuries after the Gnostics we have the Manichean world made by the darkness of evil (matter) impinging upon the light of goodness (spirit), in which angelic spirits, captured by Satan, have been imprisoned in material bodies.[2] A Manichean hymn called "The Soul's Fate" laments,

> I am a god, of the gods I was born.
> But now I am made to know pain.[3]

1. Irenaeus, *Ante-Nicene Fathers, 1*, 323.

2. The primary connection Gnosticism had with Christianity was its use of a redemption; but the redemption of Gnosticism was from a world inherently evil, not from man's own original disobedience as Christians believe. The Gnostic Christ could not, of course, become involved in matter, and so was merely a spiritual illusion of a man, and returned to the Pleroma about the time of his arrest.

3. Quoted by Denis de Rougemont, *Love in the Western World* (New York, Doubleday, 1957), p. 56.

Matter, as Valentinus points out, "is incapable of salvation" [4]—"it must of necessity perish, inasmuch as it is incapable of receiving any *afflatus* of incorruption" (p. 323). Man, being a blend of spirit and matter, can incline in either direction; and so some men have more spirit than others, enough to overcome the material part, and these are the "elect."

Here lies the basic opposition between Gnosticism and Christianity: the Gnostic "elect" is of the same spiritual substance as God, and so all he can do is seek to rejoin the spirit from which he came, find union with the One and escape from the body in which he is imprisoned and from the suffering multiplicity of this earth. He is self-sufficient and does not need to perform "good works" like the members of the church: "as to themselves," writes Irenaeus, "they hold that they shall be entirely and undoubtedly saved, not by means of conduct, but because they are spiritual by nature." [5] No church is required for a Gnostic: it is a personal problem of getting back into the One. All goodness residing in unity, not multiplicity, in spirit, not flesh, it would lower him further into matter to attach himself to his fellow creatures, who are both individual and material. Profane love is "an impossible and blamable attachment to an imperfect creature." [6] Only death is a total release for him, and some Gnostic offspring like the Cathari helped their desire for death with ground glass and the *endura;* or at least they unmercifully purged their priests to minimize the material part. [7]

4. Irenaeus, p. 324.

5. Ibid., p. 324. Cf. Parker's criticism of the dissenters: "an action is not thought gracious so much because it is agreeable to the Law of God, as because it issues from a child of God" (*Reproof,* p. 58).

6. De Rougemont, p. 150.

7. Rebecca West, *Black Lamb and Grey Falcon* (New York, Viking, 1953), p. 173.

With this mythological background in mind, as well as the uncomfortably literal interpretation given it by its devotees, it is possible to see a metaphoric source for many of the clichés that were current in the camps of both moderns and religious fanatics. We should remember, for example, that there was a striking resemblance between the Gnostic cosmology and the world picture offered by deistic reason, of a world started running by God and then abandoned; all the separate acts of creation were left to man, the remaining creative force in the world. The Puritan's clamor to "get into Christ," [8] his feeling of "election," or his view of his body as "nothing else but a prison [to the soul], and that most strait, vile, stinking, filthy" [9] may be regarded as the last breath of clichés whose origin was the Gnostic picture of man as a bit of God trapped in flesh and aspiring toward reunion with the One. At the same time, the religious metaphor includes the moderns who claim to be free of reliance upon the ancients. Thus Swift seizes, in the manner of Eachard and Marvell, upon the cliché of self-sufficiency and takes it back to the Gnostic idea of a body which contains all that is of any value within itself. The reader is made to see, on the one hand, a close relationship between the boast of sufficiency and the taunt of "puffed up with pride" or "windbag"; and on the other hand, he is made to see that from the idea of the self-sufficient body it is only another step to the image of a lone body feeding on its own excrement. Throughout the *Tale* Swift plays with the relationship between clichés and their possibly Gnostic sources, using the human body as a convenient, and

8. See South, *False Foundations*, in *Sermons, 2,* 346; or Glanvill, *Essay Concerning Preaching*, in *Critical Essays*, ed. Spingarn, 2, 277; or the general emphasis on the value of spirit over flesh in a Puritan like Milton (e.g., *Of Reformation*, passim).

9. John Bradford, "Seventh Meditation," *Writings* (Philadelphia, n.d.), p. 412.

logical, symbol to express a theme which is concerned with the nature and proper role of man.

We shall concentrate on two inferences which can be drawn from the Gnostic myth, that of dualism and that of sufficiency. The first of these, which will be developed in greater detail in Chapter 4, is that matter is worthless, a hindrance if not an actual evil, and spirit is good.[1] Thus, the Aeolist pumps himself full of his God (wind), although it distorts his body to the size and shape of a tun; and Jack mortifies, exploits and gives in to his body in the many ways shown in section II. Body being sufficiently weakened, spirit is engendered with delirium, "as Houses are said to be haunted, when they are forsaken and gone to Decay" (283); and Jack eats fire to be like lanterns, "which the more Light they bear in their Bodies, cast out so much the more Soot and Smoak, and fuliginous Matter to adhere to the Sides" (282). The point appears to be the engendering of more of the "good," at whatever expense to the "evil," which ends, in terms of the whole person, in a marked disharmony, a sickness and deformation.

As this reference to disharmony suggests, there are contrasting views of body implicit in the *Tale*. For the present it is sufficient to say that one, the Gnostic, claims that the body is dualistic, and that the good part should be allowed to dominate—by pumping in more of it, as the Aeolists do, or by abusing the bad part, as Jack does.[2] Opposed to

1. This idea does, of course, go back much further than the Gnostics, being in fact one of their appropriations. See E. R. Dodds, *The Greeks and the Irrational* (Boston, Beacon Press, 1957), pp. 139ff. Essentially the same distinction between body and soul is made in Cartesian dualism.

2. The French Quietist, Madame Guyon, upon occasion "found herself so full of this mysterious influence [spirit]" that a friend "had to oblige by unlacing her corsage" (Knox, *Enthusiasm*, p. 330). A physical swelling of the stomach is often reported as a characteristic of spiritual seizure, as in the cases of the Quakers and the convulsionaries of Saint Médard (e.g., ibid., pp. 356, 378). Cf. Eph. 3:19: "that ye may be filled with all the fulness of God."

this view is, on the one hand, the Christian view and, on
the other, what we might call the social view; [3] both of
these picture a harmoniously integrated body.

The more radical Protestants, following St. Paul, were
inclined to connect the body with sin, while the traditional
Catholic view is closer to that of St. Augustine, who, while
admitting that man is helpless and miserable, emphasizes
the essential unity of body and soul and the essential goodness of *all* that God created. "Though from this corruption
of the flesh," he writes in his *City of God,* "there arise certain incitements to vice, and indeed vicious desires," "it
was not the corruptible flesh that made the soul sinful,
but the sinful soul that made the flesh corruptible." We
must not, warns Augustine, permit ourselves "in our sins
and vices [to] accuse the nature of the flesh to the injury of
the Creator"—"it is sin which is evil, and not the substance
of flesh." [4] Blaming all of evil on the flesh is simply associating oneself wholly with spirit and disclaiming responsibility
for one's acts.

The Gnostic and the Christian views are both present
in the allegory of the coats in section 2 of the *Tale,* where
the original coats (the Christian religion) given the brothers
by their father (Christ) are plain and decent and "will grow
in the same proportion with [their] Bodies, lengthening
and widening of themselves, so as to be always fit" (73).
The will (the New Testament) gives instructions for wearing them and keeping them plain and uniform.

These coats are a representation of an external law, the
"visible church"—that by virtue of which one is not oneself but a part of a community. A suit and a will (a church

3. See below, Ch. 4, sec. VII; this amounts to a secular humanist view, and
is based on the Renaissance ideal of the harmonious body and body politic.
4. Tr. Marcus Dods (New York, Hafner, 1948), Bk. XIV, ch. 3, *2, 5*; ch. 5,
2, 8; Bk. X, ch. 24, *1*, 415.

and a Bible) make up the authority which represents "the desire for union" and "the knowledge that the individual by himself is bound to be wrong." [5] At the same time, the idea of dress expressed in the story is the Renaissance-Christian one of the body as the vesture of the soul.[6] Therefore, dress is not adornment but part and parcel of the self, an indication of what one *is*. Ideally, dress and self are mutually informing; but the clothes philosophy based on fashion to which the brothers yield makes the Gnostic distinction we have seen between body and soul (reminiscent of the Ramist distinction between form and content). Neither body nor soul can be said to bear any responsibility for the other.

The tendency toward heresy is symbolized by the tailor, whose sitting "in the posture of a *Persian* Emperor" implies, one suspects, his connection with the Asiatic origins of the Gnostic heresy, and particularly with Persian Zoroastrianism and Manicheism.[7] The tailor represents the separation we have seen between outer and inner, the tendency of the Gnostic mind to think that it can cut the exterior (the body, or the physical world) to the size of its own vision (the soul), whether by altering the institutional aspects of Christianity or by stripping them away altogether and going naked like

5. Charles Williams, *The Descent of the Dove* (New York, Meridian, 1956), p. 38. Price (*Swift's Rhetorical Art*, p. 105), speaking in somewhat more general terms, sees clothes as "the necessary emblem of the *human* animal, the necessary restraint placed upon the passions of the body."

6. Cf. Donne, Sermon XXIII, "Preached . . . Ascension-day, 1622," in *XXVI Sermons Preached by that Learned and Reverend Divine John Donne* (London, 1661, folio), pp. 319-20. See also, e.g., John Selden, *Table Talk*, ed. Sir Frederick Pollack, London, Quaritch, 1927: "Religion is like the fashion"—all men wear clothes, but "Wee differ about the trimming" (cited in Haller, *Liberty and Reformation*, pp. 234-5).

7. Mani (or Manes) was supposed to have been Persian; Marcion and Bardasarres were represented by tradition as Persian. The Gnostic mythos bears close affinities with that of the Zendavesta, the doctrine of Zoroaster.

the Adamites; or, in more general terms, that it can change
the style with the season.[8] Thus one heresy suggests that
clothes can be taken off at the wearer's convenience, another
that the clothes of the Lord-Mayor *make* the Lord-Mayor,
regardless of the person under them (79); yet another sees
the clothes as soul, and the body without its soul as "only
a sensless unsavory Carcass" (80). Peter shows that he sees
no connection between clothes and person when he seeks
to alter his status by tacking on shoulder knots and silver
fringe.

Section 2 of the *Tale* shows that, like the fat man's body
(46), various aspects of religion can grow beyond "a reasonable Compass," until the clothes are simply an image of
the "Nastiness and Lewdness" they cover. The plain, decent suit is the level of reason and decorum; what is added
represents the invention of the Gnostic mind, which takes
one detail (as in heresy, one detail of doctrine) and magni-
fies it beyond all bounds. The brothers wear shoulder knots
which are "as large and as flanting ones as the best" and gold
lace which is the "largest *Gold Lace* in the Parish" (84, 86);
Peter begins to "look big" (105). Here the ideal of physical
beauty as harmony and decorum has been lost in the
swelling, eccentric shape, which will finally evolve into
the Aeolist in section 8. But, we must not forget, this is
a deformity or disharmony which is "good," because it
emphasizes that part which is oneself and sets one off from
his materially alike neighbors. Thus the excessive weight
of modern posteriors (225) is, to a modern, a pleasing deviation from the harmonious norm, like the dwarf's genitals
(147) and the modern theory of indices and digressions
(145). Bentley, "the most deformed of all the *Moderns*,"

8. A common figure in literature is the "English tailor crazed i' the
brain / With the study of new fashions" (*Duchess of Malfi*, IV.2). The dualistic view of body expressed in terms of clothes is developed at length by
Carlyle in *Sartor Resartus*, where a strong preference is shown for the
naked body (the soul) over the clothing (the body).

has a "crooked Leg, and hump Shoulder" (251), and Wotton, it is stressed, bears *"Distortion* of Mind and Countenance" (169). The fat man in the crowd is a deviation from the norm of formal beauty, as are the Hack and Jack when they are beaten up, or the dissenter whose ears are cropped. The alarmingly deformed body of the Goddess Criticism is also such a deviation.[9]

With this physical deformity there is, of course, Wotton's overturned brain, the suggestion of mental deformity, and the repeated avowal of their reciprocal relation: in the same passage we have Wotton's *"Distortion* of Mind and Countenance," his "appearance ordain'd for great Designs, as well as Performances," and "Qualifications of Body and Mind" (169). The diseased body is also in evidence, whether on the inside or the outside, as with the Hack's and the Banbury Saint's poxed bodies. The dirty body is apotheosized in Jack's outrageous behavior: he does not remove his clothes to defecate and refuses to clean himself after his accident, and whenever he jumps into a puddle he comes out dirtier than he went in.

These people, shapes, and acts, together with the Hack's commendation of them, show that the world the Hack is busy arranging is based on Gnostic assumptions, rather than Christian.[1]

The second inference from the Gnostic myth, then, is

9. Cf. "On the Death of Dr. Swift," ll. 467–8, where Swift explains that "He spar'd a Hump or crooked Nose, / Whose Owners set not up for Beaux."

1. The foregoing discussion should, I think, answer the most damaging of the charges made against the *Tale* on religious grounds, those of Empson in *Some Versions of Pastoral* (p. 60). Empson has blamed Swift for exploiting gross physical equivalents for the terminology of the Christian religion, such as wind for spirit. But, as I have shown, Swift's point is that wind *is* physical, that it is a perversion of spirit. A reader of satire should not be tempted by the appearance of distorted physiognomies to interpret a satire as an attack on faces; Swift's satire always presents the perversion of a good, which should not be open to misunderstanding since it is based upon the Christian definition of evil.

the idea that if the "spirit of God" is already in one and
one's own "Nastiness and Lewdness" is all that is valuable,
there is no need for reliance on anything outside one's own
body. This sufficiency is expressed in the *Tale* by the body
which pretends to be autonomous, or at least demands
autonomy. The tailor, an idol raised on an altar, is such
a body; his creating by "a kind of Manufactory Operation"
(76) suggests the same sort of productivity found in the
spider in the *Battle of the Books,* who moves ("four Inches")
in only a slightly greater radius than the immobile tailor,
and produces as solely from himself. The theme of sufficiency is summarized by the bee, who says:

> So that in short, the Question comes all to this;
> Whether is the nobler Being of the two, That which
> by a lazy Contemplation of four Inches round; by an
> over-weening Pride, which feeding and engendering
> on it self, turns all into Excrement and Venom; pro-
> ducing nothing at last, but Flybane and a Cobweb:
> Or That, which, by an universal Range, with long
> Search, much Study, true Judgment, and Distinction
> of Things, brings home Honey and Wax [232].

In the bee we have those who rely on tradition as well as
themselves—the humanist mode of learning, which presupposes more than one person. Thought is expressed in conversation, an interchange and an adaptation of one's own
ideas within a context of the ideas of others. But the spider
is boorish to visitors and, from the looks of his surroundings,
a solitary.[2]

The Mechanical Operation of the Spirit contains the

2. See Walter J. Ong, "Ramus and the Transit to the Modern Mind,"
The Modern Schoolman, 32 (1955), 309: Father Ong notices a shift in
dialectic from an art of discourse, "an interplay of personalities, a give and
take in an existentialist situation," to an art of thinking or reasoning
"carried on in the privacy of one's own head."

image of the quilted cap, which holds in perspiration and keeps out any outside force such as the spirit of God that might try to get in. Under the cap the brain is filled with little animals, whose bites determine whether one will write poetry or whatnot: and the heat of the quilted cap makes them active enough to do their biting (277).[3] There is obviously no further need for God when these animals determine one's course instead.

Moderns, the Grub Street Hack tells us, "deal entirely with *Invention*, and strike all Things out of themselves" (135). Earlier he has explained that the modern's mind is like a mirror of brass: "For, *Brass* is an Emblem of Duration, and when it is skilfully burnished, will cast *Reflections* from its own *Superficies*, without any Assistance of *Mercury* from behind" (103). Being perfectly autonomous, the modern finds his praise within himself too: "*Praise* was originally a Pension paid by the World: but the *Moderns* finding the Trouble and Charge too great in collecting it, have lately bought out the *Fee-Simple;* since which time, the Right of Presentation is wholly in our selves" (47).[4] Phrases like "in our selves" or "out of themselves" suggest submerged metaphors only; but such hints tend to bloom out more specifically into the idea of *within a body,* as when the Hack speaks in section 10 of his own writing as the "whole Stock of Matter I have been so many Years providing," and admits that "Since my *Vein* is once opened, I am content to exhaust it all at a Running" (184); he sum-

3. They cling together, we are told, "like the Picture of *Hobbes's Leviathan*, or like Bees in perpendicular swarm upon a Tree, or like a Carrion corrupted into Vermin, still preserving the Shape and Figure of the Mother Animal" (277). Thus these animals are like the spirit that must usurp the brain, or what is left when the brain is as ruinous as a haunted house. They are only the appearance of a brain, as Hobbes' Leviathan or a carrion corrupted into vermin are only appearances of the body they have replaced.

4. The extent to which the Hack associates himself with moderns can be noticed in his shift from the third person to the first.

mons up the picture of a vessel being emptied, and he is
the vessel.[5] His writing is the contents of his own body,
and he is, he feels, literally pouring himself out on the page
when he writes. He ends section 10 with a significant quotation from Irenaeus, which sums up the image of all being
produced from one's own body:

> But then he [who will interpret this book] must be-
> ware of *Bythus* and *Sigè*, and be sure not to forget the
> Qualities of *Acamoth; A cujus lacrymis humecta prodit
> Substantia, à risu lucida, à tristitiâ solida, & à timore
> mobilis* [187]. (From whose tears she brought forth
> liquid matter, from whose laughter all that is lucent,
> from whose sadness all that is corporeal, and from
> whose fear all that is mobile.) [6]

As the world is contained within Acamoth, so all of human
knowledge (the Hack implies) is contained within him and
has flowed out into his book.

Thus, both the spirit-hoarding religious fanatic and the
self-sufficient modern are covered by one metaphor, which
carries ultimately religious connotations. It is significant
that the same vocabulary was coming into effect in literature, and the Longinian theory of poetry as inspiration was
moving in the direction suggested by the German word for

---

5. Cf. the Aeolists, whose bodies are "Vessels" (153); pulpits are also
considered "Vessels" (58, 156) in this world. Cf. also Temple, who writing
of man's limitations remarks that "There is a certain degree of capacity in
the greatest vessel, and, when it is full, if you pour in still, it must run out
some way or other, and, the more it runs out on one side, the less runs out
at the other" (*Essay*, in *Works*, 3, 458). He could be writing of the Aeolists.

6. My translation; for the equivalent passage, see Irenaeus, p. 321. John
Dunton affords an example of the sort of writing Swift was specifically
parodying here: "and my pregnant Brain labours with so many painful
pangs to be obstetricated, that I verily fear I shall *burst* before I come to
disgorge it thro' my fruitful *Quill* . . . "; or "this were the way to *write his
Guts out*": *Voyage*, *1, 2, 7.*

expression, *Ausdruck,* by Wordsworth's "Poetry is the spontaneous overflow of powerful feelings" and by Byron's "[poetry] is the lava of the imagination whose eruption prevents an earthquake." [7] Seen in this light, the images which the nineteenth-century critics (as well as Voltaire) saw as disrespectful to revelation are, on the contrary, representations of pseudo-revelation. The difference between Gnostic and Christian views of mysticism is, in fact, implicit in these images.

Since the Gnostic feels himself to be of the same spirit as God, he can aspire to perfect union in *essence* with Him. The whole object of life being to escape the evil multiplicity of this world, the union is an end in itself.[8] Although the imagery of ascent, and even of love, is often employed, there can never be a union in essence for the orthodox Christian mystic: the mystical experience is not man reaching up to God, it is God putting a hand down to the individual, a momentary contact or a descent of Grace. The validity of the experience accordingly depends upon what the mystic has learned, and how he uses his knowledge to help others. St. Teresa expressed this view as follows: "In order to please God, and in order to receive great benefits from Him, these benefits must—such is His Will—pass *through the hands* of holy mankind in whom, as He Himself has said, He finds His satisfaction." [9] Thus, the mystic experience can be either a hoarding within, or an outward movement, or communication with others. There are those "who want to be not only God's equals, but God Himself," [1] and there

7. See Abrams, *Mirror and the Lamp,* pp. 47–9.

8. Dean Inge calls Gnosticism "degenerate Mysticism": William R. Inge, *Christian Mysticism,* 1899 (New York, Meridian, 1956), p. 82.

9. Quoted by de Rougemont, p. 150n. See also I Cor. 14:2ff.

1. Jan van Ruysbroek; quoted by de Rougemont, p. 158. Meister Eckhart explains that when "the soul escapes from its nature, its being and its life, and is born into the Divinity, no distinction remains but this: the Divinity is still God, and the soul is still a soul" (quoted by de Rougemont, p. 157).

are those like the bee who want to spread "Sweetness and
Light."

Thus, the inspiration of those parody mystics, the Aeolists, consists of pumping in more wind of the sort they
already contain, which is very like the madman who "reinfunds" his own ordure, "which exspiring into Steams,
whirls perpetually about" (178).[2] The speaker of the *Mechanical Operation* explains that what he means by spirit
is not "a supernatural Assistance, approaching from without" but something "proceeding entirely from within"
(271). The spirit that came to the apostles descended upon
a group of men gathered *"with one accord in one place,"*
instructing them "in the Gift of speaking several Languages" (that is, enabling them to communicate their experience to others through teaching). On the other hand,
since the moderns lack "Agreement in Opinion, and Form
of Worship," as well as any form of communication with
each other, and moreover wear quilted caps, it is obvious
that the spirit they speak of proceeds "entirely from within."

From what we have seen of the body metaphor so far,
we can make two inferences: that "modern" literature and

2. Although Longinus speaks of imitation of the ancients, it is an imitation which is closer to divine occupancy, and derives from the "mad poet"
of Plato (*Ion*, in *Dialogues, 1,* 289); Longinus explains that "many men are
carried away by the spirit of others as if inspired, just as it is related of the
Pythian priestess when she approaches the tripod, where there is a rift in
the ground which (they say) exhales divine vapor. By heavenly power thus
communicated she is impregnated and straightway delivers oracles in
virtue of the afflatus" (Smith and Parks, eds., *The Great Critics*, p. 80).
In the *Tale* we read that the Aeolists are like the "antient Oracles, whose
Inspirations were owing to certain subterraneous *Effluviums* of *Wind*"
(157). Temple's remarks on the oracle should be noted as reflecting the
norm behind Swift's passage: the moderns, Temple says, misinterpreted
"the Priests of Delphos, who like those of Egypt, were a college or society of
wise and learned men in all sorts of sciences, though the use of them was in a
manner wholly applied to the honour and service of their oracle" ("Some
Thoughts," *Works, 3,* 477; see also G-S, p. 161n., for the controversy over
Delphos-Delphi).

religion have no other source but oneself; and that it is the collecting of the grain of something (wind for the Aeolist) within the person, which reveals the individuality of the person (or his "election") by the altered shape of his body or of his silver-fringed coat or, in the preachers and writers, by its exit as a book like the *Tale*.

There is at least a suggestion that this source of the individual in man is intended by Swift to be original sin. The Aeolist finds the replenishment of his "grain" in storms (which the note tells us is to represent sedition, 153), and from a northern chink in his pulpit (Scotland; but the Devil, in ancient tradition, also lives in the north—156). The vapors which rise from the "lower" parts, where the Aeolist grain resides, to cloud the brain are like the "Mists [that] arise from the Earth, Steams from Dunghils, Exhalations from the Sea, and Smoak from Fire" (163), an image which is reminiscent of one used by St. Augustine to characterize original sin: "out of the muddy concupiscence of the flesh, and the bubblings of youth, mists fumed up which beclouded and overcast my heart, that I could not discern the clear brightness of love from the fog of lustfulness." [3] The Troglodyte Philosopher calls this grain a "grain of Folly" which is common to all people—"*only the Choice is left us,*" he writes, "*whether we please to wear them* Inlaid *or* Embossed" (183). In the *Mechanical Operation* the "grain of Folly" becomes "the great Seed or Principle of the *Spirit*" (283, repeated 287). From the account we are given of the fanatic sects it is only too clear that "Seed" is used in its sexual sense. Finally, we encounter the Banbury Saint, who presented with desire "felt his *Vessel* full

3. *The Confessions of Saint Augustine,* tr. Edward B. Pusey (New York, Pocket Books, 1952), Bk. II, p. 20. Cf. the general gist of the "Digression on Madness," which substantiates the resemblance. Another analogue is Rabelais' reference to "the dimming or casting a kind of mist over your animal spirits" which is caused by "windy victuals" (*Works of Rabelais,* p. 263).

extended in every Part (a very natural Effect of strong *In-spiration;*)" (281); swelling with enthusiasm like the Aeolist or with "matter" like the Hack is no more than tumescence. The spirit one finds in oneself, far from being heavenly, is, as we have suspected, carnal. When we use this grain as the foundation of our being, shamelessly building onto it instead of controlling it as best we can, we are re-enacting Adam's sin.

If we look back at the spider and the bee, it is clear that the bee controls his grain of folly, keeping it inlaid, by gathering antidotes from a variety of people and places. The modern, believing that his own individuality is the most important thing he can have, collects and augments this grain, until finally he evacuates it in writing or some other pursuit. Finally, if we regard the idea of sufficiency with which we began as the sort of cliché Eachard or Marvell picked up, it becomes clear that the worth of man's "grain of Folly" is manifest in the logical conclusion of the meta-phor Swift has developed. If the individual's writing comes only from within himself, then metaphorically it is his excretion. The critic, compared to a serpent, emits a poison-ous scent and a poisonous vomit (100); and the Aeolist's communication is through belches. The literature the critic studies is ordure (93), and the confessional Peter estab-lishes is for the "Eructation, or Exspiration, or Evomita-tion" of the crowd (those who cannot write or orate—108). The Hack, as a true modern, is so preoccupied with excre-ment that he misquotes Lucretius in connection with the critic's poisonous scent:

Est etiam in magnis Heliconis montibus arbos,
Floris odore hominem retro consueta necare. Lib. 6 [100].

The footnote translates this as *"Near* Helicon, *and round the Learned Hill, Grow Trees, whose Blossoms with their Odour kill."* The translation omits the adjective "retro,"

which is the misquotation. In the original it is "taetro,"
foul: the flowers' foul odor; but "retro" (which appears
in editions 1–5 of the *Tale*) means "from behind." [4] In the
Mechanical Operation the various excretory organs are
alluded to one after the other, whether directly or by pun:

> Thus it is frequent for a single *Vowel* to draw Sighs
> from a Multitude; and for a whole Assembly of Saints
> to sob to the Musick of one solitary *Liquid*. . . . A
> Master Work-man shall *blow his Nose so powerfully*,
> as to pierce the Hearts of his People, who are disposed
> to receive the *Excrements* of his Brain with the same
> Reverence, as the *Issue* of it. Hawking, Spitting, and
> Belching, the Defects of other Mens Rhetorick, are
> the Flowers, and Figures, and Ornaments of his [279].[5]

The distinction is made, it should be noticed, between
"*Excrements*" and "*Issue*." In other words, the mouth can
be used to emit words or excrement; one purpose of the
quilted cap is to prevent perspiration "from evaporating
any way, but at the Mouth" (277). Accordingly, communication can be either the result of a digestive process or of a
mental process. The "Manufactory Operation" of the tailor
and the "drawing and spinning" of the spider both suggest
the mindless nature of the former.

Excretion will, moreover, reflect the individual's interior
state. We are told that "Physicians discover the State of the
whole Body, by consulting only what comes from *Behind*"

4. In this connection we should notice Swift's exploitation of the ambiguous nature of words pertaining to mysticism: "flatus" and "afflatus"
have the same stem, "wind" and "spirit" are used alternatively in the
Bible, and "eructatio" means both prophesy and belch. With such a set of
terminology, it takes only a slight twist for the whole idea of the mystical
experience to be perverted into the grossest self-reliance.

5. For the punning present in the *Mechanical Operation*, see John Holloway, "The Well-Filled Dish: An Analysis of Swift's Satire," *Hudson Review*,
9 (1956), 24–6.

(145), and this appears to be the case with the spider's flimsy web and filthy surroundings. *"A certain Rottenness or Corruption ensues"* (100) from the serpent's (critic's) vomit. The critics in the "Author's Apology" blow *"Dirt-Pellets"* from their *"envenom'd"* mouths (10); *"envenom'd"* mouth suggests rotten teeth or poor digestion, something wrong inside, with this a sign of it, like the fumes rising from fissures in volcanic earth. Thus, the satirist with rotten teeth gives out only his own breath, the sign of his poisonous insides; he hurts without instructing, and only reveals himself, not his victim.[6] The state of one's insides will, however, depend on his diet, and so pursuing the digestive metaphor to its end, we find that a poisonous breath is admirable because it comes of dining on his own excrements.

But, we ask, where did he get the food he first digested? The bee tells the spider:

> You, boast, indeed, of being obliged to no other Creature, but of drawing, and spinning out all from your self; That is to say, if we may judge of the Liquor in the Vessel by what issues out, You possess a good plentiful Store of Dirt and Poison in your Breast; And, tho' I would by no means, lessen or disparage your genuine Stock of either, yet, I doubt you are somewhat obliged for an Encrease of both, to a little foreign Assistance. Your inherent Portion of Dirt, does not fail of Acquisitions, by Sweepings exhaled from below: and one Insect furnishes you with a share of Poison to destroy another [232].

Here, in unequivocal terms, we are told that one cannot, as the moderns claim, produce a thing out of whole cloth:

6. The degree of poisonousness will depend, presumably, upon the individual's spleen, i.e. the receptacle for waste matter. The Goddess Criticism has a spleen "so large, as to stand prominent like a Dug of the first Rate" (240).

there is no such thing as sheer inspiration from within. If you do not go to the ancients, you must go to the moderns (your contemporaries) and absorb your own environment. Even the Hack admits this when he says moderns strike things "out of themselves"—"or at least, by Collision, from each other" (135). The Hack himself plagiarizes from his contemporaries, retailing their styles, metaphors, subjects, and ideas.[7] Even the broken-down noses and bodies, which offer the best homes for spirit, are shown to have resulted from intercourse with poxed contemporaries (e.g., 283).

The modern's insistence on living off of himself or his immediate environment brings us back again to the Aeolist who will pump in more air or the Gnostic who wants only more of the Pleroma he feels to be in him. In these examples we have seen the assumptions behind a view of man as self-sufficient. It should also be noticed that in the body we find a metaphor which parallels the form of the *Tale,* its bulging digressions and its excessive introductory sections. The Gnostic body is the physical equivalent of the tendencies we traced in Chapter 1, which Swift has taken as just one aspect of the expanding mind which destroys form and body in order to give its spirit expression.

Finally, we must answer the question: can we explain away Swift's preoccupation with the scatological by reference to the Gnostic myth or a metaphor of sufficiency? And we might answer by asking why it is a general characteristic of satire to emphasize excretion—whether as a mode of vituperation or as simply a diminishing device? This is particularly blatant in Rabelais, from whom it might be thought Swift inherits much of his concern with the excremental. The answer is that Swift, like Rabelais, is attacking

---

7. His actions, he explains proudly, are based on "due Deference and Acknowledgment to an establish'd Custom of our newest Authors" (132). In the introduction he says that in wit and style "as well as the more profound and mystical Part, I have throughout this Treatise closely followed the most applauded Originals [i.e. the moderns]" (71).

a view of man that finds him, by virtue of his reason, to have unlimited capabilities. By constantly referring to natural functions they remind man of his human condition. Scatology is particularly useful when the satirist is attacking an overemphasis on mind and reason. In the same way, the most general function of the body metaphor is to reduce mind to its proper level—the moderns and religious enthusiasts exalt mind or spirit, so they are reminded that they have bodies, that their bodies are only reflections of their minds and spirits.

IV. The "Converting Imagination"

The one aspect of Gnostic sufficiency we have yet to examine is the most important for the *Tale of a Tub*. I said in section III that the Gnostic myth was an example of both the Gnostic view of man and the Gnostic imagination. We have discussed the first of these: now if the Gnostic owes no allegiance to a creator or to the world he lives in, reality becomes whatever his own mind determines it to be. For example, the story of Acamoth and the creation was based on Valentinus' interpretation of the Scriptures. His authority for the passion of Acamoth when she is deprived of the Pleroma is Christ upon the cross, when he said, "My God, my God, why hast Thou forsaken me?" [1] Her anguish was indicated when he said, "My soul is exceeding sorrowful, even unto death"; her fear by "Father, if it be possible, let this cup pass from Me"; and her perplexity by "And what I shall say, I know not." [2] In the terms of a metaphor, a tenor is simply attached to any convenient vehicle. The Gnostics, we may conclude, see only what they *want* to see in any word or object. The Marcosian's search

1. Irenaeus, *Ante-Nicene Fathers*, *I*, 327; Matt. 27:46. For the whole passage see Note A, p. 236 below.
2. Irenaeus, p. 332; Matt. 26:38, 39; John 12:27.

for numbers is much the same thing: "whatever they find in the Scriptures capable of being referred to the number *eight*," Irenaeus explains, "they declare to fulfill the mystery of the Ogdoad" (p. 343).

When we saw the Hack refer with admiration to the commentators "who proceed Prophets without understanding a Syllable of the Text" (85), it appeared that words had a different meaning for him than for his readers.[3] Likewise, when the Hack calls Bedlam an "Academy" (166) and suggests that its inmates would be successful lawyers, doctors, fanatic-preachers, and soldiers if released, he means something else by "Bedlam" and "Academy" than we do. He is, in fact, illustrating the Gnostic view of language.

The epigraph—Basima eacabasa eanaa, etc.—offers us the key at the outset to this view of language, and accordingly to the Hack's relation to reality. As we saw, it is a series of meaningless words to which the Gnostics attached an altogether arbitrary meaning. In short, words are divorced from any inherent meaning of their own and made to be simply counters behind which the Gnostic can put any meaning that comes into his head.

In terms of the Gnostic myth, if the world has been botched by a demiurge and the Gnostic himself is of the true God, he can create according to the True; however odd, his creation will be the True. Thus the Gnostic's words create the object they represent, rather than coincide with it. Since the object itself has no reality except as a reflection of his mind, he elevates, as Coleridge expressed it, "Words into Things and living things too." [4] By creating the word, he creates the object.

The Christian religion, accepting a modified Realism,

3. As did "purging the brain" in the passage from Irenaeus we saw above, Ch. 2, sec. v.

4. *Unpublished Letters of S. T. Coleridge*, ed. E. L. Griggs (London, Constable, 1932), *I*, 156.

has usually placed the word somewhere between the speaker and the object. Hooker emphasizes this distinction when he writes, "But for as much as words are resemblances of that which the mind of the speaker conceiveth, and conceits are images representing that which is spoken of, it followeth that they who will judge of words, should have recourse to the things themselves whence they rise." [5] This view leaves God's role as creator untouched: the word only represents God's created object. But if we accept the word as the thing itself—as indeed we must if we accept the Gnostic relation between spirit and matter—there is no recourse, and man has usurped God's function. Thus the clear implication of the dissociation of word and object is the immeasurable enlargement of man's opinion of himself. This view of language is typically Gnostic in its seeing no need for an intermediary between man himself and the world.

The Gnostic imagination is in evidence when the Grub Street Hack interprets the story of Reynard the Fox to contain "a compleat Body of Civil Knowledge, and the *Revelation,* or rather the *Apocalyps* of all State-*Arcana*" (68). It is also in evidence when he sees Posterity as a prince and Time, his tutor, as a baby-killer who is synonymous with death. "Be pleased to remark," he tells us, "the Length and Strength, the Sharpness and Hardness of his *Nails* and *Teeth:* Consider his baneful abominable *Breath,* Enemy to Life and Matter, infectious and corrupting" (32). In terms of this interpretation of facts, the writings of moderns are willfully destroyed by the monster in his "inveterate Malice," and the Hack, accordingly the enemy of all things which have sharp edges, sees in Reason another monster with "Tools for cutting, and opening, and mangling, and piercing" (173). Wits are warlike "Levies . . . all appointed . . . with Pen, Ink, and Paper . . . and other Offensive Weapons" with which to "pick Holes in the weak

5. *Laws of Ecclesiastical Polity,* Bk. v, ch. 19, sec. 3, in *Works,* ed. Keble, 2, 85.

sides of Religion and Government" (39–40), and the Hack, in return, seeks "an Art to sodder and patch up the Flaws and Imperfections of Nature" (174). The intensity with which he names Time a villain or Reason a dissector clearly indicates the point at which the Metaphysical metaphor becomes the Gnostic truth and imagination becomes reality. His most casual remarks are based on such misconceptions: paper is poetry, weight is worth, and obscurity is profundity.

At the same time, the line is crossed between interpreter and creator; or the "false critic" (in the Hack's topsy-turvy identification) becomes the "true critic." As individual words in a scriptural text grow to be unconnected symbols, so humble objects like tubs, gallows, and stages come to represent considerably more than their wooden frames might suggest.

> NOW this Physico-logical Scheme of Oratorial Receptacles or Machines [says the Hack], contains a great Mystery, being a Type, a Sign, an Emblem, a Shadow, a Symbol, bearing Analogy to the spacious Commonwealth of Writers, and to those Methods by which they must exalt themselves to a certain Eminency above the inferiour World. By the *Pulpit* are adumbrated the Writings of our *Modern Saints* in *Great Britain,* as they have spiritualized and refined them from the Dross and Grossness of *Sense* and *Human Reason.* . . . THE *Ladder* is an adequate Symbol of *Faction* and of *Poetry.* . . . UNDER the *Stage-Itinerant* are couched those Productions designed for the Pleasure and Delight of Mortal Man . . . [61–3].

The stories of Reynard and Tom Thumb are other examples of the small object blown up into a great meaning, or, as it may be more convenient to express it: a simple vehicle given an extravagant and unconnected tenor.

Once a misidentification is made or an idea materialized,

it can next be universalized, and the idiosyncratic is made law. The *Tale* itself, we see on the title page, is for "the Universal Improvement of Mankind," and we read of "an universal System in a small portable Volume" (125), or of Peter's "universal *Pickle*" which will "infallibly" take away lice and scabs (109). With universals superlatives go hand in hand: we encounter the "noblest Writers," the "dirtiest Person" (103), and "the noblest Act" (belching, 153). With size goes vagueness, and ultimately mere obscurity and fanciful typography are required to produce a profound meaning: "where I am not understood," the Hack tells us, "it shall be concluded, that something very useful and profound is couch'd underneath: And again, that whatever word or Sentence is Printed in a different Character, shall be judged to contain something extraordinary either of *Wit* or *Sublime*" (46–7). Thus we may conclude that running parallel to the growth of the tenor is the disintegration of the vehicle. We go from words to wind (*"Words are but Wind; and Learning is nothing but Words; Ergo, Learning is nothing but Wind"*—153), from wind (a belch) to complete silence, the most sublime of all, because from it the most can be inferred.[6] As the Hack's intellect searches ever upward, words finally fail him altogether. "The present Argument," he says in the "Digression on Madness," "is the most abstracted that ever I engaged in, it strains my Faculties to their highest Stretch." Thus he expresses it:

THERE is in Mankind a certain   *   *
*   *   *   *   *   *   *
Hic Multa   *   *   *   *   *
desiderantur. *   *   *   *   *
*   *   *   *   *   *   *
*   *   *   And this I take to be a clear Solution of the Matter [170].

6. Cf. *Mechanical Operation*, where "Hawking, Spitting, and Belching, the Defects of other Mens Rhetorick, are the Flowers, and Figures, and Ornaments of" the enthusiasts' (279).

And the attempt to communicate sublimity ends in silence, the inexpressible.

The Hack's preoccupation with Rosicrucian jargon and his cabbalistic concern with numbers are pointers to the specifically Gnostic nature of his imagination; [7] but the most obvious example of the Gnostic imagination in the *Tale,* as it was in Valentinus' mythos, is the modern's metaphor of the sufficient body. The Hack's own definition of this imagination comes at a point so late in the *Tale* (section 11) that his use of the third-person plural hardly covers the self-portrait with which we have grown familiar. His passages dealing with Jack, he tells us, "will furnish Plenty of noble Matter for such, whose converting Imaginations dispose them to reduce all Things into *Types;* who can make *Shadows,* no thanks to the Sun; and then mold them into Substances, no thanks to Philosophy; whose peculiar Talent lies in fixing Tropes and Allegories to the *Letter,* and refining what is Literal into Figure and Mystery" (189–90). In short, the imagination interprets in whatever way is necessary at the moment: the fable of Tom Thumb is *symbolically* "the whole Scheme of the *Metempsychosis*" (68), while the spiritual person (because of the nature of modern bodies) is interpreted so *literally* that the poxed body is the best vessel for inspiration (66–71, 283).

What is "Figure and Mystery" on the level of the Hack

7. See the appendix on dark writers in G-S, pp. 353–60. The nineteenth-century Rosicrucian apologist, Hargrave Jennings, claimed that they "adopted as their matter the advice of one of their number, one of the Gnostics of the early Christian period": *The Rosicrucians, Their Rites and Mysteries* (London, 1879), p. 21. Rosicrucianism and Gnosticism are connected in the *Tale* (187), where the "Brother of the *Rosy Cross,*" the *Opus Magnum* and the Rosicrucian Eugenius Philalethes (Thomas Vaughan) are linked with Bythus, Sige, and Acamoth. The aim of both Rosicrucian and alchemist was, like the Gnostic, to ascend toward the source of spiritual and material power (what they called the Sephirotic ladder). The alchemist did this by spells, symbols, and concentration. See particularly A. E. Waite, *The Real History of the Rosicrucians founded on their own manifestoes, and on facts and documents collected from the writings of initiated brethren,* London, 1887.

is a concrete drama in the allegorical narrative. Every action
of the brothers spells out on a stage the metaphorical movement of the Hack's imagination. As he creates symbolic
pulpits out of tubs, Peter creates permission for the wearing of silver fringe from his father's will. But while the
brothers' adventures are a dramatization, they are also a
historical chronicle, and this is the aspect which is most
important to an understanding of the *Tale;* for, in effect,
the allegory reveals Gnostic imagination to be at the bottom
of the split church, the cause of the destruction of unified
Christendom.

Peter's interpretation of the will according to his own
lights, and Jack's according to his, represent the corruption
of church doctrine which caused, and which resulted from,
the Reformation. All the fashions of shoulder knots and
silver fringe to which Peter succumbs, dragging his brothers
after him, are the "heresies" of the Roman Church; [8] the
attempt to remove these excrescences, most conscientiously
carried out by Martin, is the Reformation; while the too
violent stripping away which damages the fabric is the sign
of the excesses of the radical Protestant sects. The excrescences on the coats or the bare skin showing through rents
in the cloth are only the outward manifestations of "converting Imagination." Whatever devious routes Peter and
Jack take, they meet, just as their different styles of dress
look the same at a distance: "For, as it is the Nature of Rags,
to bear a kind of mock Resemblance to Finery; there being
a sort of fluttering Appearance in both, which is not to be
distinguished at a Distance, in the Dark, or by short-sighted

8. Swift would seem to be suggesting a view like that of Adolf Harnack
in his monumental study of dogma, who declared that the church's harden-
ing of dogma as a reaction against the Gnostic heresies led ultimately to
the absorption of most of the Gnostic doctrine, in one form or another,
within the church, and that what became the Roman Church was essentially Gnostic in character. See Harnack's *Outlines of the History of Dogma,*
tr. Edwin Knox Mitchell, Boston, Beacon Press, 1957.

Eyes: So, in those Junctures, it fared with *Jack* and his Tatters" (200). Because of the importance given to this history in the *Tale,* we must examine the respective imaginations of Peter and Jack in the light of their historical counterparts.

Peter's brand of Gnosticism is centered on interpretation and criticism. He brings scholastic as well as cabbalistic methods to bear on the will in order to find his own meaning in it, a sanction for the wearing of individualizing ornaments. He is the "learned" brother, said to be "well skill'd in Criticisms," and he interprets in a *"Mythological,* and *Allegorical* Sense" (88) like the critic. Thus Peter's intellectual Gnosticism in sections 3 and 4 is paralleled by the critic's interpretation of texts in section 3; and the critic's Bentleyan quoting from the fifth book, eighth chapter, of an author "whose Works have many Ages since been entirely lost" (102) prepares us for Peter's interpreting himself to be God and bread to be mutton and claret in section 4. The Bentleyan critic is essentially the historical critic, as opposed to the cognitive, or exegetical, critic. Bentley brings to bear chronological, linguistic, and stylistic tests on the work of art; but, he tells us, "What force of wit and spirit in the style, what lively painting of humour, some fancy they discern there, I will not examine nor dispute." [9] He completely ignores its intrinsic merit, and so its intrinsic meaning, making its value and meaning depend rather on who wrote it, when, and where. To Swift, his scholarship and criticism would appear tools without an end, since they did not derive meaning from the work itself. The true critic (92) searches as deeply into the cheese or the nut, but is interested in the meat rather than the maggots or the worm, in the moral to which it points rather than in questions of whether it was written by Phalaris or a medieval monk. It

9. Richard Bentley, *Dissertation on the Epistles of Phalaris,* 1695 (London, 1816), p. 361; cited in *Critical Essays,* ed. Spingarn, *1,* lxxxviiin.

is another way of connecting religion and learning to show that the Bentleyan critic is as important a figure in the modern world as the tailor is in the world of Peter, Martin, and Jack, and the two are, in fact, equated (102).[1]

As the parallel between Peter and the critic suggests, the emphasis in these sections is made to fall less on bodies of dogma or particular theories than on the attitude that produces them. It was this attitude which caused the schoolmen to be called "moderns" from the first, as opposed to the "ancients" or *"antiqui theologi,"* the fathers.[2] The ancients, the writers of the patristic tradition we discussed in Chapter 2, believed that reality can only be established by analogy, that is, in terms of other people, other times, other ideas. Thus, they made their teaching a matter of studying texts, a word-by-word, line-by-line exegesis which they considered the best way to impart doctrine. But while excellent for guiding conduct, this method lacked the requirements necessary for the systematizing of doctrine. The scholastic revolt of the twelfth and thirteenth centuries (Peter's madness) attempted to remedy this situation, necessarily bringing into play dialectic, the ordering power of the mind, which assembled diverse texts and tried to make one consistent structure out of them, but, like the Bentleyan critic, in the process destroyed the autonomy of the work itself. The revolt of Erasmus and, more important, of Luther

1. This is also evident in the Hack's extreme deference, in his calling critics "my *good Lords*" (92) and "my Patrons" (104); and the head of the ass, which we shall see is connected with the Gnostic God, is lifted from the Phalaris controversy and placed firmly on the critic's shoulders. Temple's classification of critics is similar to Swift's: "Some Thoughts," *Works, 3,* 491. Significantly, Temple compares detracting critics to the levelers (p. 492), once again linking religion and learning. Wotton, too, links the two themes, of the critic and the theologian, concluding his *Reflections* with chapters on philology and theology as two aspects of the same thing (chs. 18, 19).

2. See Wotton, *Reflections*, p. 376; and H. M. McLuhan, "Edgar Poe's Tradition," *Sewanee Review,* 52 (1944), 28.

came as an attack on three centuries of scholasticism which had sacrificed instruction in morality for doctrinal organization, what the Book says for a "system." [3] They advocated a return both to grammatical exegesis and to the simpler orientation of the early fathers. It is significant, however, that Calvin, while disregarding the fathers as well as the schoolmen, built his own system on the scholastic dialectic, and associated himself in seventeenth-century Anglican eyes with those other "Goths of the Sorbonne," the Roman Catholics. Hooker could say of the Puritans that they saw what they *wanted* to see in any object; "when they read the Scripture," he wrote, "they may think that every thing soundeth towards the advancement of that discipline [i.e. of their own], and to the utter disgrace of the contrary." [4]

The intellectual respectability for Puritan epistemology came from another "Goth of the Sorbonne," Peter Ramus, who "purified" Aristotelian logic until it became a kind of intuition. While Aristotle regarded logic as "a product of the mind and not of things," Ramus' Puritan followers claimed a dogmatic Realism for their logic; if the mind corresponded exactly to the laws of nature, they argued, then what it arrived at had an objective reality in nature. "When we define," Alexander Richardson said, "do we not lay out the thing? *ergo*, if *genus* were onely mental, it could not give essence: so *causa, effectum,* and all other arguments are things real in nature, howsoever my Logick takes hold of them." [5] An example of the mind's power to create

3. Swift expresses his view of these dialecticians and philosophers in his "Letter to a Young Clergyman": even pagan philosophers, he says, have some value because they deal with moral problems; but not scholastic theology—"Neither did our Saviour think it necessary to explain to us the Nature of God; because I suppose it would be impossible, without bestowing on us other Faculties than we possess at present" (*Irish Tracts,* p. 73).

4. Hooker, preface, ch. 3, sec. 9, in *Works, 1,* 183.

5. Quoted by Miller, *New England Mind,* p. 147; see pp. 146ff.

or order reality is Ramus' theory of dichotomous division, or the dividing of every idea or substance into two components—not three or five, but two; as the Hack divides the oratorial machines into not seven or nine, but three. Men are divided into drinkers and nondrinkers, or godly and ungodly. Bacon commented on how the Ramists "torture things with their laws of method, and whatever does not conveniently fall in these dichotomies, they either omit or pervert beyond nature." [6] On a less intellectual level, this assumption of correspondence took a less literal, but just as meaningful, form. The Puritan saw in every snake the devil, in every stubbing of his toe a test, and in his every action he thought of himself as engaged in a contest of good and evil. To the Puritan settlers of New England the "wilderness" they entered was the "Wilderness" in which the ancient Hebrews wandered for forty years, and King James was the Pharaoh. [7] According to Ramist rhetoric, metaphors are mere decoration for a logical structure; but there is a difference maintained between tropes or metaphors and *types*, the former being decorative because of human and perhaps eccentric origin, the latter being essentially *true* because they come from God's imagination. [8]

6. *Works of Francis Bacon*, ed. Spedding, Ellis, and Heath (London, 1857–74), *1*, 663; quoted by P. A. Duhamel, "The Logic and Rhetoric of Peter Ramus," *Modern Philology*, *46* (1949), 169. For a more comprehensive view of Ramus, see the articles by Walter J. Ong: we have alluded to "Ramus and the Transit to the Modern Mind"; another is "Ramus' Rhetoric and the Pre-Newtonian Mind," *English Institute Essays*, 1952 (New York, 1954), pp. 138–70. Father Ong stresses the importance of the spatial relation for Ramus' dichotomies (they were usually represented on charts).

7. See Charles Feidelson, Jr., *Symbolism and American Literature* (Univ. of Chicago Press, 1953), p. 80.

8. See Jonathan Edwards, *Images or Shadows of Divine Things*, ed. Perry Miller (New Haven, Yale Univ. Press, 1948), p. 6; and Haller, *Liberty and Reformation*, pp. 26–7. Haller traces this view to Foxe for its popular expression: all history, Foxe claims, is occupied with the struggle of Christ and Antichrist for the souls of men. "The climax of that struggle began

Thus, we can see that to an Anglican like Swift, the Puritan who firmly believed that the snake he encountered was a type of the devil, or he himself in his martyrdom was a type of the saints, or even of Christ, would appear to be *creating* meaning. Satan then would be any enemy, such as Charles I.

These symbols are essentially Ramist "arguments"— "whatever is affected to the arguing of something else." [9] Thus, cause argues effect, or a snake argues Satan, and the Ramist believed that presentation was all that was necessary for this to be intuitively perceived. In Ramist logic, as in Gnostic, the "test of conclusions" was "not so much by evidence or utility as by the soul's immediate approbation or revulsion." [1] The mind was bound to assent to a true proposition when presented with one, Ramus believed. [2] But in practice this involves a certain conditioning. For example, as P. A. Duhamel has pointed out, Aristotle saw a dichotomy as "a fallacious begging of the question; it is a weak syllogism with the third term omitted. The division of men into smokers and nonsmokers is a thesis, a proposition to be proved" (p. 170). In order to see this as so apparent as to require no proof and in order to create the argument in the first place, one has to belong to an "elect," of the sort the Hack presupposes as his ideal readers. [3] For other people, this would appear a movement toward what the Gnostic called Secret Meaning, and to such an ex-

---

with the Reformation and is destined to end in Christ's approaching final triumph in England" (p. 47): a parallel to the scientific optimism of the moderns.

9. Quoted by Miller, *New England Mind*, p. 124.

1. Ibid., p. 22.

2. The central point of Ramus' "purification" of Aristotle was his reduction of the Aristotelian syllogism to a corroborative function; it would be brought into use only as a check in his "arguments." The similarity between the epistemology of Ramus and Descartes is obvious.

3. Notice that the same nomenclature runs through all of the Gnostically inclined groups: only the Calvinist "elect," the Gnostic "spiritual," the Catharist "perfecti," the Rosicrucian "initiates" can understand.

pression of transcendent significance as "Basima eacabasa
eanaa irraurista." To the Puritans, for example, "visible
church" means something that it does not mean to Anglicans, just as "Bedlam" means something to the Hack that
it does not mean to us.

Thus both Peter and Jack represent the epistemological view Anglicans attributed to the schoolmen which assumes an exact correlation between the mind's ideas and
the objective world, and this assumption is shown to be the
beginning of all the trouble since the primitive simplicity
of the early days, when the brothers simply slew giants and
dragons.

But while some Puritans could be included in the scholastic trickery of intellectual Gnosticism, the general contrast Swift sets up in the *Tale* finds all radical Protestants
in the camp of Jack. This second kind of Gnosticism has
the same effect as that which we have discussed, but its
source of authority is different; it attributes the power to
see truth to the spirit rather than to the intellect. Spiritual
Gnosticism is born in section 6 of the *Tale,* where Jack's
handling of his coat is based on passion rather than slyness,
calculation, or erudition; Jack is, in fact, motivated more by
"Hatred and Spight" of Peter than by the rule of the will
(137). Moreover, as we see in section 11 where Jack's
escapades parallel Peter's inventions in section 4, Jack refuses to use his mind, letting God's predestining guide him
wherever it will.

The Gnostic ideal, it has been pointed out, "always
swings between a self-centred ideal and one of complete
abandonment or surrender to fate or a higher power." [4]
How then, we might ask, can the abhorrence of learning
and intellectual pretensions of Jack and the radical Protestants—their Montanism—be classed with the intellectual
pride of a Peter or of the scholastics? Hooker noticed the
Puritan's tendency to believe that "to be ripe in faith were

4. D'Arcy, *Mind and Heart of Love,* p. 60.

to be raw in wit and judgment; as if Reason were an enemy
unto Religion, childish Simplicity the mother of ghostly
and divine Wisdom." [5] The Puritan Sydrach Simpson's
contention, in a sermon before the University of Cambridge,
was "That Humane Learning is not a preparation appointed
by *Christ,* either for the right understanding or right teaching the Gospel." [6] Ronald A. Knox has contrasted Gnosticism and enthusiasm as opposites, the one intellectual and
dogmatic, the other free of dogma. The difference for our
purposes, however, lies in the distinction between thought
and feeling: the Gnostic, Monsignor Knox says, "offered to
outbid the Christian message by subtleties, by over-refine-
ment of theology"—by too much thinking; while the Montanist and Donatist [7] tried to clear away learning and speculation—by a reliance on feeling, or by faith as opposed to
reason.[8] But the latter, saying that one relies on Christ as
opposed to a visible church, is ultimately more subjective,
though less strictly intellectual, than relying on one's own
reason.[9]

5. Hooker, Bk. III, ch. 8, sec. 4, in *Works, 1,* 462. There is only a slight
transition from the virtue of "simplicity" to madness, as Hooker shows:
"Shew these eagerly-affected men their inability to judge of such matters;
their answer is, 'God hath chosen the simple.' Convince them of folly, and
that so plainly, that very children upbraid them with it; they have their
bucklers of like defence: 'Christ's own apostle was accounted mad: the best
men evermore by the sentence of the world have been judged to be out of
their right minds'" (preface, ch. 3, sec. 15, ibid., *1,* 191; the quotation is
Acts 26:24).

6. Quoted by William Dell, *Tryal of Spirits,* London, 1653; cited by
Mitchell, *English Pulpit Oratory,* p. 126.

7. Montanism was the use of prophecy and spiritual seizure as modes of
knowledge; Donatism sought to make the validity of priests contingent upon
their personal goodness, not their consecration, a subjective decision which
leads to an "elect" or to an "invisible church" (see Ch. 4, sec. II).

8. Knox, *Enthusiasm,* p. 25.

9. The enthusiast's cry, "I am for Christ," meant, as Monsignor Knox
points out, "that you were appealing away from ecclesiastical authority to
the validity of a private revelation" (ibid., p. 13). See Hooker's attack on
the Puritans for hiding behind the "law of Christ" to satisfy their own
desires (Bk. VII, ch. 16, sec. 1, *Works, 3,* Pt. I, 312).

The answer is that often behind the Gnostic's freedom of invention was a similar distrust of learning, based on his trust in the spiritual essence he shared with God, for which authority was found in the New Testament virtue of "simplicity."[1] As Irenaeus explains it, "they adduce the following passage as the highest testimony, and, as it were, the very crown of their system:—'I thank Thee, O Father, Lord of heaven and earth, because Thou hast hid these things from the wise and prudent, and hast revealed them to babes.'"[2] Abhorrence of learning removes the last vestiges of one's dependence on tradition, on others, on anything outside oneself, and leads to the height of intellectual arrogance; for, as Swift writes, "it is a Sketch of Human Vanity, for every Individual, to imagine the whole Universe is interess'd in his meanest Concern" (275–6).

These, then, are the two kinds of self-sufficiency which figured importantly in world history for a seventeenth-century Anglican; the Hack and his friends, who demonstrate their imaginations in the digressions, serve to place the historic error in a timeless present. That it might happen again at any moment is half of the inference; the other half

1. Here we can see where Swift differs from Erasmus. The latter is attacking the scholastics and wishing for a return to the primitive simplicity of the Church Fathers. But he has fallen into the opposite error, Montanism, and so, as far as Swift is concerned, he is painting another form of intellectual arrogance in pretty colors. Swift, with the Church of England, agreed in desiring a return to primitive simplicity of doctrine; but they did not confuse this with simplicity of mind.

For an example of the difference, cf. *Praise of Folly* (commending): "the spirit, as conqueror and the more vital, will overmaster and absorb the body . . ." (Erasmus, p. 123). *Mechanical Operation:* "All Endeavours must be therefore used, either to divert, bind up, stupify, fluster, and amuse the *Senses,* or else to justle them out of their Stations; and while they are either absent, or otherwise employ'd . . . the *Spirit* enters and performs its Part" (269–70)—which is no very admirable part, we are assured. See Note C, p. 249, below.

2. Irenaeus, p. 345. The quotation is Matt. 11:25.

is: it has already happened and look where it has left us. The fable of the brothers is to the Hack's world as Adam's fall is to the larger picture which includes both of these.

We have thus seen, in metaphor and in allegory, the assumptions upon which the Gnostic illusion is based; we have yet to see its results and what we may call its *underlying* assumptions, which will be the subject of our final chapter.

v. The Appeal to the Senses

Before we see what the results and wellsprings of Gnostic sufficiency are, we must summarize the distinctions that may have appeared between the Hack's world and the real world. It is convenient to call the latter real; it is, however, the world Swift has created and put the Hack into with his alien assumptions, like dropping a bit of the Pleroma into matter.

While the Hack's world is an Idealist world in which external reality is an image of the mind, Swift's world is a Realist, a Lockean world in which external objects are the only reality. An example of their contact is the view of communication we have seen expressed in the Hack's straining of his faculties "to their highest Stretch," which ends in a row of asterisks: in Swift's world this view leads to an occasion like that when Jack was "not able to call to mind . . . an Authentick Phrase for demanding the Way to the Backside," and so his accident resulted (191).

By the standards of the real world there is very little communication in the Hack's world. The modern's words do not stay posted long enough for anyone to read them. No communication is possible between members of Parliament, one sleeping while the other talks and vice versa (57); there is no attempt at communication on the part of the senators "who are silent in the *House* [where they are

supposed to communicate], and loud in the *Coffee-House*"
(75).[1] Only adepti can understand the *Tale,* the Hack implies. His book, he says, will be valuable to the superficial
reader (i.e. the critical reader, who "will be strangely pro-
voked to *Laughter*"), and to the ignorant reader (i.e. the
normal reader, who "will find himself disposed to *Stare*").
"But the Reader truly *Learned* . . . will here find sufficient Matter to employ his Speculations for the rest of his
Life" (185). The latter is, of course, of the "elect," who
can appreciate what has been "spiritualized and refined
. . . from the Dross and Grossness of *Sense* and *Human
Reason*" (61–2).

With human reason we tend to see something else. As
we saw in Chapter 2, while the Hack is pointing at and
describing his world, the reader sees the accustomed objects
of the real world. The "Dedication to Prince Posterity,"
the Hack's first appearance, virtually tells the reader how
to read the *Tale;* it is riddled with the Hack's verbs of
showing or looking at, gestures which, when followed, reveal not at all what the Hack expects them to. He begins
by saying, "I here *present* Your Highness with," etc., and
tells the prince that his virtues "make the World *look
upon*" him, and that it is his "inherent Birthright to *in-
spect*" and *"peruse"* the works of the moderns. The prince
should command Time to *"show"* him these works. We
have already noticed the physical destruction the Hack
invents to explain their absence: he beseeches the prince
"to *observe*" Time's terrible scythe, "to *remark*" his nails
and teeth, to *"consider"* his poisonous breath, and to *"reflect"* whether anything could stand up against him (30–2).[2]

1. Much of the conversation we overhear consists of profanity, language
beginning to lose its meaning. Assigning *"damn'd Sons of Whores, Rogues,
Traytors"* (121) to inoffensive objects, calling one what he is not with
indeterminate titles, is another way to nonmeaning.

2. I have omitted Swift's italics and substituted my own in these excerpts
for emphasis.

But when the reader does remark, consider, and reflect, he notices that the criminal does not fit the crime, which the Hack has described as follows:

> Who has mislaid them? Are they sunk in the Abyss of Things? 'Tis certain, that in their own Nature they were *light* enough to swim upon the Surface for all Eternity. Therefore the Fault is in Him [i.e. Time], who tied Weights so heavy to their Heels, as to depress them to the Center. Is their very Essence destroyed? Who has annihilated them? Were they drowned by *Purges* or martyred by *Pipes?* Who administered them to the Posteriors of ———? [32].

The Hack's verbs—"mislaid" and "sunk"—suggest an accident rather than a murder; nor is their drowning related to the cutting capabilities ascribed to Time. If the reader follows the train of thought, from Time to tutor, to regent, to Death with scythe, to dragon, to "Usurping *Maitre du Palais*," to a Herod-like massacrer of innocents, to Moloch (33), to Immortality's priest who intercepts her sacrifices (34)—if we follow these changes of identity, which are paralleled by the changing of the modern writings themselves into toilet paper, pie papers, and window panes (36), the determining element becomes not malice but natural mutability, with the shifting water in which the works disappear its symbol.

It becomes apparent that "common sense" gives a different answer from the Hack's to "where are they?" In terms of sensory proof, before a day has passed "there is not one [of the modern works] to be heard of"; these productions "are never likely to reach [Prince Posterity's] Eyes" (33). When searched for, they "delude our Sight" (34), and one must be sent "for ocular Conviction to a *Jakes*, or an *Oven*" (36).

We can see emerging here the split between speaker's

and reader's awareness we noticed in Chapter 2. Swift gives us a specific image of this relationship a page later:

> If I should venture in a windy Day [says the Hack], to affirm to *Your Highness*, that there is a large Cloud near the *Horizon* in the Form of a *Bear*, another in the *Zenith* with the Head of an *Ass*, a third to the West-ward with Claws like a *Dragon;* and *Your Highness* should in a few Minutes think fit to examine the Truth, 'tis certain, they would all be changed in Fig-ure and Position, new ones would arise, and all we could agree upon would be, that Clouds there were, but that I was grossly mistaken in the *Zoography* and *Topography* of them [35].

When the Hack says he sees a dragon with claws one min-ute which is gone the next, only the cloud remaining, we see, if we have not already, that the shifting shapes from tutor to dragon are in the Hack's mind. The watery ele-ment and the cloud are on one level of reality, and the bodies that *appear* to be in them are on another.

The progression from image to image is like that we followed in Marvell, but with the reader's mind left to make the connections. Taking the image of the cloud for example, the reader may recall the "vast flourishing Body" the Hack a few pages before claimed the moderns to be (31). The adjectives "vast" and "flourishing" imply a vege-table quality which may remain in the reader's mind when he is asked why the books sink of their own weight. In the second place, the "vast flourishing Body" may be recalled when the reader reaches the "large Cloud" which like the modern writings is without form and without substance, changing and vanishing with every draft and yet impressive in a large cloudy way. Finally, there appears to be a rela-tion between the bear, the ass, and the dragon the Hack sees in the cloud and the names with which he ends his proof. Having to abandon the writings themselves, the Hack ends the section affirming the physical existence of "a certain Poet called *John Dryden* . . . another call'd *Nahum Tate* . . . a Third, known by the Name of *Tom Durfey* . . . also one Mr. *Rymer,* and one Mr. *Dennis* . . . a Person styl'd Dr. *B - - tl - y* . . . the Person of *William W - - tt - - n,* B.D." (36–7). These objects, like books "called" or "styled" certain names, are the sensory reality under the cloud of modern writing.

The images in the "Dedication to Prince Posterity" thus amount to a distinction between the two worlds of the Hack and of the *Tale,* and an announcement of the correct way to read the book. The three assumptions necessary for the reader are the employment of common sense, of common analogy, and of consistency.

First, "sense" in the *Tale* can mean perception through the intellect ("common sense") or perception through organs of sensation. "But when a Man's Fancy gets *astride* on his Reason, when Imagination is at Cuffs with the Senses, and common Understanding, as well as common Sense, is Kickt out of Doors . . ." (171): in this passage "Senses" carries the meaning of "through organs of sensation," as opposed to "through the imagination"; thus, there appears to be a distinction between "Senses" and "common Sense," as well as between the latter and "common Understanding." The words "common" and "Sense" tie the three groups together. "Sense" as "common Sense" comes to mean the perception of reality as based on the generally accepted and on a normal perceptive apparatus; while "Understanding" suggests reflection based on the same factors. They represent the two aspects of perceiving and understanding reality.

The opposite of sensory perception is, in the Hack's parlance, "Delusion." "Those Entertainments and Pleasures we most value in Life, are such as *Dupe* and play the Wag with the Senses" (171). To the Hack the objects not "con-

veyed in the Vehicle of *Delusion*" are "fade and insipid."
The senses without the understanding can be duped, as the
Hack says approvingly: "The two Senses, to which all Objects first address themselves, are the Sight and the Touch;
These never examine farther than the Colour, the Shape,
the Size, and whatever other Qualities dwell, or are drawn
by Art upon the Outward of Bodies" (173). Thus there are,
first, the deluded senses with which the Hack deals; and,
second, there are the senses as testers of the Hack's false
reality, which are left to the reader. Here we must add a
third meaning to "Sense": meaning. "Senses" to the Hack
lose their "sense" (their meaning), which is to perceive accurately.[3]

Thus to the reader the rhetoric of the oratorial machines is the noise of wind; reduced to the sounds we are
familiar with, enthusiast communication becomes mere
flatulence. The reader's senses of taste, smell, and touch are
evoked to give a less favorable interpretation to the excreta
that interest the Hack and are cherished by moderns. The
"Edifices in the Air" are "out of sight, and even out of hearing"—beyond the common mode of apprehension by which
the world of the Hack's imagination is tested. Peter's "universal *Pickle*," which "for its many Sovereign Virtues was
a quite different Thing" (109), however, appears "to the
Taste, the Smell, and the Sight" just pickle. In the same
way, Peter's bread, which is supposed to be mutton and
claret, *tastes, smells,* and *feels* like bread (116ff.).

Second, following from the standard of common sense
which is set up in the *Tale* is the standard of common
analogy. What the reader sees in the "Dedication to Prince
Posterity" are two metaphors, the Hack's and the author's.
The Gnostics, we have seen, created a metaphor by simply
giving a thing a name that belongs to something else. By
this system any name and object can be associated at will.

3. For a fourth meaning of "sense"—sensual—see below, Ch. 4, sec. VI.

Most of the Hack's metaphors are of this kind: Time is a monster, Reason vivisects, "Wisdom is a Fox" or " 'Tis a Sack-Posset." A true metaphor is the association of two objects by an analogy of some sort between them. Wisdom and a fox seized unwarily are both dangerous, and sack-possets, like wisdom, can be intoxicating. The reader will see this analogy, based on reason and experience. What Swift does is let the Hack create metaphors on the basis of his own "secret analogy," allowing the more common analogy to remain and act as commentary.[4]

Third, there is the reader's search for consistency, which produces a second level of meaning. In Chapter 1 we saw that the Hack's inconsistency was based on the opportunist impulse of the seventeenth-century writers. Each of his moments expresses his meaning, but, as in an acrostic, these moments can be put together and a different meaning arrived at than the Hack's. The reader connects "vast flourishing Body," the chaos of modern writing in relation to time,

---

4. Another convenient way to regard the general relationship between his meaning and the words' meaning is to imagine that he, having Puritan inclinations, is a Ramist in his logic. We have seen that the Ramist logic of presentation is not syllogistic so much as "argumentative," or, as the Hack says, "by uncontroulable Demonstration" (34). The human mind is expected to assent automatically to a true proposition when presented with one. The Ramist argument tends to take the form of interminable lists of examples, like those the Hack gives of ways Time-Death destroys books, indiscriminately chosen from history or poetry and removed from their contexts, because of the correspondence assumed between reality and the human mind. To prove that the "true Critick" is "Antient and Illustrious," the Hack gives examples from ancient writers who talk about asses and serpents. Although the literary context of these asses and serpents is lost to an ordinary reader, their everyday context is not. Rather than assent to the proposition as stated, the reader associates the critics with stupidity (the ass) and guile or danger (the serpent). From the Hack's practice we may infer that the flaw in this sort of logic is that the reader is liable to draw another conclusion than the one the author draws. The reader, with an ordinary sense of reality—based on the normal, accepted, and understood facts of life—reads the Hack's "arguments," which are superlogical, and, like Sancho Panza, sees the windmill the Hack takes to be a giant.

and the shifting cloud in a single statement, to the effect
that modern writing is a matter of appearance under which
there is little of value. In this sense the *Tale* is, as Kathleen
Williams has suggested, a quest for the reader, full of traps
to make him reorder his own stale ideas or beliefs, and full
of various touchstones, ideals and extremes.[5]

But while I have been emphasizing the reader's perception, we must not forget that, as we saw in Chapter 2, the
impression the reader is left with in the *Tale* is not so much
one of his own exploration of the Hack's reality as that of
reality's assertion of itself as an objective entity which refuses to be perverted.

That a view of the world in which order can be expected
to assert itself, and correct the errors and perversions of
bungling humans, is an important aspect of the *Tale of a
Tub* is apparent if we look back at the sections concerning
Gnosticism. The Hack, we saw, regards man as capable of
creating his own reality because the physical objects that surround him are worthless. Christian doctrine tells us (1) that
God alone has created all things, and (2) that whatever God
created is good. Once these suppositions are accepted, the
Hack is left with the ordinary tools for committing a sin.
Thus he is equipped with words or objects which in themselves are good, or, in a more secular term, are *real*. He cannot create their meaning; he can only use them wrongly.

The second important fact about the world the Hack has
been put in is that it is a Christian world—specifically, an
Anglican world. Thus the examples we have seen in this
section of reality reasserting itself are not merely advice to
the reader of the *Tale;* they represent an important part of
the *Tale's* theme.

5. See Williams, *Jonathan Swift and the Age of Compromise,* p. 136: "if
there is less incentive, and less urgency, in working out meanings [than in
Swift's other works]—as in Swift's satire we are always required to do—
there is also more difficulty; because of the utter incoherence of the
[speaker] it is harder than usual to recognize where Swift is leading us."

CHAPTER FOUR

THE CHRISTIAN VIEW OF MAN

> Let us then for the nonce consider man alone,
> without outside assistance, armed only with his
> own weapons, and destitute of the divine grace
> and knowledge, which comprise all his honour, his
> strength and the foundation of his being. Let us
> see how he will hold out in this fine equipment.
> —Montaigne, *Essays*

1. Gnosticism in Practice

In the remainder of this study we shall
see what the Gnostic assumptions the Hack employs mean
in terms of the world Swift has put him in: what they
amount to in practice. There are four main approaches to
the critique of sufficiency in the *Tale:* through (1) the allegorical narrative, (2) the Grub Street Hack, (3) *The Battle
of the Books* and *The Mechanical Operation of the Spirit,*
and (4) metaphor. Although it is only a third of the *Tale,*
the narrative of the brothers has the advantage over the
digressions in that for once the Hack is held down to facts;
whatever his interpretation (e.g., he is less fond of Martin
than of Jack), he has an "author" and sources to follow, and
Swift is careful that every step of the history is labeled.[1]

1. Swift's printing of Wotton's notes (in the 5th ed.) makes the meaning
so explicit that the reader is left with little doubt of the historical line of
development.

From this simple historical core, we can work our way out to the digressions and, finally, to the independent parts of the book, the *Battle* and the *Mechanical Operation,* and to the pattern that is produced by the over-all interaction of the parts and the metaphorical structure.

In this exploration Irenaeus will again give us some idea of what to expect. I remarked in section II of the last chapter that part of Irenaeus' importance to Swift lay in his method of juxtaposing his account of the Gnostic's imposing, if imaginative, picture of man's place in the world with Gnosticism as he knew it in practice, where "every one of them generates something new, day by day, according to his ability; for no one is deemed 'perfect' who does not develop among them some mighty fictions." [2] To a man brought up in the tradition of the Church of England the picture of every man on his own, out for his private salvation, would appear chaotic; to Swift, we shall see, it suggested the image of a crowd, a fat man pushing to get ahead of his neighbor and crying, "Lord! what a filthy Crowd is here; Pray, good People, give way a little, Bless me! what a Devil rak'd this Rabble together" (46). [3] Irenaeus' prototype for the milling crowd is his picture of heresy growing out of heresy.

The Gnosticism Irenaeus knew manifested itself in eccentricity, magic, veerings from absurd asceticism to sexual excess, and the figure of the "elect" who "struts about as proud as a cock." [4] He fastens particularly upon the debased antics of Marcus and his followers, as the reality under the appearance of the Valentinian godlike man. Marcus "the magician" is "the Christian swindler," [5] who is Peter and

2. Irenaeus, *Ante-Nicene Fathers, I,* 343.

3. See sec. VII of this chapter for a discussion of the image of the crowd as employed by Swift in the *Tale.*

4. Irenaeus; quoted by Inge, *Christian Mysticism,* p. 82.

5. Harnack, *History of Dogma,* p. 64. It is a piece of Marcosian jargon, it should be remembered, that Swift uses as his epigraph.

Jack rolled into one, and who very likely gave Swift hints toward both.

> He is a perfect adept in magical impostures [writes Irenaeus], and by this means drawing away a great number of men, and not a few women, he has induced them to join themselves to him, as to one who is possessed of the greatest knowledge and perfection, and who has received the highest power from the invisible and ineffable regions above. . . . For, joining the buffooneries of Anaxilaus to the craftiness of the *magi*, as they are called, he is regarded by his senseless and crack-brained followers as working miracles by these means [p. 334].

Like the Aeolists, these enthusiasts are "puffed up," and at another point are referred to as "inflated wise folly" (p. 341). To Irenaeus as to Swift, the air represents both the bogus spirituality and the derangement of mind which creates what is not evident to the senses. But here the derangement is a deception, and the point Irenaeus makes over and over has to do with false appearance. Error, he says, "is craftily decked out in an attractive dress, so as, by its outward form, to make it appear to the inexperienced . . . more true than the truth itself" (p. 315).

Marcus, a degraded Valentinus, makes it only too explicit that the source of inspiration resides in the senses. Marcus converts women, telling them to prophesy.

> On the woman replying, 'I have never at any time prophesied, nor do I know how to prophesy;' then engaging, for the second time, in certain invocations, so as to astound his deluded victim, he says to her, 'Open thy mouth, speak whatsoever occurs to thee, and thou shalt prophesy.' She then, vainly puffed up and elated

by these words, and greatly excited in soul by the expectation that it is herself who is to prophesy . . . idly
as well as impudently utters some nonsense as it happens to occur to her, such as might be expected from
one heated by an empty spirit. (Referring to this, one
superior to me has showed, that the soul is both au-
dacious and impudent when heated with empty air.)
Henceforth she reckons herself a prophetess, and expresses her thanks to Marcus for having imparted to her
his own Charis. She then makes the effort to reward
him, not only by the gift of her possessions (in which
way he has collected a very large fortune), but also by
yielding up to him her person, desiring in every way
to be united to him, that she may become altogether
one with him [pp. 334–5].

As we found sensual attraction involved in the seventeenth-
century literary forms we studied in Chapter 1, we can now
add to the egocentric basis of spirituality the sensual, which
is dramatized for us here and in other of Marcus' exploits.

We have noticed in the example of the brothers and
their coats that a dualistic ethics can lead to a view that the
soul has no responsibility for the body. The doctrine that
all matter is evil can lead to an ascetic repression of carnal
instincts or, as Monsignor Knox says, "it may lead to a dangerous contempt of those instincts as belonging to matter,
and therefore possessing only a material significance." [6] If
one is too holy to be polluted by them, there is no danger—
there is contempt—in deliberately dabbling in material
sins; "to the pure all things are pure (even things forbidden). . . . Somehow or other, they are not true actions;
it is the lower self that is responsible for them, and the
lower self does not count." [7] This "perfectionism" is only a

6. Knox, *Enthusiasm*, pp. 102–3.
7. Ibid., p. 141; see also p. 104.

step from predestination; and the "elect" are not sinful.[8]
The Gnostics, according to Irenaeus, believe "it is impossible that spiritual substance (by which they mean themselves) should ever come under the power of corruption, whatever the sort of actions in which they indulged. . . . [Accordingly,] the 'most perfect' among them addict themselves without fear to all those kinds of forbidden deeds of which the Scriptures assure us that 'they who do such things shall not inherit the kingdom of God.' " [9] Thus the reality Irenaeus presents under the doctrine and theory of Gnosticism is one of dissidence and immorality. At the same time that he is echoing their jargon, he is judging them by the commandment of the Christian religion, "Love thy neighbor," and finding their pretensions to vanish in the strong light of this appraisal.

II. Visible and Invisible Churches

It has been noticed by critics that the allegory of the coats is strikingly unreligious, almost secular in tone. Speaking of religion in terms of suits of clothes has seemed impious, and certainly nothing that can be called religious sentiment is to be found in Peter, Martin, or Jack. The brothers are, however, in constant contact with each other and with other people; and this is itself a level of religious significance. If religion is a coat, its practice will be in terms of manners

8. Perfectionism is the belief that man can attain a condition of sinlessness on earth. As Monsignor Knox says, this "may lead to a contempt for the decencies; nay, to a cultivation of indecency, as proving how far it is possible for the perfect to neglect all the usual safeguards of modesty, without having their passions evoked thereby. Thus the Beghards 'looked upon decency and modesty as marks of inward corruption, as the characters of a soul that was still under the dominion of the sensual, animal, and lascivious spirit'" (p. 125). Cf. Jack's lack of common decency, his inability "to eat his Victuals *like a Christian*" (192), etc.

9. Irenaeus, p. 324. He goes on from here to describe their lusts and their seductions of the women they had lured into the faith.

and morals; and Swift suggests that this is the level upon which the results of mystical experience or pious words are tested. Thus the airy pretensions of Peter's interpretation *totidem literis* and Jack's reforming zeal are contrasted with their acts ("Drank, and Fought, and Whor'd, and Slept, and Swore, and took Snuff"—74), with their desires (to be "at the very Top of the Fashion"—81), with Peter's "high-crowned Hats" and the "damn'd Kick in the Mouth" he gives those who will not kiss his foot, and with Jack's relieving himself in the eyes of passers-by (115, 195).

Swift is, of course, invoking a certain kind of religion by this parable. The Christian humanist tradition to which we have referred from time to time focused its attention on man, his conduct and morality, and consequently placed its emphasis on results rather than motives which, like that shifty word "conscience," can never be pinned down. The Church of England traditionally thought in terms of morality and civil obedience.[1] Thus, in the *Tale* speculative religion is held down to concrete deeds, and religion (as a definition) is restrained to the level on which learning operates, so that both can be seen as ordering and humanizing agencies.

In the second place, Swift follows the Christian historians of Gnosticism in attributing the corruption of the early church to the sort of ambition and self-seeking we see in the actions of Peter and Jack.[2] More than on either re-

1. Jeremy Taylor's view in *Rules and Advices to the Clergy of the Diocese of Down and Connor* (Dublin, 1661) is expressive of their concern. He advises the clergy of his diocese not to spend their "sermons in general and indefinite things, as in exhortation to the people to get Christ, to be united to Christ, and things of the like unlimited signification; but tell them in every duty, what are the measures, what circumstances, what instruments, and what is the particular minute meaning of every general advice": *The Whole Works of the Right Rev. Jeremy Taylor*, ed. R. Heber and C. P. Eden (London, 1849–54), *1*, 107.

2. See C. W. King, *The Gnostics and their Remains* (New York, 1887), p. 12. Like Irenaeus and Epiphanius, Swift represents Gnosticism as an offshoot

ligious doctrine or church history, the emphasis of the brothers' story falls upon a historical *process* which is based on a particular view of the nature of man. This process is close to the one suggested by Temple as occurring in the state not governed by "law": the speculative individualist, in order to have his freedom or his opinion, deviates from the law; following revolution is reaction, the need to impose his opinion on others; this provokes another revolution, which when successful is obliged to defend its opinion by force.[3]

The two sections of the history of the brothers which show the parallel activity of Peter and Jack emphasize this aspect rather than any other. Peter finds that once he has conceived his fancies (which disregarded the law of the will) he has to make his brothers see them the way he does, to prove that they exist: and so he forces Martin and Jack to eat bread which he claims to be mutton and claret, and makes them give up their wives for concubines. On the other hand, Jack, seeing that he has torn off too much of his suit, tries to force Martin to do the same, crying, "*Strip, Tear, Pull, Rent, Flay off all*" (139), and consequently Martin secedes from the narrative.[4] Jack's type of imagination is not discussed until section 8, when its epistemological significance has been replaced by its significance as a way to violence; and Jack's "inventions," which parallel Peter's in section 4, do not come up for consideration until section 11, when they show the functioning of Jack's imagination and the proliferation of sects to be synonymous. Here he

and corruption of Christianity, rather than (as it claimed to be—and in some respects was) an older mythology than Christianity.

3. Temple, "Of Popular Discontents," in *Works, 3,* 40.

4. Martin has no further place in the darkening world that follows section 6 (though he makes a brief reappearance on p. 204). It is also important to notice that Peter's madness and Jack's madness are balanced in these sections; the symmetrical quality of the action should be kept in mind when we follow the parallels operating in the digressions.

leaps "over Head and Ears into the Water" like a Baptist (196), believes in predestination like a Presbyterian, and carries a flame in his belly like the Quaker with his "inner light" (192). His every eccentric act spawns a sect.

The progression Swift traces is thus a redaction of the history of sects in the seventeenth century, which climaxed in the capital illustration of the Civil War and was resumed in the hardly less bloody Popish Plot scare. The *Tale* is only one of scores of works that played upon the persistent reiteration by Englishmen of the parallel between the events of 1641 and those of the present, whether the present of 1665 or 1680 or 1688. It is therefore necessary for us to fill in some of the background of the conflict which Swift uses as his "objective correlative." As early as the sixteenth century, when Anglican doctrine was still largely Calvinist, Hooker dissected the Calvinist idea of church government until the roots of doctrine itself were laid bare. The conflict he saw was, at bottom, between a visible church and an invisible (or charismatic) church. The visible church is, like Temple's state, governed by "law": salvation is contingent upon belonging and behaving properly to one's neighbors. In the invisible church, as in the state, the authority is the arbitrary rule of the charismatic preacher, or finally as schism follows schism, of the individual himself. The invisible church is, thus, the "elect"; the individual feels that he has some sort of direct contact with God, whether, like the Gnostic, he raises his intellect to God's level, or, like the Montanist, he lowers God to the occupancy of his intellect. Hooker traces the progression of dissidence from the individual's seeing what he wants to see in a Scriptural passage to "a higher point, which is the persuading of men credulous and over-capable of such pleasing errors, that it is the special illumination of the Holy Ghost, whereby they discern those things in the word, which others reading yet discern them not." [5] After that, he continues, "they must profess themselves to be all (even men, women, and children) Prophets" (p. 187). And finally, he points out that "when the minds of men are once erroneously persuaded that it is the will of God to have those things done which they fancy, their opinions are as thorns in their sides, never suffering them to take rest till they have brought their speculations into practice." [6]

Thus the Presbyterians who had clamored for freedom of religion and the heads of the tyrants Strafford and Laud sought as rigorous a discipline as the one they had overthrown, only on Presbyterian lines. As early as 1645 Thomas Edwards was telling Parliament, "You have made a Reformation, but with the Reformation have we not a Deformation, and worse things come in upon us than ever we had before?" [7] Ironically, Edwards, a Presbyterian, found himself using the old Anglican arguments (including an encyclopedia of heresies) for a visible church; he shows how close the Presbyterian point of view had come to the Anglican in the 1640's when the Presbyterians were trying to impose their own structure. But what they had started was already out of control, with the Independents carrying their assumptions to the logical conclusion of an invisible church, where one man can be a congregation. The Independents, winning the army, won the Civil War, and

5. Hooker, preface, ch. 3, sec. 10, *Works*, ed. Keble, *1*, 186. As he recognized, this produced an "elect": "This hath bred high terms of separation between such and the rest of the world; whereby the one sort are named The brethren, The godly, and so forth; the other, worldlings, time-servers, pleasers of men not of God, with such like" (p. 188). The Gnostics believed that every "spiritual" person is able to prophesy: "Every one of them," Irenaeus writes of the Gnostics (p. 398), "imagines, by means of their obscure interpretations of the [Scriptural] parables, that he has found out a God of his own."

6. Hooker, preface, ch. 7, sec, 12, *Works*, *1*, 236.

7. Edwards, *Gangraena*, Pt. 1, "Epistle," page unnumbered.

the great proliferation of sects followed. These were sects, some very small and some extinct by Swift's time, such as the Seekers, Ranters, Quakers, Familists, Brownists, Millinaries, Behmenists, Sabbatarians, Muggletonians, Sweet Singers, Bourignonists, and Fifth Monarchists. The secession of disciples from George Fox to James Nayler is only one of the more famous examples of the schism that produced such a proliferation. The nature of Gnosticism being to splinter into other sects, it is not surprising that by the Restoration the general terms "dissenter" and "nonconformist" covered all the radical sects.

To understand the extraordinary profusion of sects, as well as such phenomena as the Hack's employment of huge tenors with scanty vehicles, or the great mystery with no one to understand it, we must take into consideration the psychological temper of the century. Descartes, a central figure in this intellectual climate, illustrates a possible answer to our question. While Descartes placed the only gauge of reality in the mind, unlike the schoolmen who never doubted the correlation between thought and object, he no longer felt able to *postulate* this correspondence. He had to approach certainty through a system of "methodological doubt," based on the assumption that outside objects can only be understood in relation to oneself. This is the significant fact about the Gnostics he loosed on Europe: the mind is still one's own gauge of reality, but there was no longer any certainty that it is anyone else's; and so the mind, as in Montaigne's essays, becomes important for its own sake, with no end in view except self-expression.

On the side of religion, once the Lutheran faith in God's mercy is passed, Calvin's arbitrary God comes into view, and there is doubt in even the most certain of the elect as to whether perhaps they are not really damned.[8] Since

8. See Haller, *Rise of Puritanism*, pp. 144-5.

his "outward behavior and gesture" told whether he was saved,[9] the individual often presented a great certainty of gesture concealing a doubtfulness of mind. To the enthusiast sects the mystical experience was often the sign of election, and here too if one believed himself to be saved, he had to exalt his own idea or action to the level of Truth. Hooker has noticed the overdemonstration this leads to "lest their zeal to the cause should any way be unwitnessed" and it not appear that they were of the elect.[1] And so, with no need for uniformity went a definite need for positive action of some sort. Since there was no insistence that God said the same thing to each person, the result was often chaotic.[2]

This is the chaos from which Hooker attempted to guide the Church of England. His *Laws of Ecclesiastical Polity* (1594) represents the clearest statement of the norm by which the *Tale of a Tub* judges Jack, Peter, and their offspring. Another encyclopedia, though its ostensible purpose is to show "with whom church authority resides," [3] it in fact presents a view of man's relation to the world

9. Thomas Taylor, *Christs Combate and Conquest: or, the Lyon of the Tribe of Judah, vanquishing the roaring Lyon* (London, 1618), p. 64: "By our outward behaviour and gesture, [God] can gather our special corruptions."

1. Hooker, preface, ch. 3, sec. 12, *Works, 1,* 189.

2. The result is, of course, what we have called casuistry, the parallel tendency in life and in art toward a "vagueness or inconsistency in ideals together with a vivid awareness of one's immediate situation and a proclivity to act on the stimulus of that awareness . . . uncertainty as to the ultimate but extreme certainty and commitment as to the immediate" (Sypher, *Four Stages of Renaissance Style,* p. 141). Sypher links this attitude, on the one hand, with the Calvinistically inclined Christian (and this included many pre-Civil War Anglicans) who "stands in a very personal and always uncertain relation to his God, which deprives him of confidence but gives a melodramatic sense of the unpredictable" (p. 133), and, on the other, with the Jesuits who adopted casuistry as a method of adjusting the law to suit a particular person at a particular moment, every situation becoming a special case (p. 137).

3. Keble, ed., *Works of Hooker, 1,* lii.

he lives in; it attempts to demonstrate that man on his own cannot find imperishable truth, that he will in fact only end in disorder and conflict if he tries. It suggests that a structure of law must restrain and protect him and guide him. Hooker characteristically speaks in terms of absolutes, opposing "truth," "first original causes," the "nature" and "reason" of things, man's "mind," "judgment," and "conscience" to the shifting "error and misconceit," "prejudice," and "passionate affection" of the Puritans.[4] He contrasts the quick revolutions of the Calvinists with "the slow and tedious help of proceeding by public authority." This permanence is law, "the deed of the whole body politic"—"which being once solemnly established [is] to exact obedience of all men."[5] "Common peace" and "orderly and quiet" are key words for an understanding of Hooker; they reflect the time-consciousness of law, which is itself a reflection of Hooker's God, "the settled stability of divine understanding."[6] Such was the influence of the *Laws of Ecclesiastical Polity* that the way of the Church of England was, essentially, Hooker's "law."

To understand Hooker's position and, to a large extent, Swift's, it is necessary to see the religious and civil state in a single context: "for God is not a God of sedition and confusion, but of order and peace," and special circumstances and private interest are opposed to the best interests

4. These characteristic words of Hooker's are listed by Stueber, "Hooker's *Polity*," p. 813. Cf. the "law" of a secular theorist like Thomas Hobbes, who in his *Leviathan* (ed. Michael Oakeshott, Oxford, Blackwell, 1946, e.g., pp. 211–12) also opposes the individual's conscience or inspiration to the law of the whole.

5. Hooker, preface, ch. 4, sec. 7, *Works, 1,* 200; ch. 5, sec. 2, *1,* 204. "Laws that have been approved may be (no man doubteth) again repealed, and to that end also disputed against, by the authors thereof themselves. But this is when the whole doth deliberate what laws each part shall observe, and not when a part refuseth the laws which the whole hath orderly agreed upon."

6. *Ibid.,* preface, ch. 5, sec. 2, *1,* 204; Bk I, ch. 3, sec. 4, *1,* 262.

of both church and state.[7] The church and the state are, therefore, reason in its concrete form: the majority opinion of the learned and wise few who have studied the problem carefully over a period of years, in the light of earlier opinions. Reason, which is the basis for "law," is an acceptance of common judgment and tradition and a minimizing of self.[8]

Ultimately Hooker's "law" is the law of cosmic order. The same harmony evident in his definition of reason informs the principles of peace and justice which hold together the whole chain of being. It is law in the sense that every individual and thing acts according to the law of its nature and end, up to and including God Himself. When the individual, not satisfied with his place in the order, breaks the law, aspiring to rights only God possesses, "division of necessity followeth, and out of division, inevitable destruction"—the order is destroyed. And "without order there is no living in public society." The cosmic order extends down to man the microcosm, with sin the disordering element both physically and mentally.[9] The man who considers himself a prophet has, therefore, lost touch with his real nature and end; if he follows his inclination he breaks the structure of order.

Not surprisingly, we find the same sort of standards in the narrative of the brothers. The will is "law" and the coats will last forever and continue to adjust to the wearer's body,

7. See ibid., preface, ch. 3, sec. 2, *1*, 179.

8. Man's reason, says Hooker, can tell good from evil. But the most usual way by which man tells the one from the other is by "signs and tokens," and the most certain of these is "if the general persuasion of all men do so account it" (Ibid., Bk. 1, ch. 8, sec. 3. *1*, 282). He names three ways of knowing besides knowledge from Scriptures: (1) "by plain aspect and intuitive beholding," (2) "by strong and invincible demonstration," (3) by "probability" (Ibid., Bk. II, ch. 7, sec. 5, *1*, 406).

9. Ibid., Bk. VIII, ch. 6, sec. 9, *3*, 507; Bk. I, ch. 2, sec. 5, *1*, 253; Bk. VIII, ch. 2, sec. 2, *3*, 426; Bk. I, ch. 9, sec. 1, *1*, 296.

while its antitype, the tailor-god, sanctions the change of fashions, like those of shoulder knots and braid, from day to day. Besides the will itself, there is Martin, representing human capability, who after an initial tear proceeds "more moderately," picking up "the Stitches with much Caution, and diligently [gleaning] out all the loose Threads as he went, which proved to be a Work of Time" (136). Martin's "Dexterity and Application" carries the same suggestion of care and desire for permanence that are expressed by Hooker, as well as obedience to the will. Contrasted with this is Jack, who becomes so "kindled and enflamed" that "in three Minutes, [he] made more Dispatch than *Martin* had done in as many Hours" (138), and by working "a little too hastily" tears the garment itself. Martin is following the law of the will; Peter and Jack are following their own inclinations.

We can conclude that if we wish to find the realistic norm of the *Tale* we must go to the actions rather than words of the characters, and, more specifically, to the history of sects in the seventeenth century. And, second, if we wish to find the moral norm by which the real actions of the characters are to be judged, we must go to the Christian humanist tradition, specifically to the Church of England. The moral values of Swift's world are based on permanence and the solidarity of the social unit. In this world the individualist is the destroyer, who perversely wishes to maintain his personal integrity at whatever expense to the group of which he is a part. Thus at the center of the *Tale* is the recognition of the historical fact that a true church was corrupted and split by self-interest.

There was, however, a third party to the religious struggles of Swift's day, the Low Churchmen, the Latitudinarians; and as late as Swift's *Argument against Abolishing Christianity* (1708) he was opposing the nominal Christianity to which he believed their reforms would lead. But when he was writing the *Tale* matters looked even darker. With Sancroft's voluntary retirement (celebrated in one of Swift's earliest poems, his "Ode to Sancroft") and with Canterbury and other important sees filled by Latitudinarians, there was a continual friction between the bishops and their priests, who were largely High Churchmen like Swift. The struggle within the Church between these two groups has been described as "an English version of the French battle of the ancients against the moderns"; [1] for the Latitudinarians, deriving from the Cambridge Platonists, were willing to cast off parts of traditional doctrine and discipline in order to comprehend dissenters. While Swift may have agreed with them on many particular points,[2] he could not agree with principles that opposed the church's taking action against heresy (the Unitarian in this case) as a "deliberate narrowing of the doctrinal standards of the Church of England"; [3] or with principles like those of Glanvill, for example, who "proposed to harmonize the best of the thought of Bacon, Descartes, Hobbes, and the Cambridge Platonists," in an "attempt to combine specific doctrines from each [which] led in the end to a heterogeneous assortment of ill co-ordinated elements." [4] Thus during the period when Swift was writing the *Tale,* around the turn of the century, "the majority of the clergy [High Church]

1. George Every, *The High Church Party, 1688–1718* (London, S.P.C.K., 1956), p. 10. I have used Every as the basis for my remarks on the immediate religious background of the *Tale;* but another useful account of the period is John R. Maybee, "Anglicans and Non-Conformists, 1679–1704: A Study in the Background of Swift's *Tale of a Tub,*" unpubl. diss., Princeton, 1942.

2. For example, Swift would have agreed with their emphasis on morality rather than doctrinal speculation, on practical results, and, following Latitudinarian preachers like South and Stillingfleet, on reform in preaching.

3. Every, p. 85. To Dodwell and other High Church extremists, Tillotson and the other newly appointed Latitudinarian bishops who filled the places of the nonjuring High Churchmen were schismatics (p. 71).

4. G. R. Cragg, *From Puritanism to the Age of Reason* (Cambridge Univ. Press, 1950), p. 82.

were convinced that the bishops [Latitudinarians] had failed
to stem the rising tide of Dissenting and unbelieving influence that threatened to overwhelm the Church. The
Church was in danger from the toleration, from the rising
wealth of the 'Commonwealth men,' Presbyterians, Quakers,
Baptists, Scots, Dutchmen. The bishops were set on ap-
peasement, on minor concessions that could not check the
flood" (p. 104).

Now if on the one side we have Peter, Jack, and all the
schismatics, and on the other Martin and the Church of
England representing order, who represents the third, perhaps most dangerous, side? The Grub Street Hack, it should
be remembered, claims to be a historian and an encyclo-
pedist, one who includes "all that Human Imagination can
Rise or *Fall* to," and while his bias is toward Jack, he includes Martin and has a few good words to say for him, and
even admires Peter's projects. He carries traces of the virtuoso, the projector, and the Rosicrucian about him, as
well as the Puritan and the enthusiast.

Throughout the book, the Hack uses the homely images of
domestic or country life, of lanterns, foxes, cheeses, jakeses,
and ovens, which echo the Puritan sermon. His approach to
life is that of the Puritan for whom the "life of the spirit"
is a "pilgrimage and battle," summoning up struggles like
the one against the Apollyon-like monster Time-Death, or
his war with the wits, or his self-identification with the
"true" critic as a warrior.[5] He carries all the images of persecution and suffering nobly for the faith, telling how he
posted the works of the moderns and was laughed at, how
Gresham and Will's betrayed and slandered him—he is
constantly slipping off into spiritual autobiography in the
best Puritan manner. He sees himself involved in a drama of
temptation and trial, from which he has emerged unscathed,
"with great Content of Mind" (106)—and to his "unspeak-

5. See Haller, *Rise of Puritanism*, p. 142. Bunyan's *Pilgrim's Progress* is
the most famous example of the "life as a pilgrimage and battle."

able Comfort . . . with a Conscience void of Offence" (71).

But if the Hack speaks bits of Puritan jargon and shows some sympathy in that direction, he also shows himself familiar with the jargon of the Royal Society and the virtuosi. The Hack's claim on his title page that he writes "for the Universal Improvement of Mankind," as well as the emphasis on benefit and usefulness which keeps cropping up in his adjectives, would have been enough to bring to mind the Royal Society's employment of phrases like "for the Advancement of experimental Philosophy," "for the Benefit of human Life," and "the Advancement of Real Knowledge"—all of which appear on the first two pages of Sprat's *History of the Royal-Society of London, For the Improving of Natural Knowledge.*[6] And so the Hack is both a Puritan sympathizer and a supporter of the Royal Society. But the phrase "for the Universal Improvement of Mankind," Guthkelch and Smith point out, is also a Rosicrucian tag, reminiscent of the supposedly Rosicrucian text, the *Allgemeine und general Reformation der ganzen weiten Welt.*[7] The Hack's concern with "Fraternities" and "Societies" is specifically Rosicrucian, and his asides to the reader are couched in mysterious terms such as *"vere adepti," "Arcana,"* or "dark points" (114). If his hero Jack

6. 1667 (London, 1734). William King used the phrase to point up a parody of the *Philosophical Transactions* in 1700:

> This noble Corporation [the Royal Society]
> Not for themselves are thus combin'd,
> But for the public good o' th' nation,
> And general benefit of Mankind.

Thus, it appears that the phrase meant to unsympathetic contemporaries an appearance of unselfishness concealing the usual self-interest. See *The Transactioneer, with some of his Philosophical Fancies, in two Dialogues,* London, 1700; cited in Carson S. Duncan, *The New Science and English Literature in the Classical Period* (Menasha, Wis., Collegiate Press, 1913), p. 121.

7. G-S, p. 353. The association of this unlikely work with Rosicrucianism came about as a result of its being printed together with the *Fama Fraternitatis* (1614), what G-S calls the "first of the Rosicrucian manifestoes."

claims that his father's will is *"the Philosopher's Stone, and the Universal Medicine"* (190), the Hack makes the claim for the *Tale* that it is the *Opus Magnum* (187), which contains ultimate knowledge including the secret of the transmutation of metals, and the universal elixir which "clears the Breast and the Lungs, is Soverain against the *Spleen,* and the most innocent of all *Diureticks"* (185).

That there was a common ground among these various groups is evident in that each of them strives for an exaltation of man above the "nasty, brutish and short" life of everyday. Science was as promising a way to this ideal as the Rosicrucian mysteries, and religion was as promising as either of these.[8]

Thus the Hack's role as taleteller would appear to be that of the collector of all that is valuable in all the sects and societies. It is in this sense that the Hack's casuistry, his willingness to accommodate all, would have linked him with the Latitudinarian, who was, to many Anglicans, the fool to the dissenter's knave. The Hack is the modern-above-all who acts the fool to the various critic, virtuoso, or enthusiast knaves, and the *Tale* he tells of the brothers accordingly draws as much significance from the manner of its telling as from the actions that take place.

III. The Hack's Battle with Reality

The speaker of the *Tale* is himself a symbol of the imagination's collision with reality, which reveals under the "Figure and Mystery" a hack furiously patching a very

8. Historically, there were men like Elias Ashmole, who were prominent members of the Royal Society and at the same time adepti in Rosicrucian mysteries. The Rosicrucians themselves were another underground sect which rose in Protestantism. In their "acknowledged manifestoes" the Rosicrucians "avow themselves a mere theosophical offshoot of the Lutheran heresy, acknowledging the spiritual supremacy of a temporal prince, and calling the Pope Antichrist" (Waite, *Real History of the Rosicrucians,* p. 97). Waite refers to the Rosicrucians as "Lutheran disciples of Paracelsus," and as "rabidly and extravagantly Protestant" (p. 209).

shoddy reality—or, in his own image, a maggot at the center of a cheese. In this section, therefore, we shall examine some of the lights that are turned upon his particular existence, and then scrutinize that existence itself.

Before he even appears on the scene we are presented with a series of norms by which to judge him: the "author," Lord Somers, and the Bookseller. It is an error to suppose that the "Author's Apology" is spoken by Swift himself; its "author" is as much a part of the fiction as the Hack.[1] For example, he is referred to in the third person (in contrast with the Hack, who always uses the first person), and the passage which apologizes for "several youthful Sallies, which from the Grave and the Wise may deserve a Rebuke" (4) is merely a parody of similar disclaimers in writers like Dryden, who wrote:

> My thoughtless youth was wing'd with vain desires,
> My manhood, long misled by wand'ring fires,
> Follow'd false lights. . . .[2]

The effect of such distancing and impersonalizing is to move both author and book in the direction of abstraction and symbol. Thus the book, the author establishes at once, "seems calculated to live at least as long as our Language, and our Tast admit no great Alterations" (3); for it was, he says, "chiefly intended for the Satisfaction of future Readers" (9). "The greatest Part of that Book," he explains, "was finished above thirteen Years since, 1696, which is eight Years before it was published" (4).[3] The care with which he

1. The "Author's Apology" was affixed to the fifth edition of the *Tale* (1710). To answer the attacks on the *Tale* and to clear up the misunderstandings that led to them, Swift evidently found it necessary to insert another standard to supplement the standard of reality he had established in the Bookseller.

2. *The Hind and the Panther*, Pt. I, ll. 72–4.

3. He goes on to say he wanted to write in a way "that should be altogether new, the World having been already too long nauseated with

gives the date of composition implies that the *Tale* was not
so occasional as might appear, that it could sit and wait (and
be pondered by its author) without losing its power.[4] He
speaks of the "Pains and Skill," "Wit, Learning, and Judgment" (10) that went into it, and, he assures us, it was "the
Product of the Study, the Observation, and the Invention of
several Years, that he often blotted out much more than he
left, and if his Papers had not been a long time out of his
Possession, they must have still undergone more severe Cor-
rections; and do they think [he adds of his detractors] such
a Building is to be battered with Dirt-Pellets however envenom'd the Mouths may be that discharge them" (10). In
short, the *Tale* itself is mockingly set up as an ideal of
permanence against the Grub Street literature that has attacked it, and whose disappearance the "author" associates
with the changing of the seasons: "They are indeed like
Annuals that grow about a young Tree, and seem to vye
with it for a Summer, but fall and die with the Leaves in
Autumn, and are never heard of any more" (9).[5] In the re-
sultant equation the *Tale*, which "cost so much time" (11),

---

endless Repetitions upon every Subject." The emphasis here is on new vs.
repetitious, not new for its own sake, as in the practice of Bayes or the
Hack.

4. It is also meant to establish the author's youth, and thus some excuse
for his freedom in the writing of the *Tale* (though its conventionality
makes this somewhat dubious).

5. The emphasis on time extends from the repetition of dates or references like "ten Years after his Book was writ, and a Year or two after it
was published" (14), to details like the mention, in the "Bookseller to
the Reader," of the work's being lent "to a Person, since dead" (28)—here
is a book which can outlive a man, a remarkable thing in this world
where authors usually outlive their works.

However, we should notice the conventionality of this stance too: Dunton,
for example, writes that his book is "none I'lle assure ye of the short-lived,
unlaboured pieces, which like the *Ephemeris* (Ah poor *Ephemeris*) is got
in Morning, *born at Noon*, and dead by Night"—he "labour'd and polish'd
the works of *sweating* thoughts, and many a *drudging* hour, tho' 'tis confest
a pleasant Drudgery" (*Voyage, 1, 3*).

is opposed to the "Rate" at which a writer like Dryden pours forth his "Merits and Sufferings" (imitated in the outpouring of nonparallel clauses), just as religion in its stability, "the best of Things," is opposed to its "Corruptions," in their instability, which "are likely to be the worst" (7).

If the "author's" *Tale* is made to represent a standard of permanence, based on care of construction, breadth of view, and strength of materials, Sir William Temple and Lord Somers represent a standard of morality which is as permanent in its own way. Temple is referred to in the "Apology" as "universally reverenced for every good Quality that could possibly enter into the Composition of the most accomplish'd Person" (11), and Somers' virtues (lauded by the Bookseller) are "Wit, and Eloquence, and Learning, and Wisdom, and Justice, and Politeness, and Candor, and Evenness of Temper in all Scenes of Life" (25). These words are part of the vocabulary of humanism: the "accomplish'd Person" is "good," and wit and reason, guided by learning, lead to wisdom. Wisdom, which according to Cicero is the knowledge of things both divine *and* human, is communicated by eloquence—the important factor which we have seen separating the humanist tradition from the solitary contemplation of scholasticism—and demonstrated in justice and politeness, which with candor and evenness of temper represent the outward signs of inward wisdom.[6]

That there is an element of permanence in the moral individual is demonstrated by the fact that out of the multiplicity of poets who take "Detur Dignissimo" to be their own one common factor can be separated: Somers, whom they all name second; just as one common factor can be separated out of the answerers to the *Tale:* the book answered. Both must be distinguished from the individuals who end as the only reality detectable in modern writing. Swift is careful to make clear that it is the book, and not the

6. Cicero, *De Legibus*, Bk. i, ch. 7, 23; *De Officiis*, Bk. ii, ch. 2.

author, which provides this form of stable order, just as it is Somers' virtue rather than Somers and, in Hooker's terms, law rather than individuals.[7] Individuals change, but order has to be permanent and unchanging.

Finally, there is the Bookseller, who appears as the author of the "Dedication to Lord Somers" and of a note to the reader. Standing at the portal of the *Tale,* he is a single point of undisputed reality, a fact to take hold of. He is the plain, blunt businessman who knows that "the Fruits of a very few leisure Hours" is a laborious piece of hack writing and "a World of Business" is the producing of more such "Fruits." [8] He establishes the presence of the real world when he admits that he is "never likely to have the Honour of being known to" the prince to whom the Hack's "Dedication" is addressed (22). The work of Grub Street *is* transitory, he admits, and, moreover, there is no such person as Prince Posterity in the first place.

The Bookseller is both sincere and a realist. He establishes his sincerity by stating the tenor as well as the vehicle of his metaphors: "I should celebrate your Liberality towards Men of great Parts and small Fortunes," he tells Somers, "and give you broad Hints, that I mean my self" (23). He is a realist who knows that "those, to whom every Body allows the second Place, have an undoubted Title to the First" (24); and he admits that the reason for delay in publishing the Hack's manuscript was that he had better work to do. And now, he admits, the style is no longer what

7. Cf. Temple: "For the scribblers are infinite, that, like mushrooms or flies, are born and die in small circles of time, whereas books, like proverbs, receive their chief value from the stamp and esteem of ages through which they have passed" (*Essay,* in *Works, 3,* 432).

8. The Bookseller does, however, represent a norm of reality only. The virtues he admits in Lord Somers represent the realization of the obvious, not praise, which would imply a moral standard. The Bookseller is merely admitting what he sees, and his remarks are a sign that no one—not even Grub Street booksellers—can miss the virtue of Somers if they, unlike the Hack, open their eyes.

it was six years ago and writers no longer acknowledge Posterity. This is why he must apologize for the *Tale* and use Somers' name. He explains what a dedication is in fact: a great name on the front that will "get off one Edition" and will help the bookseller along to an aldermanship; the information in dedications is unreliable ("a good Historian will not be apt to have Recourse thither, in search of Characters"), and many are used over and over with different titles. They are, he admits, "tedious Harangues." Money is the motivating force in this world: the hacks receive fifty shillings for sheets of praise, and when a wit writes in praise of himself he works gratis. The wits, it appears, are egoistic (each thinks the "Detur Dignissimo" refers to him), they work for the Bookseller, and they live at the top of "a prodigious Number of dark, winding Stairs" (26, 24).

When the Bookseller's dedication is placed alongside the Hack's which follows it, we have some idea of the relation between fact and fancy; and with the "Apology" in mind, we see a vivid contrast between permanence and a shifting, chaotic present.[9] What this juxtaposition shows most clearly is different attitudes toward the real and the ideal, or *what is* and *what should be.* First, there are the hacks of the real world, who accept reality and laugh at the Hack when he comes to look for the writings so recently posted. Second, there are the people like Somers and the "author" who accept reality and abide by it, but, by a sensible utilization of *what is* in a context óf permanent values, seek *what*

9. The notes added to the fifth edition represent one more ray of light cast upon the *Tale* proper. They are by "W. W-tt-n, B.D. and others," and as such offer a fussy and pedantic commentary by one modern on another, Wotton on the Hack. Wotton's notes offer a sort of exantlation of significance, doing for the Hack what the Hack did for Reynard the Fox and Tom Thumb; the unsigned notes, as Guthkelch and Smith have shown, censure the author, disagree with him, correct him, and "explain why there are chasms in the manuscript" (G-S, p. xxii). Though the author they censure is the Hack, they also, it should be noted, reiterate the date of the book's composition (e.g., 86, 208).

should be. Third, there is the Hack, a modern who gives battle or attempts evasions.

We have seen how the Hack attempts to impose the image of a malignant slayer on the flux of time; this refusal to recognize the fact of change or to acknowledge an alternative in permanence causes the comic collision with reality which reduces him, by the end of the "Dedication to Prince Posterity," to offering proofs of the physical existence of men themselves with as much specificity of time and place as an alibi. When he writes, "With these Eyes I have beheld the Person of *William W - - tt - - n,* B.D." (37), what he is emphasizing is his attempt to convince himself and others that he *did* see Wotton, that there is such a person.[1]

As to the Hack himself, we might notice the descending spiral of his claims concerning the origin of the *Tale* he is writing. He says in his preface that he has "had the Honour done" him to be chosen by the "Grand Committee" to divert the wits (41); but it seems more likely that he is telling the truth when, in his *apologia pro vita sua,* he records that he wrote *"Pro's* and *Con's* upon *Popish Plots,* and *Meal-Tubs,* and *Exclusion Bills,* and *Passive Obedience,* and *Addresses of Lives and Fortunes;* and *Prerogative,* and *Property,* and *Liberty of Conscience,* and *Letters to a Friend. . . .* Fourscore and eleven Pamphlets have I written under three Reigns, and for the Service of six and thirty Factions" (70). At this moment he is seeking sympathy (against the attacks of his enemies of Gresham and Will's), and he has forgotten his earlier statement, if the reader has not. While the Hack sees himself as a server of church and state, we see him as an opportunist, and, materializing the metaphor of his

---

1. Notice the Hack's use of the perfect tense, the tense auxiliary having the function of stressing the idea of the reality of the attainment. (An example is "Why don't you go to town?"; "I have gone to town.") In the Hack's example there is, besides the note of desperation, just a trace of sarcasm in the auxiliary, as in "Well, you *have* done it now." The person of William Wotton was something one had to brace himself to look at.

venality, he is "thread-bare and ragged with perpetual turning" (70); which is one interpretation of his Latitudinarian tendency.

Another explanation for the composition of the *Tale* is, however, forthcoming: "finding the State has no farther Occasion for me and my Ink, I retire willingly to draw it out into Speculations more becoming a Philosopher . . ." (71). Commercial matters have been set aside, perhaps of necessity, and the Hack has decided to do his best to write a book worthy of the modern ideal.

The focus of reality for the Hack seems to be the completion of his book, or publication day; for as that time approaches his explanations become franker, until he admits pathetically that writing is itself mere diversion, that a writer writes as an outlet for the frustrations of his human state:

> If it were not for a *rainy Day, a drunken Vigil, a Fit of the Spleen, a Course of Physick, a sleepy Sunday, an ill Run at Dice, a long Taylor's Bill, a Beggar's Purse, a factious Head, a hot Sun, costive Dyet, Want of Books, and a just Contempt of Learning.* But for these Events, I say, and some Others too long to recite, (especially *a prudent Neglect of taking Brimstone inwardly,)* I doubt, the Number of *Authors,* and of *Writings* would dwindle away to a Degree most woful to behold [183].

And finally, having seen the Bookseller and being wholly in the real world again,[2] the Hack admits that he wrote the book to make some money ("considering my urgent Necessities"—207); and he is willing that the bookseller say it is written by whatever author is at that particular moment in vogue, in order to sell it.

2. This is one of the inconsistencies we noticed in Ch. 1. The Bookseller has claimed that he never saw the author of the manuscript that was given to him (28).

The facts of his existence that show through indicate that the Hack is, in short, a hack. What is revealed is a fact about Puritanism which Ian Watt has demonstrated in relation to Defoe's novels: that the energy and enthusiasm of the Puritan was by the early eighteenth century largely secularized and turned into economic channels.[3] As Robinson Crusoe's spiritual flights scarcely conceal his acquisitiveness, so the Hack's pretensions scale off until only the scurrying businessman remains. Although he claims to have "just come from having the Honor conferred upon me, to be adopted a Member of that Illustrious Fraternity" of Grub Street (63), it is clear from the autobiographical references he makes that he is no newcomer to this fraternity. He lives high up in a garret (169), and, though he maintains that it is a Longinian preparation for writing, we can take it for a fact of his existence that he often goes hungry and is often plagued with "a long Course of Physick, and a great want of Money" (44). He is not so young any more ("the poor Remains of an unfortunate Life"—70), has had "a certain

3. Ian Watt, *The Rise of the Novel* (Berkeley and Los Angeles, Univ. of California Press, 1957), pp. 80–5. The Hack's milieu, Grub Street, would have had certain connotations for a contemporary. The street, whose name came from a refuse ditch (a grub) which ran alongside it, lay outside the old walls, in Cripplegate, and like other of the areas lying outside the immediate jurisdiction of the city became a haven for wanted men. Through the seventeenth century it carried a reputation for harboring dissenters, who took their printing presses there to escape more active surveillance; and, in fact, both Cromwell and Milton lived there. All sorts of scurrilous writing, pornographic as well as seditious, was spawned in Cripplegate and along its main street. It had already passed its peak of prosperity by 1700, and by the time Pope attacked it, and the *Grub Street Journal* flourished, and Samuel Johnson lived there, its population of hacks had dwindled to only a fraction of its former size. Thus, to the Londoner of 1704, Grub Street would have suggested dissenting and scurrilous literature; and the word Grub might have further suggested a refuse ditch and a verb meaning "to dig up, to destroy by digging," as well as "a small worm that eats holes in bodies" (Johnson)—all connotations which Swift exploits in the course of the *Tale*.

Domestick Misfortune" (54), has a broken head and a poxed body (70), and has spent some time in Bedlam (176). Finally, as if the whole world would conspire against the Hack, a glance back at the Bookseller's note to the reader shows that the objective world "can give no manner of Satisfaction" as to the Hack's very existence (28). No name appears on the title page, perhaps a result of the same accident which deprived us of several more titles (71).

If, however, we compare the "Dedication to Prince Posterity" with the sections that follow it, the Hack's strategy for refusing to accept and attempting to change these facts (his strategy for diversion) becomes clear. In the preface he is ostensibly discussing the functions of a preface, how other moderns write them and with what assumptions. But the reader notices that the writings the Hack posted and could not find the next day in the "Dedication" are echoed here by the jest "that is no where intelligible but at *Hyde-Park* Corner" (43). Having acknowledged that meaning has been reduced to "Circumstances of Time, Place and Person" (43), he simply concludes that, because the present moment is all a modern can hope to establish, he "cannot imagine why we should be at Expence to furnish Wit for succeeding Ages, when the former have made no sort of Provision for ours" (44). Thus he addresses not "future Readers" but those at hand "this present Month of *August,* 1697."

That the Hack is exalting this limitation into a matter for pride is plain if we compare a passage from the "Dedication" and one from the "Digression in the Modern Kind":

> I profess to *Your Highness,* in the Integrity of my Heart, that what I am going to say is literally true this Minute I am writing [36].

> But here I think fit to lay hold on that great and honourable Privilege of being the *Last Writer;* I claim

an absolute Authority in Right, as the *freshest Modern,*
which gives me a Despotick Power over all Authors
before me [130].

In the second passage the anxiety we notice in the "Dedication" has become belligerent pride. We are shown the anxiety first, and it is never entirely absent from the second; but
the Hack's object is to raise this limitation of the shoddy into
law for all. And so he explains in the "Digression on Madness" that the difference between a madman and a genius,
between Empedocles and Decius, depends ultimately on
the moment of action. "Thus one Man chusing a proper
Juncture, leaps into a Gulph, from thence proceeds a Hero,
and is called the Saver of his Country; Another atchieves
the same Enterprise, but unluckily timing it, has left the
Brand of *Madness,* fixt as a Reproach upon his Memory"
(175). This then is the principle behind the casuistry we noticed in the Hack's style and mode of thought in Chapter 1; and it is this which allows the reader who seeks
consistency to find a meaning the Hack had not intended.
What the Hack's stand amounts to is a demand upon the
reader that he *not* seek consistency, that he stop at this
moment—"*August,* 1697"—and, to facilitate this, he describes what he went through as he wrote the *Tale,* which
the reader must go through in order to "understand" it:
"Whatever Reader desires to have a thorow Comprehension
of an Author's Thoughts, cannot take a better Method, than
by putting himself into the Circumstances and Postures of
Life, that the Writer was in, upon every important Passage
as it flow'd from his Pen; For this will introduce a Parity
and strict Correspondence of Idea's between the Reader and
the Author" (44). The Hack's point in giving the reader as
many dates, facts, and clues as possible is thus to make sure
that the "peculiar *String* in the Harmony of Human Understanding" (167) is going to be "of the same Tuning" as

his, so that he will be a Decius rather than an Empedocles.

Thus twin threads of challenge and response run through the *Tale*. In section 10 we are told that writing itself is due to "Accidents and Occasions" (182), and in the "Conclusion" the matter of timeliness has been extended to the books which "must be suited to their several Seasons, like Dress, and Dyet, and Diversions. . . . I am living fast, to see the Time," the Hack continues, "when a *Book* that misses its Tide, shall be neglected, as the *Moon* by Day, or like *Mackarel* a Week after the Season" (206). The Hack's solution to this particular challenge, we have seen, is to let the Bookseller attach to his book the name of the author who *is* in season.

The Hack's *Tale* itself is an evasion: we have seen how he asserts that it contains all knowledge, is the *Opus Magnum* and grand elixir; he implies that it holds the secret of how to get by in this wretched world of ours. But, he tells us elsewhere, the aim of such Grub Street writing as his is to kill the monster Time; it has "clipt his Wings, pared his Nails, filed his Teeth, turn'd back his Hour-Glass, blunted his Scythe, and drawn the Hob-Nails out of his Shoes" (63). The *Tale* is, we may infer, a diversion for mankind as the tub is a diversion for the whale, a way of softening realities and creating illusions that will make life bearable for the shifting crowd to which he addresses himself. Diversion is his elixir; he proves "that, as Mankind is now disposed, he receives much greater Advantage by being *Diverted* than *Instructed*" (124), by evading rather than facing the facts of existence; and he has already set up three main diversions, the pulpit (for spiritual), the gallows (for political), and the stage, under which fall Grub Street writings. As the pulpit becomes the dissenter's tub, so each has its purpose shifted from instruction to entertainment.

To summarize: first, modern writing can be understood at just the one moment of composition and only by the writer himself, and these conditions must be reconstructed for communication to take place. Second, if we look back at the "Dedication to Prince Posterity" it will be clear now why the Hack lists the authors—Dryden, Tate, and the rest —as the *one* fact he can produce in favor of the existence of the works which have disappeared. The author's being, in a sense, *has* to be established, because the book has no other criterion to be judged by, no other context of existence. It fits into no framework but that of the author's mind.

Finally, the precariousness of the moment can be seen as one source of a tendency which extends from a need to "put it over" on the reader to an outright aggression which demands that the reader be like the author. This is a tendency which anticipates and runs parallel to the aggressive activity of Peter and Jack in the narrative, and like that activity can be divided into two kinds: it is the forcible "exantlation" of one's own interpretation from any object; and, on the other hand, the forcing of this view on others. The Hack promises in his introduction that, to get *his* meaning (which in this case is *any* meaning at all) out of a Grub Street production, he will "lay open by Untwisting or Unwinding, and either . . . draw up by Exantlation, or display by Incision" (67).[4] Then, illustrating the Hack's metaphor, Peter draws out his meaning from the will by force in section 2, and in section 4 imposes this meaning on his brothers. The Hack echoes Peter's aggression toward his brothers in the "Digression in the Modern Kind," where he claims that being "the *freshest Modern*" gives him "a Despotick Power over all Authors before me" (130). We have noticed his exorbitant demands on his reader, whom he compares to "a lazy, an impatient, and a grunting" horse (203). The

---

4. Cf. Swift's reference in the "Apology" to his enemies' drawing meanings unfavorable to him out of the *Tale:* e.g., "There are three or four other Passages which prejudiced or ignorant Readers have drawn by great Force to hint at ill Meanings . . ." (8).

Hack's ordering of chaotic reality is a similar act of aggression: he explains in the introduction that by "reducing, including, and adjusting every *Genus* and *Species* within that Compass [of his interpretation], by coupling some against their Wills, and banishing others at any Rate" (57), he will reduce all nature to the number three, destroying its rivals, the numbers seven and nine. In theory, these acts exemplify man's ability to categorize and order his world. But the violence of the act, hinted at in these instances, is made clear in the "Digression in the Modern Kind" (immediately following Peter's violent expulsion of his brothers in section 4), where the Hack cuts up the "Carcass of Humane Nature" in order to prove his point.

Ultimately, this is an attempt to reduce "the Notions of all Mankind, exactly to the same Length, and Breadth, and Height of his own" (166). The "Digression on Madness" serves as a focus for this attempt. Here the Hack, who has spent some time in Bedlam, makes all the greatest men out to have been madmen, much as Jack tried to make Martin join him in the shambles to which he had reduced his coat (section 6). In doing so, the Hack makes a brave attempt to implicate the reader too in his madness, ending in the well-known passage about the "Fool among Knaves"—an attempt which has worked with more than one critic.[5]

Now if we turn back to an example of the Hack's aggression, his claim of "Despotick Power" in the *"freshest Modern"* passage, we shall see that it is to prove a rather small point: "In the Strength of which Title [freshest modern], I do utterly disapprove and declare against that pernicious Custom, of making the Preface a Bill of Fare to the Book" (130-1). Similarly, by dissecting Human Nature, the Hack proves the mild fact that the greatest public good

---

5. Since this strategy, and our "smoking" of it, tend to sum up all that we have been saying about the way reality and the Hack's mind work on each other, I shall discuss it in some detail in the next section.

is performed by diversion. The matter on which self-aggrandizement is based is minuscule, and must be if there is to be a new "Despotick Power" every minute. Next minute the index may be the bone of contention, or the number three. The power is the important thing—the matter on which it is gained can be of no consequence, can be something the Hack a moment before has disapproved of: for he has himself, we have seen, made his own preface the "Bill of Fare" to his work, telling the reader exactly how he wants everything interpreted. Certainly he does as he says Dryden does: assures the reader that it is a great book.

Accordingly, the greatest actions performed by single men, which are listed in the "Digression on Madness," are *"The Establishment of New Empires by Conquest: The Advance and Progress of New Schemes in Philosophy; and the contriving, as well as the propagating of New Religions"* (162). These are *new* empires, schemes, and religions in the same sense that every moment the *"freshest Modern"* supersedes a predecessor. The Hack himself is shown, in his introduction, to be not quite a modern.[6] The brotherhoods of true moderns, Gresham College and Will's Coffee House, refuse to acknowledge him; or rather, since like Time they are probably unaware of him, refuse to acknowledge their source in Grub Street. The inference we can draw from this fact is that they are not true scientists or wits but rather have transferred Grub Street to Gresham and Will's, and now are ashamed to own their former ties; they represent the sort of schism we noticed in the narrative of the brothers. In a hurt tone the Hack claims that "Their own Consciences will easily inform them, whom I mean," and he admits that many of his own kind have "already deserted to them, and

---

6. He admires them immensely—"Our illustrious *Moderns*" and "the great Modern Improvement" are words never far from his lips (92, 143); and he hopefully calls himself one: "We whom the World is pleased to honor with the Title of *Modern Authors*" (123).

our nearest Friends begin to stand aloof, as if they were half-ashamed to own Us" (64, 65).

In the Hack's world man has usurped Time's function, and his terror of Time is a terror of himself, or a manifestation of his aggressive nature; in this sense it is man himself who causes mutability, by feverishly overthrowing all that is present, superseding, and being himself superseded. The tailor being god, fashion is ultimately what the Hack fears, not Time, which is impersonal.

Thus the Hack is reduced to a squabbling, funny, faintly dangerous little man—dangerous because he is cornered. To preserve his illusion of sufficiency he grasps at straws, if necessary impinging upon the lives of other people. He demonstrates that the swelling of the brothers' coats leads ultimately to the incision in one's neighbor, and his own development from illusion to pride to aggression, we have seen, makes a single progression with that of the brothers in the allegorical narrative.

iv. The Hack and the Nature of Man

The view of the nature of man that is expressed in the actions of Peter, Jack, and the Hack is a part of the skeptical tradition, whether in religious or secular thought. In religious thought this is fallen man without the guide of a church, and in secular thought this is simply man, without any recourse. We shall try to determine in which of these traditions the *Tale of a Tub* is written.

The skeptical view appears conveniently schematized in Temple's "Of Popular Discontents," an essay which, we have seen, presupposes a disintegration in the state without law very like the one Swift demonstrates in his history of the church. Both Temple and Swift state this disintegration in terms of time. When the value of the past, or tradition, is denied and value becomes solipsist, then of course the

present moment becomes crucial to man's knowledge of reality.[1] According to Temple, dissatisfaction with the present
and love of change, the need for diversion and for restless activity every minute, are the sources of self-assertion and
individualism.[2] Temple's most famous statement of the
view of man he predicates is at the end of his essay "Of
Poetry": "When all is done, human life is, at the greatest
and the best, but like a froward child, that must be played
with and humoured a little to keep it quiet till it falls
asleep, and then the care is over."[3]

Pascal, one of Temple's probable influences, believes that
if a king "be without what is called diversion [*divertisse-
ment*], he is miserable, and more miserable than the least
of his vassals who can play and amuse himself." Accordingly,
the moment is all that matters. "However full of sadness he
may be, he is happy for the moment if you can get him to
take up some amusement; and, however happy he may be,
he will soon be vext and wretched if he is not amused and
mastered by some passion or pursuit which prevents the
development of ennui." The object, then, is to leave not "one
hour in the day when [men] can think about themselves"
—"be always occupied."[4]

Man's chief source of diversion is his imagination, which

1. For a brilliant account of the tradition of the moderns, particularly
as regards time-consciousness, which developed the Richardsonian novel,
see Watt, *Rise of the Novel*, passim. The connection is so striking that the
Tale could almost be called a parody-in-advance; it is possible that Sterne,
when he came to satirize these very aspects of the Richardson novel, had
the *Tale* in mind (see *Tristram Shandy*, Bk. IX, ch. 8).

2. Temple, "Of Popular Discontents," *Works*, 3, 34–7.

3. "Of Poetry," *Works*, 3, 429. He develops the idea in his epistle "To
the Countess of Essex, Upon her Grief occasioned by the Loss of her only
Daughter": "We bring into the world with us a poor, needy, uncertain life,
short at the longest, and unquiet at the best; all the imaginations of the
witty and the wise have been perpetually busied to find out the ways how
to revive it with pleasures, or relieve it with diversions; how to compose it
with ease, and settle it with safety" (pp. 506–7).

4. *Pensées*, No. 110, p. 55; No. 116, p. 63; No. 122, p. 67.

"governs all . . . creates beauty, justice, and happiness which are mankind's whole aim." Ultimately, it is "this deceitful faculty" which "enlarges trifles" and leads man to pride in himself and the abandonment of his natural state. If pride is one implication of the desire for diversion and the "deceitful faculty" of imagination, a second implication is man's littleness in the face of his upper potentiality, the angelic: "This man, born to know the universe," Pascal writes, "to pass judgment on everything, to govern a whole state, is engaged and wholly taken up with the business of catching a hare." A third, and most important, implication is that one man's search for diversion will impinge upon another's, or a third person's will exploit the search of the other two; in short, it leads to aggression.[5] The manifestation of man's insecurity, Temple points out in "Of Popular Discontents," is restless ambition (p. 35)—the "perpetual and restless desire of power after power, that ceaseth only in death" which Hobbes erected into a system.[6] The two key words of Temple's essay are "restlessness" and "faction" and the transition from one to the other carries us back to the world of schism and sedition.[7] One conclusion we can draw from the Hack's murderous proving of rather

5. Ibid., No. 75, p. 43; No. 86, p. 49; No. 118, p. 65. The ego, Pascal believes, "is essentially wrong since it makes itself the centre of everything; it is a nuisance to others because it tries to enslave them, for each 'ego' is the enemy and would fain be the tyrant of all the rest" (No. 146, p. 79). Cf. Temple in "Of Popular Discontents": "For the animosities and hatred of the factions grow so great, that they will submit to any power, the most arbitrary and foreign, rather than yield to an opposite party at home" (Works, 3, 45).

6. Leviathan, ed. Oakeshott, p. 64.

7. See Temple, "Of Popular Discontents," Works, 3, 34: "a certain restlessness of mind and thought," p. 35: "This restless humour," p. 37: "naturally restless, and unquiet," p. 42: "ever restless to get into public employments," and p. 43: "restless passion." Temple discusses "faction" on pp. 35 and 45; on p. 36 he speaks of "those streams of faction, that, with some course of time and accidents, overflow the wisest constitutions of governments and laws."

trifling points is that the aimlessness and meaninglessness of his aggressive tendencies suggest that at bottom it is merely a desire for diversion that drives him. The illusion he creates as a way to diversion for the crowd hides an expression both of aggression and of mere restlessness on his own part.

The characteristic form these observations take in the writings of Temple and others is the skeptical reduction. When Montaigne, having presupposed a man who is independent and proud of his sufficiency, asks, "Is it possible to imagine anything more ridiculous than that this miserable and puny creature, who is not so much as master of himself, exposed to shocks on all sides, should call himself Master and Emperor of the universe, of which it is not in his power to know the smallest part, much less to command it?" [8] he is engaging in the skeptical gambit; we have seen the same in Temple's attack which begins "We are born to grovel upon the earth, and we would fain soar up to the skies": man's pretensions are set up and knocked over.[9] Pascal uses the same form, citing what amounts to the theory of vapors to prove man's insecurity and insignificance. Instead of Henry IV and Louis XIV (Swift's examples), he uses the example of Oliver Cromwell at the height of his power: "the royal family was ruined, his own securely established, were it not for a tiny grain of sand which found its way into his bladder." Another example is "the mind of yonder sovran judge of the world": "a fly is buzzing in his ear; that is enough to make him incapable of sound judgment." He concludes: "The power of flies: they win battles,

8. "Apology for Raimond Sebond," *Essays, 1,* 441. This passage follows the passage I have used as epigraph for this chapter; taken together they present the full skeptical reduction. The metaphor of man armed with "only his own weapons," while implicit throughout the *Tale,* is made explicit in the armed moderns of the *Battle* (228).

9. Temple, *Essay,* in *Works, 3,* 459.

hinder our minds from acting, devour our bodies." [1] In the
Tale of a Tub the skeptical reduction is also at least implicit in Swift's juxtaposition of the ideal and the real in the
Hack, and particularly in his reduction of man to the tool
of a vapor in the "Digression on Madness."

There is a whole literature on man's incompetence. If
we go back to its source, we must call it skeptical; but
Pyrrho was more interested in man's flawed perception than
in the flawed moral sense to which the Church Fathers
adapted the skeptical method. The general pattern of man's
condition is the same in Montaigne and Temple, in Pascal
and Jeremy Taylor—in skeptic, libertine, fideist, and Anglo-
Catholic. But once having proved man's incompetence, the
writer can go in one of these several directions. The skeptic
stops with the reduction and the middle ground to which
man is restricted by his capabilities; he is willing to accept
man's weakness as an excuse for inaction. And it is hardly a
step from Montaigne's refusal to commit himself (his *que
sais-je?*) to hedonism or libertinism. If men cannot know extremes and are limited to a middle area, and if Montaigne's
answer is "Let us be detached," it is a logical inference to
add "Then let us enjoy." The pleasures of the middle area
are the simple ones of eating, drinking, and wenching,
which, as far as Swift is concerned, are merely other methods
of diversion. Libertinism is implicit in Temple's "froward
child" passage, which makes the end of life simply to live
without pain and, if possible, to enjoy oneself.

If the skeptic says that since there is no hope of knowing
anything, the best we can do is remain imperturbable, the
fideist, who is equally condemned by the church, says that
since we can *know* nothing we must blindly *believe*. The

1. Nos. 97, 102, 103, p. 53. For Swift's knowledge of Pascal, and for other
verbal echoes, see Emile Pons, "Swift et Pascal," two articles: one in *Les
Langues Modernes*, 45 (1951), 135–52, and the other in *Etudes Anglaises*, 5
(1952), 319–25.

orthodox Christian view, whether Anglican or Roman, is
that grace and the church (or, stated differently, tradition)
act as a pair of glasses to adjust man's faulty vision, and with
them he can see the world more accurately.

The distinction between skeptic and Anglican is evident
in the metaphors used by both: while the skeptic talks of
following a "middle" road, the Anglican talks of a "common" or "straight" road. Hooker employs this metaphor
when he writes that "Goodness in actions is like unto
straightness. . . . For . . . the straight way is most acceptable to him that travelleth, because by it he commeth to his
journey's end." [2] This is the same metaphor Swift uses at the
beginning of section 11, where the Hack says, "If a Man
is in haste to be at home, (which I acknowledge to be none
of my Case, having never so little Business, as when I am
there) if his *Horse* be tired with long Riding, and ill Ways,
or be naturally a Jade, I advise him clearly to make the
straitest and the commonest Road, be it ever so dirty"
(188). Thus Martin did not choose his middle way simply
because it was halfway between Peter and Jack, but rather
because it followed the will, while remaining within the
bounds of human possibility (some of the silver thread was
too deeply sewn to remove); and the Church of England
went back only to the early *organized* church—while the
Independents advocated no church or organization, regarding everything after the apostles as corruption [3]—not because this was a middle way but because the visible church
presupposed order as an ideal.

2. *Laws of Ecclesiastical Polity*, Bk. I, ch. 8, sec. 1, *Works, 1,* 281. It is,
of course, arguable that Montaigne is himself orthodox, however delicate
a balance he maintains between Christianity and skepticism; and, in this
connection, it is interesting to notice that his metaphor is the same sort
Hooker used: pride "turns a man aside from the common path . . . makes
him embrace novelties" instead of following "the straight and beaten
road": "Apology," *Essays, 1,* 493.

3. Hooker, preface, ch. 4, sec. 2, *Works, 1,* 194–5.

Thus when we turn to the matter of Swift's picturing man as a tool of vapors in the "Digression on Madness," we must conclude that this is not man's only possible situation. Rather, this digression establishes the Hack's relationship to the ordinary man, whose perception we have seen to be the standard of the *Tale's* reality; therefore, it is particularly important that the ordinary man not be tripped up at this point by the Hack's casuistry.

One reason why the "Fool among Knaves" passage is crucial to an understanding of the *Tale* is that it is a likely spot on which to base a charge of nihilism if a critic is looking for one; another is that by misreading it on the Hack's (the subject) level the reader can infer that Swift is saying that all men are to some extent mad; a third is that the *Tale*, which is already a partaker of the skeptical attitude toward man's pretensions, can be accused of advocating the skeptical conclusion as well. If a reader accepts the view that Swift thinks we are all mad, it is possible to interpret the satisfaction the Hack expresses at being a "Fool among Knaves" as a denial of the possibility of action —Montaigne's *que sais-je?*

It can be argued in favor of this view that the "Digression on Madness" shows enthusiasm to be simply a disease,[4] in fact one which can be located in Burton's *Anatomy of Melancholy*. The particular kind of melancholy relevant to the *Tale* is "hypochrondriacal, or Windy Melancholy." The symptoms are very like those of the Aeolist: "continual, sharp, & stinking belchings, as if their meat in their stomack were putrefied, or that they had eaten fish, dry bellies, absurd & interrupt dreams, & many phantastical visions about their eyes, vertiginous, apt to tremble, & prone to Venery." [5]

---

4. See Clarence M. Webster, "Swift and Some Earlier Satirists of Puritan Enthusiasm," *PMLA, 48* (1933), 1141–53.

5. Ed. Floyd Dell and Paul Jordan-Smith (New York, Doran, 1927), pp. 323, 326. Other familiar symptoms are "heat in the bowels, wind and

The cause, in Burton's words, is the "keeping in of our ordinary excrements"—a common malady of moderns, we
have seen, and this is "sometimes . . . a sole cause of Madness" (p. 203). However, if any "evacuation stopped" is a
cause of melancholy, the obvious cure is an "artificial evacuation." "They saw one wounded in the head," Burton
writes, "who, as long as the sore was open, was well; but
when it was stopped his melancholy fit seized on him again"
(p. 205). This is the effect Ravaillac's knife has on Henry
IV when the inconvenient withdrawal of the woman into
another country made him subject to "omission of venery." [6]
The "artificial evacuation" is also the physiological reason
for the Hack's opening of his vein "to exhaust [the accumulation of his grain of folly] all at a Running" (184),
as it is for the Aeolist's belches.[7]

But if the enthusiast is a sick person, it will tend to free
him from responsibility for his acts. Burton's opinion tends
in this direction,[8] and he also gives some support to the

---

rumbling in the guts, vehement gripings, pain in the belly and stomack
sometimes . . . the veins about the eyes look red, and [they] swell from
vapours & wind" (p. 350).

6. G-S, p. 164; Burton, pp. 204–5.

7. The discharge is required, the Hack explains, by "a *rainy Day, a
drunken Vigil, a Fit of the Spleen* . . ." etc. (183). Like Swift, Burton parallels
physical causes with a perturbation of the mind: sorrow, fear, envy, malice,
hatred, anger, discontent, misery, desire or ambition (pp. 217ff.).

8. He says that the conditions for religious melancholy "are so ridiculous
and absurd on the one side, so lamentable and tragical on the other; a
mixt Scene offers itself, so full of errors, and a promiscuous variety of
objects, that I know not in what strain to represent it" (Burton, p. 896).
Webster, p. 1144, points to similar views in Meric Casaubon's *Treatise
Concerning Enthusiasme as It is an Effect of Nature; but is mistaken by
Many for either Divine Inspiration, or Diabolicall Possession*, 1655 (cf.
Mechanical Operation, 267: the ways of transporting the soul beyond the
sphere of matter are by "the immediate Act of God, and is called, *Prophecy
or Inspiration* . . . the immediate Act of the Devil, and is termed *Possession* . . . [and] natural Causes"); and in Henry More's *Enthusiasmus
Triumphatus*, 1656. Webster points out that part of Swift's "real contribution was to be found in his analysis of the zeal and fervor which made all
men irrational" (p. 1141). He seems to see a pitying quality in Swift's
treatment which I do not detect.

view that we are all mad: "we have all been mad at one time or another," he writes; "you yourself, I think, are touched, and this man, and that man, so I must be, too" (p. 615). These add up to the skeptical position: man is ultimately helpless, and so the best solution may be to refrain from committing yourself.

Now to look at the text: the Hack has explained that enthusiasm is a disease, and it is an accident whether a man so afflicted is acclaimed a genius or a madman. The source of the vapor does not matter, only "in what *Angles* it strikes and spreads over the Understanding, or upon what *Species* of Brain it ascends" (169). The second point ("what *Species* of Brain") is, of course, the crucial one; he begins to develop it, but it is too abstruse or too dangerous and only a hiatus results. The possibility of placing some sort of responsibility on the person for his madness is passed up.

The Hack resumes by explaining how the process works after the vapor has taken hold, which leads him to observe, shifting his terms a bit, that " 'tis manifest, what mighty Advantages Fiction has over Truth; and the Reason is just at our Elbow; because Imagination can build nobler Scenes, and produce more wonderful Revolutions than Fortune or Nature will be at Expence to furnish" (172). Thus the Hack equates madness and imagination, giving the former a more respectable sound than it usually has. He offers the case Erasmus' Folly offers, and in almost as persuasive a way: he tells of fiction's "mighty Advantages," imagination's "nobler Scenes" and "wonderful Revolutions"—it is the exaggerated diction of the gesturing Hack, slightly absurd, amusing, but ingratiating. By equating memory and imagination he makes the product of the imagination appear to be real: memory holds the past, and the past was real; thus what the imagination holds is also real. When he remarks "How fade and insipid do all Objects accost us that are not convey'd in the Vehicle of *Delusion?* How shrunk is every Thing, as it appears in the Glass of Nature?" (172), the

reader is aware that there is a sense in which the objects
of nature are shrunk, and in which "delusion" is a good
thing. The reader may notice slips like the substitution of
"delusion" for "illusion," but the Hack appears to be coming clean and presenting in fairly respectable terms the assumptions upon which his behavior up to the present has
been based. Then he gives us the alternative to his proposal:

> IN the Proportion that Credulity is a more peaceful
> Possession of the Mind, than Curiosity, so far preferable
> is that Wisdom, which converses about the Surface, to
> that pretended Philosophy which enters into the Depth
> of Things, and then comes gravely back with Informa-
> tions and Discoveries, that in the inside they are good
> for nothing . . . [The sight and touch] never examine
> farther than the Colour, the Shape, the Size, and what-
> ever other Qualities dwell, or are drawn by Art upon
> the Outward of Bodies; and then comes Reason of-
> ficiously, with Tools for cutting, and opening, and mang-
> ling, and piercing, offering to demonstrate, that they are
> not of the same consistence quite thro' [173].

It is possible for the reader, however, to miss two points:
first, the Hack has made the dichotomy of curiosity and
credulity, reason and imagination himself; and second, the
Hack's Reason which mangles and cuts is as much a creation of his imagination as was Time-Death.[9] For example,
we have just noticed in the case of Henry IV (164) that cutting can cure. If the reader misses these points, he finds
himself forced to accept one of the alternatives which are
offered. First, he is lured by the Hack's picture of nature
transformed and the monster Reason into revealing a natural desire for comfort and fear of pain. What Leavis says

9. See sec. v of Ch. 3 for a discussion of true reason. Another indication
that the Hack has created his own view of reason is his discovery, *"A
Universal Rule of Reason, or Every Man his own Carver"* (130).

of Swift we can perhaps say of the reader: after the passage about the woman flayed, it is beyond doubt "that Swift feels the strongest animus against 'curiosity.' " There is even a sense in which "credulity" represents "the 'common forms' —the sane, socially sustained, common-sense illusions" as it does in Erasmus' Folly.[1] "Such a Man ["as you," the Hack implies] truly wise, creams off Nature, leaving the Sower and the Dregs, for Philosophy and Reason to lap up. This is the sublime and refined Point of Felicity, called, *the Possession of being well deceived;* The Serene Peaceful State of being a Fool among Knaves" (174). When this comfort is shown to be "the Serene Peaceful State of being a Fool among Knaves," it has become self-indulgence. But having accepted the Hack's assumptions, there is no way out: if the refusal to cut and mangle is cowardly, the opposite is cruel, painful, and useless. Thus, as Leavis asks, "What is left?" (p. 84).

The reader who succumbs to this brilliant rhetorical play will conclude that any real choice is impossible, and that the skeptical solution is all that remains. The Hack's object has been to reduce his reader to the same state of madness and inaction which is his, and to make him accept the accompanying conclusion that such madness is chance and we bear no responsibility for it. It is true that the reader is to some extent implicated in the Hack's madness—this is Swift's point, how easy it is to settle for being a fool among knaves. But when we recognize the two points I mentioned earlier, it becomes clear that the choice is a false one, concocted in the Hack's imagination.[2] Actually, this dilemma is apparent only to the man like the Hack who is on his

1. Leavis, *The Common Pursuit*, p. 83. For other interpretations of the "Fool among Knaves" passage, see Elliott, "Swift's *Tale of a Tub*," pp. 450–5, and Kelling, "Reason in Madness," pp. 212–22. Note C, below, p. 249, connects the passage with Erasmus' *Praise of Folly*.

2. Significantly, this passage is immediately followed by a description of the kind of bodies the vapors do their work in ("waste and empty Dwellings"), suggesting some little preparation on the part of the individual (174).

own and who can create it. The "author," Somers, and the Bookseller have already defined the Hack's position so that we see him as what man would be like if he were, as the skeptic assumes, "alone, without outside assistance," a Robinson Crusoe of Grub Street. The reader, whose normal perception is Swift's standard, must not forget the suit of clothes, or the church, or tradition, which acts as mediator and guide through such false dilemmas, and in fact eliminates them.

Of the inferences we can draw from this example the most important is that the Hack's reduction is to the level of his own perversion, not—as Swift's hostile critics have supposed—to the level of the human condition. Man does not have to be like the Hack. While we are so weak that our actions can be influenced by a little thing like a vapor, still we do not need to be overwhelmed by this, or, on the other hand, to exult in it and help the vapors along as the Aeolists do.

v. Other Views of Reality

Although we have examined metaphors which appear in the *Battle* and the *Mechanical Operation* and mentioned certain episodes from time to time, thus far we have talked primarily about the *Tale* proper. The *Tale* is the first, longest and most puzzling part of the book called *A Tale of a Tub,* and the other two parts illuminate it in such a way as to be largely dependent upon it. In this section we shall discuss the views of reality a reader obtains from these other parts and the relationship they bear to each other.

It is at once apparent that the *Tale, Battle,* and *Mechanical Operation* differ greatly in technique, particularly in their points of view. While the speaker of the *Tale* is clearly a Grub Street Hack, the speaker of the *Battle* is not so easy to identify. On the one hand he is a modern writing

an up-to-the-minute "Full and True Account" of what happened "last Friday . . . in St. James's Library" (211), and
on the other he is an ancient writing an imitation of an
epic. The ostensible detachment of the historian or epic
poet actually masks, in this case, a partisan of the ancients.
When the speaker calls Wotton "a Person of great Valor,
but chiefly renowned for his *Humanity*" (224), he is con-
forming to the nonpartisanship of his convention; but this
sort of epithet being attached equally to ancients and moderns has the effect of showing up the discrepancy between
them. To call Homer "a Person of great Valor" is to praise
a great book or an abstraction like Goodness or Greatness,
but Bentley and Wotton are merely names of men. By the
end of the *Battle,* when the speaker is making up epic
similes of Bentley and Wotton as mongrel curs (253), he has
become virtually a spokesman for Swift. The result is a
relatively straightforward presentation of the same theme
that is obliquely portrayed through the Hack in the *Tale.*

The new perspective found in the *Mechanical Operation*
is brought about by the scientific detachment of the speaker,
of a sort only suggested in the *Tale* at moments like "Last
Week I saw a Woman flay'd." [1] He is so detached as to become at times godlike. However, at other times he is as
immersed in the moment as the Hack, and there is at least
one indication that the Hack is meant to be the speaker:
the speaker claims to be the author of an essay upon "the
Art of *Canting, Philosophically, Physically, and Musically*

1. James L. Clifford has shown how critics have generally ignored the
Mechanical Operation, either out of prudery or misunderstanding. Arguing
against this indifference, he has recognized that it is obviously climactic
in a "shocking" or "stinging" way; but while referring to the "verbal con-
nexions, the hidden allusions which subtly lead the reader back and forth
from one theme to the other, until they almost fuse" in section 8 and the
"Digression on Madness," he does not discuss the *Mechanical Operation*
as a thematic climax: "Swift's *Mechanical Operation of the Spirit,*" in
Pope and his Contemporaries, Essays Presented to George Sherburn, ed.
Clifford and Louis A. Landa (Oxford, Clarendon Press, 1949), p. 144.

considered" (279), the exact title of one of the "Treatises wrote by the same Author" (2); all but two of the others are claimed by the Hack.[2] But in the *Tale* the Hack is the symbol of the world he describes, to some extent an autobiographer, and a certain consistency is necessary. In the *Mechanical Operation* (as in the *Battle*) the speaker is only a voice, but the point of view is an odd variation of the Hack's: this speaker appears to be the Hack stripped of (or having cast off) illusions, praising the mechanism he sought to hide beneath his rhetoric before.

For example, the "methods" the speaker of the *Mechanical Operation* talks about are the mechanical rationalization of the aggressive trends we have seen in the Hack's unexpressed, perhaps even subconscious, intentions. Here we have a frank admission that the teacher exploits his auditory, as the speaker explains that enthusiasm is "improved by certain Persons or Societies of Men, and by them *practiced upon* the rest" (266).[3] As in the *Tale*, the senses

2. Throughout the discourse enough of the Hack's vocabulary—the "illustrious and right eloquent Penmen, the modern Travellers," "most universal Notion," "gross Ignorance," "most horribly confounded"—is employed to indicate his probable presence. It is hard to say to what extent the echoes of the *Tale* are intended to remind us of the Hack and how much of just the *Tale*. But the preface to the *Mechanical Operation* demonstrates that this is "fashionable" modern writing: the speaker employs the form of a letter to a friend (cf. the Hack's "Letters to a Friend"—70) because he can find no other "which holds so general a Vogue" (262). He makes it clear that the form he chose is only for appearance's sake, adding the conventional *"Pray, burn this Letter as soon as it comes to your Hands"* at the end, but establishing his intention at the beginning: "(For, let me say what I will to the contrary, I am afraid you will publish this *Letter,* as soon as ever it comes to your Hands;)"—262-3. Cf. the Hack's reference to a work of his "(which, perhaps, the World may one day see, if I can prevail on any Friend to steal a Copy, or on certain Gentlemen of my Admirers, to be very Importunate)"—124. Like the Hack, he makes his excuses for the writing—haste and illness (cf. 30, 182); and he asks the reader to make an excuse for him whenever a bad passage appears: "if any other Modern Excuses, for Haste and Negligence, shall occur to you in Reading, I beg you to insert them" (263). Cf. the Hack's instructions to his readers, 46-7.

3. My italics. The whole passage, containing the list of specific countries

have to be corrupted for imagination to hold sway, and the two passages are parallel:

> Those Entertainments and Pleasures we most value in Life, are such as *Dupe* and play the Wag with the Senses [171].

> All Endeavours must be therefore used, either to divert, bind up, stupify, fluster, and amuse the *Senses* . . . [269–70].

Reason has to be overthrown in both cases; but the end of the first is the *"Possession of being well deceived,"* while in the second it is bluntly to overthrow "the Fort of *Reason,"* and a persuasive argument has been replaced by a military metaphor.[4] A plea for madness is veiled and made to be appealing in the first, while in the second the process of going mad is catalogued.

It is important to see that the epistolary form in which the *Mechanical Operation* is written is a parody of a report to the Royal Society, addressed to a friend at the Academy of New Holland, as Leeuwenhoek, for example, wrote to the Secretary of the Royal Society from the continent.[5] The speaker, unlike the Hack, is actually, or claims to be, a member of the Royal Society. The *Mechanical Operation* is, therefore, a scientific explanation, addressed to the Society, of what was presented as a diversion, addressed to "Mankind," in the *Tale*.[6]

---

where revolutions are to take place, parallels the passage we have already looked at in the "Digression on Madness" (162): in both, the greatest activities of man are conquests, philosophies, and religions employed as areas of influence.

4. The metaphor is reminiscent of the one used in the "Digression in Praise of Digressions" to show how the digression conquers the book (144).

5. See *Philosophical Transactions*, e.g., No. 159, *14*, 568.

6. Since, as we have seen, the underlying (or masked) views expressed in

A second characteristic of both *Battle* and *Mechanical Operation* is the echoing of phrases or ideas of the *Tale* proper. The changed viewpoints allow these to be presented with an emphasis which clears much of the ambiguity we have remarked in the *Tale*. Sometimes these are merely reminders, as in the idea expressed in the *Battle* that moderns have greater antiquity than ancients, which echoes a similar sentiment in the "Digression on Critics." [7] There are verbal echoes, such as the effect of the Goddess Criticism's throwing a monster into Wotton's mouth "which, flying straight up into his Head, squeez'd out his Eye-Balls, gave him a distorted Look, and half over-turned his Brain" (243), which echoes the tailor's stitching up of Jack's collar which "squeezed out his Eyes at such a Rate, as one could see nothing but the White" (199), and Jack's "Intellectuals" which "were overturned" (162). But it also offers an explanation of the fact, mentioned in the "Digression on Madness," that Wotton's "Brain hath undergone an unlucky Shake" (169). Another passage in the *Battle* answers the Hack's question in the "Dedication to Prince Posterity": why do modern writings sink when "in their own Nature they were *light* enough to swim upon the Surface for all Eternity" (32)? The answer is that "being lightheaded, they have in Speculation, a wonderful Agility, and conceive nothing too high for them to mount; but in

---

the *Tale* are the same as the expressed attitudes of the *Mechanical Operation*, it might be possible to assign it to the Hack again, making it another example of casuistry. If we think of him as threadbare and ragged enough "with perpetual turning," we could also credit him with the *Battle*, one of his pros and cons. The over-all structure of the book would then have a certain hilarity of opportunism about it that we have noticed to be a strong characteristic of moderns. Whatever the answer, the prefatory note demonstrates the realism of approach the *Mechanical Operation* takes. The speaker devotes two short paragraphs to an imitation of epistolary style— asking about mutual friends, the Iroquois virtuosi, and the literati of Tobinambou—and then excuses himself from the formal restrictions, making no further effort at the appearance of a letter until his hasty closing.

7. Cf. *Tale*, G-S, p. 93; *Battle*, G-S, p. 227.

reducing to Practice, discover a mighty Pressure about their Posteriors and their Heels" (225).

The same can be said of the *Mechanical Operation*. For example, a passage in section 8 of the *Tale* speaks of the Aeolists' creating a devil by singling out "some Being . . . which was in most Antipathy to the God they had framed" (159), from which we can infer that the Aeolists create a god after their own image and, then, a devil after their opposite. The *Mechanical Operation* is more specific: "Men have lifted up the Throne of their Divinity to the *Coelum Empyroeum*, adorned him with all such Qualities and Accomplishments, as themselves seem most to value and possess . . . they have sunk their *Principle* of *Evil* to the lowest Center, bound him with Chains, loaded him with Curses . . ." (274–5). There are more echoes here than in the *Battle*, perhaps because of its climactic position. For example, the *Tale* reads: "For, to enter the Palace of Learning at the *great Gate,* requires an Expence of Time and Forms; therefore Men of much Haste and little Ceremony, are content to get in by the *Back-Door*" (145). The gist of this progression, we recall, was to get from *index* to *back* to *posterior.* So now the speaker makes the leap in the same sentence: "These are the Men, who pretend to understand a Book, by scouting thro' the *Index,* as if a Traveller should go about to describe a *Palace,* when he had seen nothing but the *Privy* . . ." (284). Or compare the continuations of these passages:

> Thus Physicians discover the State of the whole Body, by consulting only what comes from *Behind* [145].

> or like certain Fortune-tellers in *Northern America,* who have a Way of reading a Man's Destiny, by peeping in his *Breech* [284].

The profusion of echoes tends to give the *Battle* and the *Mechanical Operation* the appearance of a recapitulation;

and it is particularly true of the *Battle* that its symbols and images are summations of the obliquely approached themes of the *Tale*. The spider who weaves his flimsy reality from his own bowels is one example of this, a sudden materialization of the practice we have seen the Hack engaged in throughout the *Tale*. But the battle itself is, of course, a concrete embodiment of all the aggressive tendencies that can be noticed in the Hack and his friends. This battle is more than a fight between ancients and moderns for the possession of Parnassus; rather, here particular men are made to stand for the various trends we saw milling about in the person of the Hack: reason and tradition against self-sufficiency. It draws our attention, in one focal symbol, to all the hints that are scattered through the *Tale*. The modern warriors explain proudly: *"For, our* Horses *are of our own breeding, our* Arms *of our own forging, and our* Cloaths *of our own cutting out and sowing."* To which Plato replies, "observing those that spoke to be in [a] ragged Plight . . . their *Jades* lean and foundred, their *Weapons* of rotten Wood, their *Armour* rusty, and nothing but Raggs underneath" (228). In the *Tale* the Hack can be surmised to be in a comparable state from the facts that slip through to the reader; here it is dramatized for us.

If the same sort of dramatization occurs in the *Mechanical Operation* it is less because of the summarizing symbols like the "quilted cap" than because of the assumption of scientific objectivity which leads the speaker to "tell all"— and to assume a position of godlike eminence from which he can reduce his own friends the moderns to nothing, without losing his aplomb. At these godlike moments the speaker coincides with Swift himself with a peculiar intensity found nowhere else in the book. For example, at the beginning of section 2, if we take a modern for the speaker, what the passage states is that there is no room for divinity in this modern world, any more than there is room for the ancients or anything else that is outside the individual. "For, I think," says the speaker, "it is in *Life* as in *Tragedy,* where, it is held, a Conviction of great Defect, both in Order and Invention, to interpose the Assistance of preternatural Power without an absolute and last Necessity" (275). Then, as he moves from conclusion to conclusion, the voice we hear is no longer either the Hack's or the scientist's; it is an apocalyptic voice, which says, "Who, that sees a little paultry Mortal, droning, and dreaming, and drivelling to a Multitude, can think it agreeable to common good Sense, that either Heaven or Hell should be put to the Trouble of Influence or Inspection upon what he is about?" (276). As if the whale suddenly reared up before the bobbing tub, Swift's voice rises and turns the speaker's exaltation of man into reduction. The speaker says that man does not *need* inspiration or possession; Swift says that God or Satan would not take the trouble to inspire or possess man. Whoever is speaking, we are here at the bottom of the reality of the *Tale.* The Hack's wonderful oratorial machines—"a Type, a Sign, an Emblem, a Shadow, a Symbol"—have become "a little paultry Mortal, droning, and dreaming, and drivelling to a Multitude."

But then we return to the unquestionable world of the speaker, and a hiatus in the manuscript: this blank space was the peak of sublimity for the Hack; but here it is imposed from the outside. The realist speaker is all too willing to give the details, but even the relatively down-to-earth Bookseller could not have this information revealed. Presumably there would have been no illusion left.[8]

Here we see the difference between the *Battle* and the *Mechanical Operation:* the one giving a straightforward,

8. The Bookseller's comment is that "it was thought neither safe nor Convenient to Print it" (276). Earlier the speaker has said, echoing the Rosicrucianism of the *Tale,* "having had the Honour to be initiated into the Mysteries of every Society, I desire to be excused from divulging any Rites, wherein the *Profane* must have no Part" (270).

and optimistic, account of what *should* happen if the forces of order and disorder were to meet; the other revealing the ugliest realities under the skin, which are a different sort of truth but a more cogent one because they are not merely true, but also existing.[9] We may conclude that it is interesting, but by no means necessary, to accept the *Battle* and the *Mechanical Operation* as examples of the Hack's opportunism; it is more important to see them as different perspectives on the problem presented in the *Tale*.[1] It is perhaps a sign of pessimism in Swift that the ugly reality should be last and the moral norm with its happy ending should remain in the middle. But the arrangement of the large parts is as important to an understanding of Swift's intention as is that of the sections and paragraphs.

VI. The Network of Association

So far we have seen that the parts of the *Tale*, as well as the *Tale* itself, the *Battle*, and the *Mechanical Operation*, are not merely juxtapositions of disparate ideas and materials but the spotlights of various points of view upon a single theme. In the last section it was suggested that their relationship to a common theme is pointed up by repeated words, pieces of metaphors, or scattered facts. These various

9. Since Swift has been careful to divide everything in his book into the Hack's cabbalistic *three* (parts, brothers, oratorial machines), we might go so far as to notice a rough parallel among the three parts of the book and the three brothers. Peter, the "Original Author of *Puppets* and *Raree-Shows*" (109), is known for his diversions, while Jack is known for his tearing away of all illusion (literal interpretation) and the revealing of the ugly. Martin is the ideal in the same way that the *Battle* shows what *should* happen.

1. They may, of course, have been written at different times (as the "author" claims). They may be regarded as two works which were written at other times and are unconnected with the *Tale* except by theme, in approximately the way Bk. IV of the *Dunciad* is connected with the earlier books. This would explain the repetitions as unintended and the recapitulations as the author's clearing up of points in his own mind, but the effect would be the same as far as the reader is concerned.

pieces are threaded together, crossed, and tangled, so that at every moment the reader is jolted into awareness of the new direction the thought is taking.[1] We saw in Chapter 2 how paratactic fragments can be organized into structures of meaning; in this section we shall examine some of the images that tie together the three parts of the *Tale of a Tub* and see how they interact. I hope to show that a portion of the meaning (or theme) is carried by leftover elements of the seventeenth-century anatomy, whether esoteric allusion, eccentric image, or the Metaphysical development of metaphor.

1. We can begin with individual words. As Robert Heilman has noted, "Repetition itself is a mode of meaning. The trivial or accidental will not be repeated by a knowing artist." [2] This is one assumption a reader must take with him when he approaches the *Tale*. A number of such words in the *Tale* are signposts for the reader which will perhaps reveal the significance of a passage for him, without however having an independent significance of their own.

One of the words that might have rung a bell in the attentive reader's mind when he examined the passage about the "Fool among Knaves" was "Revolutions"—imagination, the Hack says, can "produce more wonderful Revolutions than Fortune or Nature" (172). "Revolution" is an example of a word that is repeated throughout the *Tale*, acquiring a particular meaning, which becomes damaging,

1. Clifford has observed ("Swift's *Mechanical Operation*," p. 143) that "a careful study of the organization of the material [in the *Tale*] will reveal the intricate and careful design of the whole piece. Like James Joyce's *Ulysses*, underneath the bewildering exterior is a carefully knit unified framework, tied together by a multitude of cryptic allusions and cross-references."

2. *This Great Stage: Image and Structure in King Lear* (Baton Rouge, Louisiana State Univ. Press, 1947), p. 9. See also W. B. C. Watkins, *Perilous Balance* (Princeton Univ. Press, 1939), p. 12; Watkins believes that Swift uses "repetitive imagery symbolically" as Shakespeare does.

or revealing, at this point when the Hack calls revolution wonderful and tries to make it respectable.

Revolution, or rotation of some sort, is normally a regular change, as in the "Dedication to Prince Posterity," where the "Revolution of the Sun" destroys the modern writings (33).[3] But the rotation of the tub in the preface (40) suggests irregular turnings at the mercy of waves and water currents, and the rotation of "Tops" (in the academy of wits—42) is a similar replacing of the regular and organic change, which is the order of the universe, by erratic movement. This is the sort of "great Revolutions" brought about by Peter (105) in his projects and his attempts to overawe his brothers; and the revolutions he carries out in the objective world are paralleled by one in his brain, which "began to *turn round* for a little Ease" (114). The result of both is the Revolution (137) which separates Peter and his brothers—the Reformation. Jack is characterized as a revolutionary: he thinks fit to give the revolution (the break with Peter) "another Turn" (141), and, if he did not invent Aeolism, he "gave it at least a new Turn" (161).[4] Like Peter, Jack's "Intellectuals were overturned," and we are told that the reason of all authors of new conquests, philosophies, or religions has "admitted great Revolutions" (162). Again, the physical revolutions are exact reflections of the revolutions in the conqueror's head (171).

Thus when the reader reaches the "wonderful Revolutions" (172), rather than seeing these as the "mighty Advantages Fiction has over Truth" or the "nobler Scenes" imagination can produce, he sees the imagination as the

3. Cf. the "Apology," where the rotation of seasons destroys the modern writings that attacked the *Tale* (9); and the Hack's reference to "Revolutions" which "may happen before [this writing] may be ready for your Perusal" (36).

4. The "first Revolutions" of Jack's brain gave rise to the Aeolists, we are told later (189).

source of the chaos these spastic motions have led to, and recognizes madness under the Hack's prettier word.

The word continues its life after the "Digression on Madness," until, as we might suspect, the Hack implies that his *Tale* too will bring about such a state: "IF the Reader fairly considers the Strength of what I have advanced in the foregoing Section [10], I am convinced it will produce a wonderful Revolution in his Notions and Opinions" (184).[5]

2. There are a number of mysterious (in the Rosicrucian sense) images in the *Tale,* like the tailor and the ass. We have seen the tailor as a probably Gnostic symbol. But the allusions that surround him and the punning of the words which describe him create an image of a markedly sexual nature. His ensign is the goose (both a tailor's iron and a colloquial expression for sexual intercourse),[6] and the description of the tailor himself ends with the following observations: "The chief *Idol* [the tailor] was also worshipped as the Inventor of the *Yard* and the *Needle,* whether as the God of Seamen, or on Account of certain other mystical Attributes, hath not been sufficiently cleared" (77). The conjunction of "Yard" and "Seamen" brings out the sexual puns in both, and a possible one in "Needle" as well. For example, a yard is, as it becomes more physical, (1) a yard-stick, used by a tailor, (2) a spar of a ship which holds sails, and (3) a sexual organ. The appearance of these puns makes the reader think twice about the word "tailor": it is derived from (1) the French *taillier,* to cut, and from (2)

5. This is followed in the next sec. (11) by the image of the reader as a horse and the Hack as the rider: "*Curiosity* [is] that Spur in the side, that Bridle in the Mouth, that Ring in the Nose, of a lazy, an impatient, and a grunting Reader" (203). "Curiosity" here should be compared with "Curiosity" in the Hack's curiosity-credulity dichotomy in the "Digression on Madness" (173).

6. See John S. Farmer and W. E. Henley, *Slang and its Analogues* (privately printed, 1893), *3,* 181–2: "A woman: whence, by implication, the sexual favor." As verb: "To go wenching" or "To possess a woman."

the Latin *talea,* a rod or stick. This aspect of the problem is emphasized again in critics' and tailors' having *"Weapons near of a Size"* (102), with the further suggestions that follow from the tailor's weapon being a needle. Finally, most outrageous of all, the worshippers of the tailor are said (in the next paragraph) to have had a system which turned upon a "Fundamental." [7]

The tailor would seem to represent, besides the cutter and arranger of reality, an arbitrary and changeable passion which is at the bottom of fashion.[8] As a symbol he therefore embodies the passion that is also at the bottom of Peter's and Jack's manipulation of reality. In either case, there is no fixed object of passion except the individual who is being passionate: the passion is for an ideal (to be at the "Top of the Fashion") which is so manifestly impossible that, as we have seen, Peter goes mad.

Perhaps because there is no object except gratification, there hovers behind this passion the suggestion of incompetence if not of impotence. Swift refers to one of the traditional sayings about tailors when he writes that "it requires at least as many [critics], to the making up of one Scholar, as of the [tailors] to the Composition of a Man" (102).[9] A quotation Swift may have had in mind when he wrote the *Tale* was Thomas Adams' gloomy picture of man

7. This word is used with ever greater frequency as the *Tale* progresses, particularly in the *Mechanical Operation,* e.g., "and from reflecting upon that fundamental Point in their Doctrines, about *Women* . . ." (287).

8. As Irenaeus had noted of the Gnostics, Hooker noted of the Puritans, that women were the best converts, and that "Affections, as joy, and grief, and fear, and anger, with such like, [are] as it were the sundry fashions and forms of Appetite" (preface, ch. 3, sec. 13, and Bk. I, ch. 7, sec. 3, *Works, 1,* 189–90 and 275). From the beginning, Puritans were linked with gross sexuality; see Clarence M. Webster, "Swift's *Tale of a Tub* Compared with Earlier Satires of the Puritans," *PMLA, 47* (1932), 175.

9. See Farmer and Henley, *7,* 61–2. In general tailors seem to have had a bad reputation: another common saying was "Thieving and tailor go together" (Ibid.). See also Carlyle's chapter "Tailors" in *Sartor Resartus* for more tailor lore.

in *Soules Sicknesse* (1630): "God hath made a man, he hath made himself a beast; and now the tailor (scarce a man himself) must make him a man again." [1]

Whether or not we take this as more than a hint, there is less doubt about the sexual implications of the Aeolist *adepti* who apply bellows to each others' breeches (153). Surely, when we remember the method of introducing the afflatus into the female *adepti*, the parallel is obvious.[2] It is interesting to note that in connection with Manicheism the charge was common that Catharist *perfecti*, maintaining their protest against physical contact with women, encouraged homosexual indulgence among their followers.[3] At any rate, the introduction of wind into the body offers

1. *The Soules Sicknesse: A Discourse Divine, Morall, and Physicall,* in *The Workes of Tho: Adams* (1630), *1*, 487. Swift may also, of course, have had in mind the numerous references to this pun in Shakespeare's plays.

2. See Dodds, *The Greeks and the Irrational*, p. 70. The prophetess, he explains, citing Herodotus, "was locked into the temple at night, with a view to mystic union with the god. Apparently she was thought to be at once his medium and his bride. . . ." See also Lewis R. Farnell, *Cults of the Greek States* (Oxford, 1896–1909), *4*, 187–9. It should also be noticed that there is an element of topical satire in the use of a priestess, perhaps aimed at the Quakers, whose women delivered sermons.

3. See A. S. Turberville, *Medieval Heresy and the Inquisition* (London, Crosby Lockwood and Son, 1920), p. 32 and n. The derivation of the common English slang for pederast, "buggerer" (see, e.g., Bailey's *Dictionary*), is from a heretical Bulgarian sect of Catharist origin (see Robert Graves, " 'Lars Porsena,' or the Future of Swearing and Improper Language," in *Occupation Writer*, New York, Creative Age Press, 1950, p. 7). There is more than a suggestion of sexual perversion in the relationship Swift sets up between Bentley and Wotton. In parallel constructions, we hear of Wotton and "his Lover" Bentley, and of Boyle and "his Friend" Phalaris. The relationship is between defender and defended, and the implication is that Wotton's defense is produced by less disinterested reasons than Boyle's (cf. Bentley as Wotton's "Yokemate"—38). The love Wotton represents has no other end than self-gratification: by supporting moderns or Bentley he is advancing himself. In the same way, one Aeolist simply employs another to fan and nourish his grain of wind, and to act as a channel of evacuation. (The learned dust which fell upon Bentley's spleen—"and some climbed up into his Head, to the great Perturbation of both"—may be the scholar's equivalent of the sex drive that inspires the vapor of the enthusiast—226.)

little hope of either physical or moral fertilization, and serves to separate these parody mystics from true mystics who bring forth deeds from their experience.

A closer look at the text will disclose dozens of half-articulated references to sex, impotence, and drought, which help to create the peculiar world of the Hack. One result of the tailor's kind of sex drive is apparent in the Banbury Saint and in the Hack himself, both of whom have poxed bodies to show for it. Other signs of venereal disease as the fruit of sexual activity among moderns are the suggestion of sweating tub in the *Tale's* title and the school of salivation in the Academy for wits.[4] On the other hand, there is no sign of fertility being connected with sex; the flowers in the "Conclusion" which are dropped among "unsuitable Company" (210) do not grow, any more than the piece of wit taken out of Hyde Park (43); the strange flower in the epigraph from Lucretius is known to none. The reason that fame, "being a Fruit grafted on the Body," cannot grow is that there is nothing there but self, and so no rooting place (185). That is, the ancients represent a fertilizing source to which one can go; but the modern man fancies himself hermaphroditic.[5]

The *Mechanical Operation* gathers together these scattered allusions and uses them to answer the question abandoned in the Hack's hiatus in the "Digression on Madness": if enthusiasm is madness, is it simply an accident or a disease which precludes individual responsibility? The speaker of the *Mechanical Operation* reveals the truth that the enthusiasts arrange things so that it is easy to go mad. Their preacher is one "way" (he is compared to a form of transportation), and so the subject of the *Mechanical Op-*

---

4. Two cures for venereal disease were the sweating tub and salivation by mercury.

5. Cf. Temple's "mighty reservoirs or lakes of knowledge" which nourish the sensible people like Thales and Pythagoras (*Essay*, in *Works, 3, 434*)

eration is "by what Intercourse between [the teacher] and his Assembly, [enthusiasm] is cultivated and supported" (265). The direction this will take is implied by the pun, which is developed through the *Mechanical Operation*: intercourse becomes sexual intercourse, as the ultimate and most conspicuous example of physical gratification. Other forms of gratification are presented, however, from the Aeolist-like holding in of tobacco smoke to the pleasure of hearing the preacher's drone. But as the latter is compared to the lover's whine, so the sexual allusions cling to these other sources of enthusiasm too.[6] If we turn back to the oratorial machines which have effect on "ears" and "raise Pruriences and Protuberances," it becomes clear that the relation between auditor and teacher has been at least metaphorically a sexual one from the beginning.[7] The

6. See, e.g., the motions of the enthusiasts' bodies and the reference to "the Art of *See-saw* on a Beam, and swinging by Session upon a Cord, in order to raise artificial Extasies" (272). The passage is riddled with sexual puns:

"See-saw": *to see* was colloquial for *to copulate* (Farmer and Henley, 6, 138); thus the extension to seesaw, as in the example from Pope which Dr. Johnson quotes: "His wit all *seesaw*, between that and this; / Now high, now low, now master up, now miss."

"Session": in the source Swift cites it means sitting (see G-S, p. 272n.), but it also suggests a court sitting, from which we get the connection with the gallows as a means to ecstasy (see n. 7, below).

For "raise" cf. 61, "raising Pruriences and Protuberances," or 288, "raise That of a Gallant."

7. The pulpit is supposed to have a "mighty Influence on human Ears" (58), rather than on minds and understandings. Thus the reference to "ears" is, first, a dig at the emphasis on sheer sound in the sermons of the period and, second, a reference to the thin line that separates the man in the pillory with cropped ears from the man in the pulpit (both are high places and allow the person to be seen and heard, and both are lodgings for dissent and faction). But it can also be taken as a reference to the connection between "ears" and sexual organs drawn in section 11. As a colloquial verb, "ear" meant to plow, with the implication of copulation (Latin *arare*): Eric Partridge, *Shakespeare's Bawdy* (New York, Dutton, 1948), p. 105.

The gallows was an example of the sensual pleasure that drew huge crowds to executions; but the implication is that the orator gets as much

preacher, whether orator or Aeolist, is the male principle, and his congregation the female, into whose mouths he drops his words.

The sexual metaphor is important in the *Mechanical Operation* because it is couched, as we have seen, solely in terms of self-gratification. There is no communication between preacher and congregation, only the search for ecstasy. Love is characterized in the fanatic sects of the *Mechanical Operation* by the garlands the couples wear "of *Ivy* and *Vine*, Emblems of Cleaving and Clinging; or of *Fir*, the Parent of *Turpentine*" (285). The relationship expressed is a sticky, parasitic one. What Augustine said of stage tragedy could apply to this level of mystical experience: "But what sort of compassion," he wrote, "is this for feigned and scenical passions? for the auditor is not called on to relieve, but only to grieve. . . ." [8] What the church disapproved of was the stimulating of emotions without any useful end, "only to drain them away into the barren sands of inactivity." [9] Augustine expressed the same view of "irresponsible amatory adventure," comparing the "self-restraint of the marriage-covenant, for the sake of issue" with "the bargain of a lustful love." [1] The sermon which only aroused emotions for their own sake, directing them toward union with a vague One instead of toward moral practice, was guilty of the same error.

We can conclude that the tailor, who symbolizes heresy in the historical narrative (at the center of the thematic structure), contains the germ of a theme which spreads by

---

pleasure out of his drop as does the audience. See, e.g., Browne (*Pseudo-doxia*, in *Works*, ed. Sayle, *1*, 289), who, mentioning the belief that man-drakes grow "under Gallowses and places of execution, arising from fat or urine that drops from the body of the dead," alludes to the belief that the breaking of the neck causes an orgasm.

8. St. Augustine, *Confessions*, Bk. III, p. 31.

9. Charles Norris Cochrane, *Christianity and Classical Culture* (New York, Oxford University Press, 1957), p. 392.

1. St. Augustine, Bk. IV, p. 46.

allusions and puns until in the *Mechanical Operation* it is made to be the last word on enthusiasm and the Hack's easy illusions. The *gratification* of the self is simply the other side of the Gnostic *reliance* on self we saw in Chapter 3, and the suggestion of sexual irregularity and impotence in the Hack's language is an expression of the perversion of the inward-turned man, who mishandles the reality of this world.

3. A second puzzling image is the ass, which is not limited like the tailor to one appearance and one mention (in connection with the critic). The ass appears at several crucial moments, being linked with those important moderns the critics (98–9) and with Bentley himself in the *Battle* (254, 257), because of the topical allusion to asses in the Phalaris controversy.[2] But the ass is not entirely explicable as simply the traditional figure of stupidity.[3] He is also associated with Jack, whose head (after he ate fire) looked "like the Scull of an Ass, wherein a roguish Boy hath conveyed a Farthing Candle" (192), and appears elsewhere as "an Asse's Head." [4] As such, I believe the ass is meant as a sort of counter-idol to the tailor, the explanation lying in the ancient belief that the ass is a false god. For example, we have a reference in one of Swift's sources for his knowl-

2. Boyle claimed that Bentley called him an ass (G-S, p. 233 n.), and adds that Bentley calls everyone an ass: "In the 11th page," Boyle pointed out, "the Sophist is *an Ass under the Skin of a Lyon*; in the 59th, *Phalaris is a meer Asinus ad Lyram*": Boyle, *Dr. Bentley's Dissertation on the Epistles of Phalaris, and the Fables of Aesop, Examin'd by the Honourable Charles Boyle, Esq.* (London, 1698), p. 220. There is a particular reference to this incident in the *Battle* (254, 257), and in general Swift equates critics and other moderns with asses. But before any of these, Temple had quoted, in his attack on man's presumption, "Vain man would fain be wise, when he is born like a wild ass's colt" (*Essay*, in *Works*, 3, 460; see also "ass's ears," p. 490).

3. See, e.g., Pope's use of an ass on the title page of the *Variorum Dunciad* (1729).

4. E.g., when it is a cloud (35), or the office of confession (108), or Jack's head (192), or simply referred to as "Ears" (when associated with the ear-fetishists—200).

edge of Gnosticism, Epiphanius' *Panarion*, where the god of the Gnostics is accused of having "the face of an *Ass*." [5] As a result of an iconographical confusion, the ass head became associated with the god of the Gnostics, and even at one point with the god of the Christians.[6] It is enough here to notice that the ass was (in Swift's knowledge if no one else's) associated with the Gnostics, and more generally associated with a false or parody god, such as the critic or Jack set up to be.

The *Tale*, however, develops one other aspect of the ass, when in the *Mechanical Operation* it becomes Mahomet's ass and later is associated with satyrs and goats, "Companions of great Skill and Practice in Affairs of Gallantry" (285). Robert Graves points to the ancient connection between asses and lust in his introduction to Apuleius' *Golden Ass*. When one of the characters "rides home on ass-back, he remarks that this is an extraordinary sight—a virgin riding in triumph on an ass. He means: 'dominating the lusts of the flesh without whip or bridle.' " [7]

It is at this point that the images of horse and rider join that of the ass, and what has been a matter of general control of oneself becomes specifically control of the passions. In the *Tale* the modern, not looking for control, "when he gives the Spur and Bridle to his Thoughts, doth never stop, but naturally sallies out into both extreams of High and Low, of Good and Evil" (157). Sometimes the metaphor expresses an inverted relationship, as when "a Man's Fancy gets *astride* on his Reason" (171), where obviously Reason should be the rider. Again, when Reason is the rider he is light and easily shaken off (180). But while in the *Tale*

5. Epiphanius asserts "that the Gnostic Sabaoth has, according to some, the face of an *Ass*, according to others, that of a Hog; on which latter account He hath forbidden the Jews to eat swine's flesh" (Cited in King, *Gnostics and their Remains*, p. 230).

6. For the story of how this came about, see King, *Gnostics*, pp. 227–31.

7. Robert Graves, ed., *Golden Ass*, by Apuleius (Penguin Books, 1950), p. 13.

proper it is simply a convenient image for a relationship between reason and imagination, control or uncontrol, in the *Battle* the horse is materialized on the ground together with his rider. Again the horse represents the imagination, but the horses of the ancients are such powerful ones as Homer's, which is "with Difficulty managed by the Rider himself, but which no other Mortal durst approach" (244–5); while the moderns ride old lean horses like that of Dryden (246), who is himself afraid to mount Virgil's horse when given the opportunity. Lucan's horse is "head-strong" but bears "the Rider where he list" (247); and Pindar directs his horse, "Never advancing in a direct Line, but wheeling with incredible Agility and Force" (248). The modern is shown to have neither true horse nor strong bridle; and the contrast is therefore underlined when the *Mechanical Operation* commences with the image of Mahomet (any modern) trying to get to heaven on his ass.

In terms of the *Battle* the ass may suggest a second-rate substitute for an imagination, and there is some indication that we are to take *ass* as a pun on *arse*,[8] which would both locate imagination and suggest an image of sufficiency: re-fusing the aid offered by heaven—the "fiery Chariots, wing'd Horses, and celestial Sedans"—Mahomet "would be born to Heaven upon nothing but his *Ass*" (264). But this remains a secondary, playful meaning, while it is soon established that the horse substitute is one of the asses we have encountered in the *Tale*—the enthusiast preacher; the *Mechanical Operation* is about *his* way of conveying men and women to heaven. Heaven, however, is a pun too,

8. See Holloway, "The Well-Filled Dish," p. 24, who offers this possibility. It is made clear, however, that the pun *is* intended when we are told (278) that the best musical instruments are made from the bones of an ass, and some critics believe this means jawbone, but others think it means *os sacrum*. See also a sermon attributed to St. Augustine, *De Cantico Novo 3*: "*caro nostra iumentum nostrum est: iter agimus in Ierusalem*" ("The flesh is the nag on which we make the journey to Jerusalem"); quoted by Cochrane, p. 446. The idea in this passage is that if our loves are evil they will lead us to hell, if good to heaven.

becoming the purely physical ecstasy we discussed earlier in
this section.

The three examples we have explored may suggest some
of the complexity of reference and cross reference that is
present in the *Tale of a Tub*. They show how words,
images, facts, and metaphors merge into larger structures
of meaning, often metaphorical, and how figures like the
tailor are compact embodiments of these various fragments
of theme. Moreover, these images run as an undercurrent
parallel to the development we have followed in the narrative and in the Hack's tampering with reality, revealing
the least respectable and most thoroughly concealed (perhaps subconscious) motives of the self-sufficient modern.
These motives are characterized by a pitiable desire for
diversion and sensual gratification; the very simplest drives
are thus at the bottom of the complicated edifice of pride
and pretence.[9]

9. Another pattern of imagery we could mention in this connection is
that of food and eating, which pervades the *Tale*—a sort of backdrop for
the sensual imagery we have discussed in this section. The diversion the
orators offer the people is *"weighty* Matter" that drops from the machines
into the "Mouths open, and erected parallel to the Horizon" (60–1). Thus,
when attacked by Gresham and Will's, the Hack is answering the accusation that there is no nourishment in this food: *"Wisdom* is a *Fox,"* he says,
". . . 'Tis a *Cheese,* which by how much the richer, has the thicker, the
homelier, and the courser Coat; and whereof to a judicious Palate, the
Maggots are the best. 'Tis a *Sack-Posset,* wherein the deeper you go, you
will find it the sweeter" (66). The foods he produces have at their centers,
the reader notices, merely dangerous, unpleasant, or intoxicating things.
Following the line of food imagery, we find the critics who "nibble at the
Superfluities, and Excrescencies of Books" (98), who are like wolves after
game (101), rats after cheese, wasps after fruit and dogs after a bone (103).
Hunger becomes one of the chief characteristics of the Hack's world; but
taste itself has no meaning for critics who are "padling in, or tasting"
ordure (93), or it is destroyed by the modern's love of olios and ragouts—
"the Fashion of jumbling fifty Things together in a Dish" (144), so that
mere *eating* is involved. Thus the reader knows how to interpret the Hack
when he refers to his book as a meal (184), or explains that "The late
Refinements in Knowledge [run] parallel to those of Dyet in our Nation"
(143).

VII. The Norm of the Harmonious Body

We have seen moral norms in Lord Somers and the *Tale* itself (as presented in the "Apology"), which tend toward the metaphorical. In the last section we saw such a norm in the rider who controls his horse; the norm was implicit in the images of horses controlling riders in the *Tale,* and became explicit in the ancients who control their horses in the *Battle.* Another such norm was the coat in the allegorical narrative, which represented a plain and decent individual, church and dogma, unrent by sin or by dissension. The norm of the original coat, followed by its corruptions, acts as a central, explicit image which is developed in the images of deformed or diseased bodies we noticed in Chapter 3. There we saw that the Gnostic finds the deformed body individualizing and therefore superior to the harmonious body; but the Christian religion, expressed in the original coat and seeing a psychosomatic relation between the inner and the outer man, finds the harmonious body its ideal. We were primarily concerned in Chapter 3 with the Gnostic's view of the individual, and so of his own body; but as the allegory of the coats suggests, the norm of the harmonious body is twofold: that of the individual's body and that of the body politic.

In this section we shall examine the norm of the harmonious body, against which the reader judges the Gnostic body, and then we shall see how Swift parallels the picture of the one man out on his own, outside and against society, with an organ of the body, or any part of a whole, that grows out of proportion and first distorts the harmony of appearance and of operation and then tries to take over control for itself. The well-functioning body will be seen to be like the body politic; when one part ceases functioning as a part, the whole organism suffers.

The church has traditionally regarded itself as the body
of Christ, and the spirit, faith, love, sacraments, word, and
ministry are the veins and arteries which bind it together.
The metaphor suggests that the body of the church on
earth is aspiring toward the body of Christ, as a child
aspires to be a man; the apostles, pastors, and teachers work
toward "the edifying of the body of Christ":

> Till we all come in the unity of the faith, and of the
> knowledge of the Son of God, unto a perfect man,
> unto the measure of the stature of the fulness of Christ:
> that we henceforth . . . may grow up into him in all
> things, which is the head,[1] even Christ: From whom
> the whole body fitly joined together and compacted
> by that which every joint supplieth, according to the
> effectual working in the measure of every part, maketh
> increase of the body unto the edifying of itself in
> love.[2]

The image of a whole, healthy body remains as a sort of
norm in the back of the Christian mind, giving to the individual body a sanctity of its own.

The same sort of analogy operated in the social context,
where the body's humours were like the four elements,
earth, water, air, and fire, and from there the imagination
could build the head into a king, arteries and veins into
rivers and highways, arms and legs into soldiers and coun-
sellors.[3] The most striking example of the metaphor of a

1. See Col. 1:18: "he is the head of the body."
2. Eph. 4:13-16. See also I Cor. 12:13-14: "For by one Spirit are we all
baptized into one body . . . For the body is not one member, but many."
See also Rom. 12:4ff.
3. It is reasonable to think that the metaphor of the body politic has its
origin in the totemic identification of a king with his country; the Fisher
King is stricken in the loins, and so the fertility of his country is impaired.
When magic becomes metaphor it does not entirely lose its spell; this may
be one reason for the choice of the body as the symbol of the church. The
body is, of course, a natural point to start from if one seeks an analogy:
our everyday speech is full of transfers like "leg" of a table or "arm" of
a chair.

body politic in Swift's time was Hobbes' *Leviathan*. Swift refers to the *Leviathan* as a whale (preface); but his use of the body metaphor reminds one of the figure of the giant composed of innumerable little men which appears on Hobbes' title page (and to which Swift alludes—277). Hobbes writes of the state in terms of a body which has currency for blood, tax-collectors for veins, and colonies for children; [4] which is prone to various diseases such as *"Tyrannophobia"* ("fear of being strongly governed," caused by the bite of "democratical writers"), epilepsy (defiance of the temporal authority by the spiritual), ague (shortage of revenue due to the subjects' stinginess), pleurisy (monopolies), or "the insatiable appetite . . . of enlarging dominion; with the incurable *wounds* thereby many times received from the enemy; and the *wens,* of ununited conquests . . . as also the *lethargy* of ease, and the *consumption* of riot and vain expense" (pp. 214–18).

Moreover, the Renaissance made the human body the symbol of the beauty and harmony it advocated. Alberti defined beauty accordingly in his treatise *On Architecture* (1452): "I shall define Beauty to be a harmony of all the parts, in whatsoever subject it appears, fitted together with such proportion and connection that nothing could be added, diminished or altered." [5] Alberti's definition is related to Swift's definition of style as "proper words in the proper places," as well as to Hooker's idea of law as harmony and beauty of proportion. If we regard a sermon or a poem, or any work of man, in the light of these implications, we shall see that the dislocation of form can be taken by a Christian as a symbol of moral failure. Hooker's view of the church as a structure of law and reason into which man fits is ultimately a matter of order, and order, for Hooker and his contemporaries, is harmony and beauty. "Goodness in actions is like unto straightness; wherefore

4. *Leviathan*, ed. Oakeshott, pp. 164–5.
5. Quoted by Sypher, *Four Stages of Renaissance Style*, p. 62.

that which is done well we term *right*. . . . Besides which
fitness for use, there is also in rectitude, beauty; as contrari-
wise in obliquity, deformity. . . . In which consideration
the Grecians most divinely have given to the active perfec-
tion of men a name expressing both beauty and goodness." [6]
The order of the inward self is accordingly reflected in the
appearance of the outward—the well-tended body, the
proper suit of clothes worn properly, as well as table manners. Hooker remarks disapprovingly of the Puritans that
"Where they found men in diet, attire, furniture of house,
or any other way, observers of civility and decent order,
such they reproved as being carnally and earthly minded." [7]
And it is a simple extension of this to Hooker's view of
their dissident position in the church and state. The un-
kempt exterior is, moreover, with dirt, disease, and deformity, a Christian symbol of sin; and the connotations of
sin naturally follow when the metaphor is extended from
the body to the body politic. As opposed to the "glorious
church, not having spot, or wrinkle, or any such thing . . .
holy and without blemish," we find Ezekiel's accusation:
"In thy filthiness is lewdness: because I have purged thee,
and thou wast not purged, thou shalt not be purged from
thy filthiness any more, till I have caused my fury to rest
upon thee." [8] This metaphor also suggests the body's inno-

6. Bk. I, ch. 8, sec. 1, *Works, I,* 281. A typical body image used by Hooker
compares his work (the *Laws*) to a "whole entire body" in which can be
found "each particular controversy's resting-place" (preface, ch. 7, sec. 7,
Works, I, 215). Though only submerged, this metaphor is very different
from the Gnostic one; he uses it to command, they use it to condemn the
body as matter. See also Bk. VIII, ch. 4, sec. 7, *Works, 3,* Pt. I, 477ff.

7. Preface, ch. 7, sec. 7, *Works, I,* 229.

8. Eph. 5:27, Ezek. 24:13. For a discussion see Roland M. Frye, "Swift's
Yahoo and the Christian Symbols for Sin," *Journal of the History of
Ideas, 15* (1954), 201–17. Frye cites corroboratory passages from Donne,
Agas, and Taylor (pp. 210–11). He tends, however, toward the Puritan view
of a strong dichotomy between body and soul, associating this view with
Swift's treatment of the Yahoos.

cence: it can be *made* dirty or diseased, it is (because of the Fall) capable of it; but the body itself is good, like all creation.

This concept of body is a natural one to attach to the image of a unified church. Isaac Barrow's *A Discourse Concerning the Unity of the Church* (1680), a well-known contemporary statement of this view, employs as a central image the church as the *"One body, into which we are all baptized by one Spirit; which is knit together, and compacted of parts affording mutual aid, and supply to its nourishment and increase;* the members whereof do hold a mutual sympathy and complacence; which is joined to one Head, deriving sense and motion from it; which is enlivened and moved by *One Spirit."* Barrow finds this metaphor bolstered and extended by Biblical reference to the metaphor of *"One spiritual house,* reared *upon the foundation of the Prophets and Apostles, Jesus Christ being the chief corner-stone; in whom all the building fitly framed together groweth into an holy temple in the Lord."* Finally, Barrow parallels both of these with the *"One family of God."* [9]

Body, house, family: Barrow may have been in Swift's mind when he wrote, since the *Tale* also starts with a body and moves toward analogous forms; the *Tale*, in fact, takes this series of unities and presents their modern versions:

9. *The Theological Works of Isaac Barrow, D.D.,* ed. Alexander Napier (Cambridge, 1859), *8*, 687. Barrow's epigraph is *"One body, and one Spirit. —Eph. 4.4."* The edition of 1680 was in Swift's library sale catalogue— Williams, *Swift's Library,* No. 505, p. (13). While Swift must have agreed with Barrow's general argument for church unity, it is unlikely that he agreed with some of the Latitudinarian proposals for bringing it about.

The metaphor of body is also used strikingly by Milton in *Of Reformation,* culminating in an image of episcopacy as the bunch of flesh, the wen, a putrifying mass, which tries to call itself the head of the church (which is the body). This is a very Swiftian image, and the interchange between the wen and the other parts of the body may have helped to suggest the spider-bee interchange in the *Battle.*

the deformed body, the haunted house, and the chaotic crowd.

We saw in Chapter 3 that the principle behind the deformed body was the encouraging of one organ or characteristic to grow beyond a "reasonable Compass." Shortly after the appearance of the fat man in the preface, the Hack warns satirists to remember "it is with *Wits* as with *Razors,* which are never so apt to *cut* those they are employ'd on, as when they have *lost their Edge.* Besides, those whose Teeth are too rotten to bite, are best of all others, qualified to revenge that Defect with their Breath" (49). As a razor is for shaving, not cutting, so teeth are for chewing food, not biting; breath is "life itself," as we read in section 8, but here it is a weapon. These are diseased organs whose original purpose has been lost, and as the fat man's size requires him to crowd for more room, so the rottenness of teeth forces the poisonous breath on the owner's neighbors, and the growth of one organ will force other organs to stop functioning.[1]

Following the picture we are given in section 2 of the fringe and lace which overwhelm the coats of the brothers, comes the critic who subsists on this excess. He eats the *"Superfluities, and Excrescencies"*—"the *Luxuriant,* the *Rotten,* the *Dead,* the *Sapless,* and the *Overgrown Branches"* (98). It is implied—in the image of the heroes who "when all *other* Vermin were destroy'd, should in Conscience have concluded with the same Justice upon themselves" (94)—that the critics too are excrescences. All human actions being divided, "One Man can *Fiddle,* and another

---

1. It is significant that this should be followed immediately by the discussion of satire, and reference to "lashes" and "pestilent Disease," to rotten teeth and foul breath, to health as "but one Thing . . . whereas Diseases are by thousands, besides new and daily Additions" (50). Knavery and atheism *"are Epidemick as the Pox"* (52). All of these reflect the satiric metaphor of body, which is the normal body diseased, and lashed for its own good.

can make *a small Town a great City,* and he that cannot do
either one or the other, deserves to be kick'd out of the
Creation. The avoiding of which Penalty, has doubtless
given the first Birth to the Nation of *Criticks*" (101). An
excrescence, then, is something for which there is no ordinary use; like the true (the Hack's false) critic, one should
step over it, not dabble in it or drag it out into the light.

More important, the excrescence which is encouraged by
the modern takes control of the body itself. The modern
preface is defined by the Hack as *"large* in proportion as
the subsequent Volume is *small"* (54), and in the "Digression in Praise of Digressions" we are shown what happens
when one part of a book is allowed, or encouraged, to grow
so beyond "a reasonable Compass" that it takes over the
book, either usurping or killing. In the modern world the
odd ingredients thrown into a ragout for their own sake
overwhelm any staple that may have been present; mercenary armies take over countries they are paid to defend;
the index takes over the book and leads into the enlargement of all that is behind or at the back. As palaces should
be entered from the rear and armies attacked from the rear,
so the physician should discover "the State of the whole
Body, by consulting only what comes from *Behind*" (145).
From this point on, the idea of the digression or of the sub-
servient organ taking control is associated with the "lower"
parts of the body: the bowels and the sexual organs.

In section 8 the digression controlling the book is extended to the excretion controlling the body, and, finally, in
the "Digression on Madness" we are left with an image of
man allowing this little thing, perhaps sexual, perhaps
excremental, to control his whole body and life. In terms of
the philosophical controversy of the day, this is the "cer-
taine glande forte petite, située dans le milieu de sa substance" where Descartes located the soul (more specifically,
the mind) of man, in opposition to the old Aristotelian

image of the soul as the stamp and the body as the wax.[2]
In this topsy-turvy world madness is given control of the
mind and we are not surprised to hear the Hack declare,
"I wake, when others sleep, and sleep when others wake"
(185).

The *Battle* gives us a final catchall image of the inhar-
monious body in the monstrous goddess Criticism, which
carries echoes of both Blackmore's fury Persecution and
Milton's Sin: [3]

> The Goddess herself had Claws like a Cat: Her Head,
> and Ears, and Voice, resembled those of an *Ass;* Her
> Teeth fallen out before; Her Eyes turned inward, as if
> she lookt only upon herself: Her Diet was the over-
> flowing of her own *Gall:* Her *Spleen* was so large, as to
> stand prominent like a Dug of the first Rate, nor
> wanted Excrescencies in form of Teats, at which a
> Crew of ugly Monsters were greedily sucking . . .
> [240].

Here we see recapitulated (1) the theme of cutting and dissecting, and (2) the image of the ass's head. The ears (recall-
ing Jack's "perpetually exposed and arrect"—195) and
the voice (the braying, which suggests the theme of noncom-
munication) are connected. (3) Her eyes are turned inward
with the spider self-interest, and both this and her fallen
teeth suggest impotence; (4) like the spider and the doctor
she lives off of her own excretion. The spleen, it should

2. *Oeuvres de Descartes,* ed. Charles Adam and Paul Tannery (Paris,
Cerf, 1904), 2, 352. Descartes describes the medium that connects the mind
(the pineal gland, or conarion) as a "vent tres subtil" (2, 129). For a somewhat later contemporary account of the conflict, see Prior's *Alma,* Canto
i, ll. 14ff.

3. If we include Criticism's speech, the parody is more specifically of
Blackmore's *Prince Arthur, An Heroick Poem in Ten Books* (London, 1695),
pp. 18–19. Like Milton's Sin (*Paradise Lost,* Bk. ii, ll. 781–802; cited in G-S,
p. 240n.), her father is also her husband and Pride is her mother; her progeny
is a crew of monsters that flocks about her.

be remembered, was a bowel which caught the salts and earthy excrements from the blood (Bailey). (5) Thus, an organ of excretion has been allowed to grow out of control, and the teats (called "Excrescencies" themselves) are once again being nibbled by critics.[4] The theme is summed up when Criticism says: *"By Me, Beaux become Politicians; and School-boys, Judges of Philosophy. By Me, Sophisters debate, and conclude upon the Depths of Knowledge; and Coffeehouse Wits instinct by Me, can correct an Author's Style, and display his minutest Errors, without understanding a Syllable of his Matter or his Language"* (241). If the spider represents the individual who considers himself self-sufficient, the Goddess Criticism represents the nightmarish result to which this attitude leads.

Finally, from the *Mechanical Operation* and its discussion of ways and means, we can infer that all of these deviations or distortions of the body—as, incidentally, of words—come from self-indulgence; whether from eating too much, wenching too much, or (we can presume with Wotton and Bentley) bending too long over books.

Swift's use of the "one spiritual house" is less specific, but perhaps more inclusive, than the metaphor of body. Twice he compares the body which is inhabited by vapor or spirit to a haunted house: these houses are "waste and empty Dwellings," "forsaken and gone to Decay" (174, 283). They are, however, only part of a complex of images revolving around the idea of the body's resemblance to a container—the Gnostic belief that the body is simply a tub for holding spirit. The ass's head, for instance, is spoken of at one point as containing a candle, and is compared to Jack's head glowing like a jack-o'-lantern (192). Jack's moral is that *"a Wise Man was his own Lanthorn,"* which is a

---

4. It should also be noticed that her chariot is drawn by "tame Geese"—presumably here geese represent stupidity; but they also contain a memory of the tailor's goose, with its appropriate connotations.

literal way of interpreting "inner light." In the *Mechanical Operation* we read that these lanterns are stuffed with "Leaves from old *Geneva* Bibles" (279), and, going one step further, we are told: "Remark your commonest Pretender to a Light *within,* how dark, and dirty, and gloomy he is *without;* As Lanthorns, which the more Light they bear in their Bodies, cast out so much the more Soot, and Smoak, and fuliginous Matter to adhere to the Sides" (282). From the idea of "inner light" taken literally, we have moved to the actual properties of a lantern; [5] after this, the speaker of the *Mechanical Operation* extends the general shape of a container of fire to a furnace, and thence to the haunted house, within which "the *Spirit* delights to dwell" (283). The *Tale* is, in fact, full of images of containers: the housewife's still, the well that is too dark for the bottom to be seen, the Aeolist's body which is a "vessel" or "tun," the barrel-shaped pulpit, and finally the tub itself.[6]

These are containers which—taking the house as our example—no longer contain anything, or do not contain what they should: instead of a sturdy structure containing people, the house is a decaying shell containing ghosts. The central image from which the others we have mentioned emanate is the tub, significantly a part of the book's title, a container which contains nothing. The tub is also, however, a container which wishes to appear as if it did contain something. It is presented in the preface as analogous to the ship of church and state (as a way to fool the whale), and in these terms it is a false appearance of a ship. Something important is missing in it: a straight course or cargo or ballast. It has only the outward appearance of a ship, "hollow, and dry . . . and wooden," while in fact being "empty, and

5. In all of these cases the property of fire that is emphasized is heat rather than light—self-gratification of the individual rather than enlightenment of others. For earlier references to lanterns, see pp. 36, 62, and 193.

6. See pp. 277, 207, 153, 58, 40.

noisy . . . and given to Rotation"—at best a parody, at worst a tub actively trying to pass for a ship. These characteristics of shape, hollowness, dryness, emptiness, and noise, woodenness, rotation—and pretense—proceed through the *Tale* summoning up the idea of tub whenever they appear.[7]

The tub is initially connected with the product of the modern's imagination, but by section 8 it has become the modern's body itself, since his writing is, we have seen, synonymous with himself. The three oratorial machines are "Receptacles or Machines" which "contain" a great mystery (61), and when the pulpit (the first oratorial machine) is called a "Vessel" (58), it is shown to be a tub masquerading as a pulpit: a mere container into which anything can be poured, including incitement to sedition.[8] In the same way, modern writing is presumably a container like the Hack's commonplace book, which he says he is able to "fill much slower than I had reason to expect" (54). In the introduction the tub as a false appearance becomes the vehicle (or fable) of the writings of Grub Street. In the Hack's defense of these writings against Gresham and Will's, the emptiness of the tub is merely echoed by the various dangerous or un-

7. Often it is a matter of word play as when, a page after the introduction of the tub, the Hack discusses his imagination in terms of a tub run dry (i.e. a tub masquerading as an imagination). He admits that because his imagination is "empty" and "drained" he cannot live up to the duty of a preface writer. The moderns, however, he says, "will by no means let slip a Preface or a Dedication, without some notable or distinguishing Stroke, to surprise the Reader at the Entry, and kindle a wonderful Expectation of what is to ensue" (42). "Kindle" is another of the active verbs that bring life to abstract language in the *Tale*. On the speaker's level of awareness "Stroke" is a good literary touch; but its literal meaning of a blow produces two countermeanings: (1) the "touch" struck the reader more than charmed him, and (2) with "kindle" parallel with "surprise" as "Stroke's" verbs, it becomes the stroke that starts the spark out of a flint. We are back to the hollow, dry and wooden, which when it has run out of imagination as liquid can consume itself with fire.

8. Cf. the Meal Tub Plot, referred to in the introduction (70), "*an Account of a* Presbyterian *Plot*," Swift's note tells us, "*found in a Tub, which then made much Noise.*"

rewarding tenors contained in the vehicles of foxholes, cheeses, sack-possets, and nuts. Neither the probing of the "penetrating Wits" nor the Hack's exantlation will reveal anything worthwhile on the inside.[9] The Hack's final example, though he is not aware of it, carries the container from the book to the author's body: like his Grub Street fables, it is beat-up on the outside and poxed on the inside (70). A page later he writes that "I have with much Thought and Application of Mind, so ordered, that the chief Title prefixed to [this treatise], (I mean, That under which I design it shall pass in the common Conversations of Court and Town) is modelled exactly after the Manner peculiar to *Our* Society" (71). His title tells us the whole story. Like the tub, the products of *"Our* Society" are hollow and empty.

The full impact of the connections we have seen made in the introduction dawns upon the reader when the Hack dissects Human Nature in order to draw out his own conclusion (123), as he promised to exantlate the Grub Street fables. When all containers have the same significance— i.e. are merely containers—by a simple extension the dissecting of a maggoty cheese or a piece of writing becomes the dissecting of a human body. From this point on the human body has become a container so far as the moderns are con-

9. We have seen (sec. vi of this chapter) that the cheeses, sack-possets, and nuts connect the metaphor of hunger and eating with that of the empty container which is a false appearance. In this passage the two metaphors are apprehended as one, creating the familiar appearance of dainties that turn to ashes when tasted, like Augustine's reference to the Manichean doctrines which seduced him as "glittering fantasies," "empty husks," dishes which turned out to be "emptiness, nor was I nourished by them, but exhausted rather" (St. Augustine, *Confessions*, Bk. iii, pp. 35–6). In the overall structure of the *Tale* this image answers the question: what is the nature of the creation that results from the Gnostic imagination? After the introduction the methods of creating these diversions and the appalling results are discussed; but the problem of the object's utter worthlessness has been settled. Thus when the reader reaches the Hack's "false Mediums" in the "Digression on Madness," he will probably associate them with the "Surface and Rind" of the introduction.

cerned—simply a container for mind or spirit; and the idea is developed in the vessel-like bodies of the Aeolists and of the vapor-dominated moderns of the "Digression on Madness."

The metaphor of body can be seen to tie together a number of the threads of the *Tale* into one coherent image of a body which eats, lusts, excretes, and destroys itself by various excesses. But we have also seen, particularly in the *Mechanical Operation,* that one individual collides with another; and this leads us to Barrow's final image, which occurs at intervals through the *Tale of a Tub.* This is the image of unity as the *"One family of God,"* which is presented to us around the father's deathbed in section 2 of the *Tale,* and is almost immediately broken up: Peter, Martin, and Jack become three different people, moving in different directions, in short no longer a family but a crowd. The image of a crowd is hardly named, but a reader will notice it as the conformation into which moderns instinctively fall. Like the tub, it may be traced through the development of shapes, and is perhaps related to the "vast flourishing Body" of modern writers and the shifting chaos of water and cloud in the "Dedication to Prince Posterity." [1]

Immediately following these images, the preface presents us with a discussion of the relationship between the crowd and its members, alternating its focus from one to the other. The quality of disorder is emphasized by the "very numerous" wits (picking holes in church and state), who are opposed to a device for "containing" them (41), an academy the Grand Committee is going to build (which, significantly, "will require some Time, as well as Cost, to perfect"—39). If the first crowd image emphasizes the mere number and undirected energy of the crowd by contrasting it with an

1. Body is often used in the *Tale* in a punning sense which suggests both a human body and a body of people; thus Swift provides another connection between the two metaphors.

image of external order, the second one shows the relationship between members of the crowd. This is the anecdote of
the fat man who pushes for more room and is told to bring
his "own Guts to a reasonable Compass" (46); it is supposed to illustrate the Hack's admiration for crowds, but
coming as it does between discussions of the exorbitant demands he makes on the reader,[2] we see that both he and
the fat man are trying to impinge upon the realities of
other people in the name of their own, and that it is, in
fact, in the nature of a crowd for every member to do so.
The Hack sees no inconsistency in believing, first, in everyone's autonomy (as when he defends the crowd against the
fat man) and, second, in his own (as when he imposes his
reality upon his readers).[3]

The third crowd image follows, contrasting the effect
of satire aimed at an individual, which is to bring down the
skies on the head of the satirist, and the effect of satire
aimed at "mankind," which is to have it merely "bandied

2. Having finished the anecdote, without pausing for breath, the Hack
explains that the assumptions behind his writing are: (1) whenever the
book is obscure, the reader will assume that it is profound, (2) whatever
is italicized or capitalized will be considered profound, (3) "*I speak without Vanity*" will be taken to mean "I praise myself" (47). These are the
"common Privileges of a Writer," and, as the Hack says later of Dryden's
practice, the purpose of a preface is to explain what the rest of the book
means (131). Thus there is hardly a transition from this imposition of significance to the fat man who crowds for more room.

3. An example appears in sec. 10, where the Hack explains that "I shall
venture to affirm, that whatever Difference may be found in [readers']
several Conjectures, they will be all, without the least Distortion, manifestly
deduceable from the Text" (185). He allows a reader almost any interpretation he desires, because he believes in the autonomy of the human mind
(and this may prove the "profundity" of his work). On the other hand,
he follows this assurance that any interpretation is deducible from the text
by spelling out in cabbalistic detail exactly where the meaning does lie;
for example: "Whoever will be at the Pains to calculate the whole Number
of each Letter in this Treatise, and sum up the Difference exactly between
the several Numbers, assigning the true natural Cause for every such Difference; the Discoveries in the Product will plentifully reward his Labour"
(187).

to and fro" like a ball. We are left to conclude that while the crowd is the individualist's playground, it also obviates any sense of responsibility he would be liable to as an individual. The man in the crowd can give rein to unlimited individualism, and he can also, like Ulysses, escape retribution by answering, *I am nobody.*

The crowd is a particularly disquieting symbol to the twentieth century,[4] and there is little doubt that it represented to Swift essentially the same myth of individual freedom together with a mindless energy waiting to be directed toward the worst ends. Discussing the Augustan idea of the "Mob" (*mobile vulgus*), Ian Watt points out that it was "the perfect antitype of proper standards: the more so as, being mobile as well as vulgar, it could naturally represent sentiment, enthusiasm, every kind of fashionable novelty, as opposed to the unchanging norms of nature and tradition espoused by the Augustans. Finally—and perhaps most significantly—the mob, as an ancient symbol of irrational forces, could stand for passion, as against reason." [5]

But the mob by itself is not enough: in the introduction the *Tale* takes up the relationship between the crowd and its director, the orator. This again is the charismatic leader, whether religious or secular, the opposite of law in any form. If we judge by the quotation from Virgil, the point is that he is above the world of common behavior—"*evadere ad auras*"—trying to reach some reality that has nothing to do with the business of living (55). The distinction is between the ground, where human action takes place, where a leader would impose some order upon the crowd, and the air, where nothing goes on but talk. There is no lead-

4. See de Rougemont, *The Devil's Share* (New York, Meridian, 1956), p. 141, who writes that the principle of the crowd is "fleeing from one's own person, no longer being responsible, and therefore no longer guilty, and becoming at one stroke a participant in the divinized power of the Anonymous."

5. "Ironic Tradition in Augustan Prose," p. 23.

ing, since the crowd merely mills about and its members
jostle each other. There is, as we have seen, no instruction,
since the relationship between orator and crowd is purely
sensual.

The crowd of unrelated and uncooperating individualists
in the preface eventually becomes, in the *Mechanical Operation,* the conventicle where no harmony can be found "between any two Heads" (270).[6] In between, we have the hungry mass that surrounds the oratorial machines, the crowd
of Aeolists, each panting for the preacher's wind,[7] and the
list of madmen in Bedlam, each of whom is oblivious of
any other madman, intent on his own private obsession.[8]
The *Battle* shows us the crowd as a mob of moderns trying
to make up an army, contrasted with the ordered ranks of
the ancients. Of the moderns we are told that "nothing less
than the Fear impending from their Enemies, could have
kept them from Mutinies upon this Occasion"; and among
the horse, "every private *Trooper* pretended to the Chief
Command" (235). In short, this idea or symbol of a crowd is
repeated in various contexts, with various casts of characters, showing that in every one of the modern sects and
societies the same pattern of individualism and chaos exists.

In this section we have seen the large-scale disorder of the
split church echoed in the metaphors of deformed bodies,

6. The crowd is the image that distinguishes the conventicle from the
congregation—the one made up of individuals each seeking God in his
own way, the other a group of people seeking God together.

7. The wind itself is a symbol of chaos, which connects with the shifting
forms of the "Dedication to.Prince Posterity." For some significant parallels,
see Job, e.g., 1:19, 7:7, 8:2, 38:1. While for the moderns (particularly the
Aeolists) wind carries overtones of pride, in Job it is used to show man's
littleness and valuelessness.

8. The Aeolist ceremony carries a vague suggestion of the Witches' Sabbath, of the inversion of religion, with wind as a non-God (the eating of
the wind suggests an infernal parody of the communion or eucharist). The
general pattern of perversion in the ceremony is the same as that of the
Sabbath. See Grillot de Givry, *Witchcraft, Magic & Alchemy,* tr. J. Courtenay
Locke (New York, Frederick Publications, 1954), p. 87.

ruined houses, and broken-up families. The Hack who reduces oratorial machines to the number three because it is his favorite number, and the digression which destroys pattern for casual insight; the moment which is exalted over eternity, and the individual's interpretation of Scripture which supersedes tradition's; the organ which destroys the body, the body which destroys the group; the words which overthrow sentences, the examples which overthrow theses, and the individual who overthrows the social structure—all of these interact in one huge metaphor of the part against the whole in a context of Christian thought where this is the ultimate sin.[9]

VIII. Conclusion

I have tried to show the importance for the *Tale of a Tub* of some of the particular literary and religious trends of the seventeenth century, and to trace some of the aspects of the rather novel, and yet traditional, form to which their influence upon Swift led.

But while there are large patterns of interconnected images that help to build up a particular sort of parody world, the reader is also sustained by each section as he moves along, in much the same way that he is carried along by each new subject in an encyclopedia, or by each of Don Quixote's adventures. Although its focus is often made clear by means of the images we have examined, each section has a particular aspect of the Gnostic problem to discuss. As I have suggested, the general impetus for the order of progression comes from the historical narrative of the brothers, which gives the reader his bearings among the

9. The ninth circle of Dante's hell is filled with those who betrayed their masters, benefactors, or cities—in effect, the commonweal which was responsible to them and to which they were responsible. Beginning with Paolo and Francesca, the sinners that circle the pit are those whose attention has been directed inward, refusing anything beyond itself.

digressions (showing him what to look for in them). We have concluded that the narrative's emphasis falls on the imagination in action rather than on doctrine (i.e. the product of the imagination), and that the progression traced starts with man out on his own and ends in a chaos of conflicting sects and open sedition.

Starting at the beginning, the "Apology" and the Bookseller's notes present various norms of morality and reality by which the reader will be able to judge the Hack's world. At this point the Hack makes his appearance, and the first impression he creates is of modern flaccidity (the style of his opening), modern conventionality (his dedication to an imaginary "Prince Posterity"), modern imagination (his invention of Time-Death), and the precariousness of modern creation (the works that vanish overnight). The subject of the "Dedication to Prince Posterity" is, accordingly, largely proleptic, created by a group of allusions and images, but it is centered on time and the modern's refusal to understand or abide by it.

The preface is about the general relationship between individuals when they have no external order to guide and control them, and we have seen that the image which governs the section is the crowd. The introduction is about the relationship between the creator or the orator and the crowd, first, as to what their mode of communication is (through senses, not the understanding) and, second, as to what the nature of the product itself may be (a cheese with maggots at its center). The introduction having presented the nature of the created object, section 2 presents the object itself, which in the Hack's terms has tremendous significance and in the reader's actually does: the narrative of the brothers is based sufficiently on history, from earliest Christianity to the present, to give reality to the argument itself. Sections 2 and 3 (the "Digression concerning Criticks") treat intellectual Gnosticism, or the interpretation performed by Peter and the critic; sections 4 and 5 ("Digression in the Modern Kind") present the necessity for compelling one's imagination upon others once it has begun to work, and sections 6 and 7 ("Digression in Praise of Digressions") follow this with the reaction of the compelled, who revolt and start to compel others themselves. The movement from the "Digression in the Modern Kind" to "in Praise of Digressions" is from a presentation of the individual against other individuals to the individual who tries to overcome the whole, of which he is a part. This is pointed up by the example of Martin, who, while forced to revolt against Peter, remains properly subordinated to the law of the will; in the digression the theme is carried on by metaphors of parts—indices, mercenary armies, digressions—which overwhelm the whole.

Section 8 concerns the basis of Jack's kind of imagination, which is even slimmer than that to which Peter is accustomed. The Aeolists are like Peter and the critic in that as these interpreters draw out their own ideas from a text, so the Aeolists make their gods in their own image (they are themselves presumably windy), and their devils in the opposite image. Section 9 ("Digression on Madness") is the reduction of the modern's pride to the functioning of a vapor, the results of which are both evil and destructive; at the same time it is the Hack's defense of the vapor, together with his attempt to implicate all of us in his own madness (the modern is shown to be the lonely fool among knaves who is constantly soliciting companions). Following this, section 10 gives instructions (as did the preface) on how to understand the *Tale*, a sort of invitation to madness; [1] section 11 shows what the acceptance of such an invitation leads to, and the "Conclusion" is an inconclusive farewell from the Hack to his readers.

There is a letdown after the "Digression on Madness,"

1. Both of these are, of course, parallel to the "author's" instructions to his readers, in the "Apology," as well as in the imagery of his opening sections.

which some critics have seen as proving that the *Battle* and
Mechanical Operation were specifically intended to follow
the *Tale* and that a breathing space had to be provided
after the intensity of this last digression. Certainly there
is no further climax after the "Digression on Madness,"
and one may be forced to conclude either that the dying
fall of the *Tale* is imitative of the modern practice (the
climax being, characteristically, in a digression), or that
the *Battle* and *Mechanical Operation* were designed as climaxes.[2] It is most reasonable, I believe, to accept both of
these, and conclude that sections 10, 11, and 12 ("Conclusion") are there to clear up a few matters that were left
over. They do, of course, considerably more than that: they
reduce the Hack to the world of reality as he approaches
the moment when someone must buy his book, and they
carry on, though in a sketchy manner, the earlier themes.
Even the tailor returns when we see the Hack's dependence
on him reflected in the *"long Taylor's Bill,"* one of the causes
of his writing the *Tale*.

Section 10, more than any other, is about the Hack's *Tale*
itself, about the Hack's own imagination, and about its
sources in Rosicrucianism and Gnosticism. In the "Conclusion" he ends by admitting, in the image of the well, that
there is nothing under all of this gesturing and posturing,
and then he commences to talk about "nothing." [3]

2. At least in the form in which Swift put it together before publication
—perhaps not its original form, where the *Mechanical Operation* may even
have been a digression. See Clifford, "Swift's *Mechanical Operation*," p. 142.
But also, note the use of "Body" in the "Author's Apology" ("Body of the
Book," 12); in a sense the *Battle* and the *Mechanical Operation* are other
examples of the appendages which contain perhaps the most important parts
of the book.

3. ". . . often, when there is nothing in the World at the Bottom, besides *Dryness* and *Dirt*, tho' it be but a Yard and half under Ground, it
shall pass, however, for wondrous *Deep*, upon no wiser a Reason than because it is wondrous *Dark*" (207–8). Here again we have the image of the
tub, with its two qualities of false appearance and dryness emphasized.
The dust is the reality which, disguised by darkness, appears to be profundity.

The object of section 11 is to demonstrate the ultimate degeneration of religion after the process of individualism, corruption, and aggression that is traced in the earlier sections and climaxes in the "Digression on Madness." Section 11 brings us up to date—to the year 1697—even to the mayoralty of Sir Humphry Edwyn. Religion has become a rabbit-like proliferation of sects in Jack's wake, and the section ends with a sort of fertility cult of "ears," and with the merciful loss of the Hack's notes on further decline (203–4). The apocalyptic visions of the Aeolist ceremonies and of Bedlam are thus echoed in a vision of the darkened contemporary world.

The *Battle* comes next to set things right. It brings the theme of aggression resulting from sufficiency down to a concrete battle between ancients and moderns, in which the moderns are routed. It presents a set-to with the spider, in which the spider is worsted; and both Bentley and Wotton, the "critics," are impaled on a single spear. It offers, in short, the happy ending to the *Tale;* if it is not as satisfactory as the other parts of the book, in spite of the brilliant passages that precede the war itself, it is perhaps for this reason. The normative function of the *Battle* is almost lost in the orgy of evening-up scores, and it is the satirist here, not Bentley, who is slinging ordure. The hiatuses and the sketchiness of the battle would suggest either that Swift cut the worst parts or that he made a perfunctory job of carrying out the metaphor of battle to which he had committed himself at the start. This part was probably written as soon as Temple was attacked; at any rate, the battle scenes have an immediacy about them that is closer to anger than to mature thought.

The *Mechanical Operation* sums up the theme of the false and the true that runs through the *Tale*—we have seen implied the true ship, the true body, the true church; here we have the true heaven presented at the beginning, to be

arrived at in the carriages of the church. Mahomet and the
modern have their own way of getting there, and the function of the *Mechanical Operation* is to show that this pseudo-
heaven turns out to be nothing more than a physical orgasm.

A number of parallels are set up between the two sections
that make up the *Mechanical Operation.* The conventicle
scene at the end of section 1 is balanced by the scene that is
implied at the end of section 2. In the first of these a religious service, with the preacher helping his congregation
toward a mystical experience, is presented in submerged
sexual terms, as we have seen. At the end of section 2 the
courting lover and the enthusiast are compared, with the
implication that the physical manifestation is the same for
both: "Nay, to bring this Argument yet closer, I have been
informed by certain Sanguine Brethren of the first Class,
that in the Height and *Orgasmus* of their Spiritual exercise
it has been frequent with them * * * * * ; immediately
after which, they found the *Spirit* to relax and flag of a sudden with the Nerves, and they were forced to hasten to
a Conclusion" (288). Parallel to this comparison is the image
with which Swift concludes the book, of the "Philosopher,
who, while his Thoughts and Eyes were fixed upon the
Constellations, found himself seduced by his *lower Parts*
into a *Ditch*" (289). The final parallel is, then, between the
ogling lover and the preacher, who share the physical orgasm, and between the Platonic lover and the philosopher,
both of whom by looking at the stars lose their footing on
earth. There appears to be little distinction between the
lover and the preacher, except that what may be expected
from the one is monstrous in the other; and so for a norm
in the passage we must look again to the earth. By inference, the ordinary man keeps his eyes on the ground,
and for him the sexual experience is natural and represents
no fall. For the platonic lover and the preacher it does represent a fall.

As a conclusion this is perhaps not so pessimistic as it may at first sound; it is, rather, an admonition: "Too intense a Contemplation is not the Business of Flesh and Blood"—and this agrees with the image of man that has been built up through the *Tale*. It is almost as great a mistake to think that Swift sees the ideal, harmonious body as possible for man as that he sees the Houyhnhnm as either possible or desirable; any more than Martin, for all his care, can have a perfect suit. Like the church, man works toward "the edifying of the body of Christ"; but, if success seems unlikely, Swift is not guilty of Flaubertian detachment; it is evident from what we have seen of the Hack that he relishes much of this world.

If we put together the various hints we are given about the modern's body—that he and his works sink, that Aeolists pump themselves full of wind, that the Hack empties himself when he writes, that moderns have an "unhappy Weight" and "a mighty Pressure about their Posteriors and their Heels" (225)—the picture we are given is of a man with a head that aspires ever upward but with a body so heavy that as soon as he gets off the ground he tumbles down again. It is therefore clearly better to walk on the earth, because in this posture and place the weight of one's lower parts acts as ballast and balance, even assists gravity, rather than acting as a handicap.[4] It should be noted that when weight is used in the proper way, like the knife, it can be good, as when "the *Weight* of *Martin's* Argument" and his "Gravity" sustain him against Jack's blandishments, and make Jack "fly out, and spurn against his Brother's Moderation" (140). In short, the human body, whatever its limitations, is God-given and good.

Swift is saying in the *Tale of a Tub* that people like the

4. "The body," writes St. Augustine, "by its own weight, strives towards its own place. Weight makes not downward only, but to his own place. Fire tends upward, a stone downward. They are urged by their own weight, they seek their own places" (*Confessions*, Bk. XIII, p. 273). Cf. Swift's poem, "The Progress of Poetry."

Hack *are* dropped into this world, that this *is* the way things are—life *is* unstable, writings vanish, and we *are* in need of diversion—but that with the church and tradition we can make the best of them; by oneself, or with the pseudochurches and diversions to which the moderns are addicted, reality is frustrating and produces only frenzied activity like that of the Hack.

Thus we are left at the end of the *Mechanical Operation* with a conclusion not unlike that at the end of *Gulliver's Travels*. It can be argued that there is a difference: in *Gulliver* the belief that man's business is to be human and that it is here on earth remains, but it is now the only standard. The standard of timelessness associated with the church and the coats is no longer present. Only an approximation remains: half way between Yahoo and Houyhnhnm, which is Gulliver himself if he only knew it, or ordinary man. But it can also be argued that there is no difference: the *Tale* is about the nature of man, and even the church (the mediating agency between man and God and man and reality) is a human organization, the presuppositions of which are (1) the possibility of change in the world, (2) the need of time to consider and work things out, and (3) the need of law to hold things together. These three assumptions, which are embodied in both the *Laws of Ecclesiastical Polity* and the *Tale of a Tub,* show a realization and acceptance of the human state. They are not skeptical because they do not deny the individual the power to choose or act; but the church they envisage is no supernatural structure—though it is based on Holy Scripture, it is man-made and adapted to human needs.

Thus, perhaps the difference between Martin and Gulliver is that Gulliver (who is very much like the Hack) does not understand the human condition. For Gulliver it can only be defined by opposites, and he, like the Hack, chooses one when the dichotomy itself is false, and the choice is among three things

The first point I have tried to prove in this study is that the *Tale of a Tub* is not simply a *jeu d'esprit*, but rather falls easily within the area of literature which is concerned with moral problems—what Leavis calls the "great tradition." The solution the *Tale* offers may or may not be acceptable to twentieth-century readers; Leavis' view that "We shall not find Swift remarkable for intelligence if we think of Blake" is a concise statement of the question of acceptability.[5] One who finds Blake "remarkable for intelligence" will not find Swift so and vice versa, because two definitions of intelligence are being used. Swift would have found Blake "remarkable for presumption," a Gnostic in a quite literal sense and an enthusiast to boot. If you define intelligence as isolated insight or as penetrating perception, then Blake carries it hands down; but it is a matter of opinion as to whether the insights commonly shared are more profound than those lone flights or dives when, like the whale, you come up with bloodshot eyes. On the other hand, it is at least possible to see images like those in sections 8 and 9 as being of a profoundly apocalyptic nature and showing a deep insight into the nature of evil.

The second point I have tried to demonstrate is that the *Tale* is a unified structure, not only about something but cunningly planned and executed. The summary of the *Tale's* outline which I have recounted in this section may suggest that the *Tale's* reliance on an anti-Ciceronian order-in-disorder finally masks a strikingly periodic order of parallel and balanced sections, subjects, and characters: a logically arranged encyclopedia of Gnostic sufficiency. For the form of the *Tale*, like that of *Gulliver's Travels* too, is the encyclopedia, a gathering of all examples and aspects of some subject. But while *Gulliver's* basic form is cloaked in the parody form of the travel book, as Rabelais' was in the form of the epic, the *Tale's* parody form is so close to its satiric form that it is hard to decide where to draw the

5. Leavis, *The Common Pursuit*, p. 87.

line between them. What Swift is presenting in the *Tale* (the "author's" *Tale*) is the general outline of an ideal—the concept of the rounded citizen, the versatile and encyclopedic individual, as well as the traditional compendium of knowledge, grammatical exegesis, saints, heresies, fools, of the Church Fathers. Thus the real form of the *Tale* is an encyclopedia of errors or fools; and its parody form is the encyclopedia of useless speculation, the modern's *summa*.

Inevitably the *Tale* must stand comparison with *Gulliver;* and I believe that Leavis is correct when he points out that the essential difference between these two works is that in *Gulliver* Swift imposes a form upon himself which restrains much of the freedom of invention which is his characteristic quality—in short, his Metaphysical wit. The difference could best be shown if we were to trace the development of key images from one book to the other; for all of Swift's work is based on a few central images. *Gulliver* makes a much more obvious use of the body image, as Kathleen Williams has shown,[6] presenting us with the real bodies of giants, pygmies, and horses, while the *Tale* relies largely on a metaphoric pattern to convey the moral picture Swift wishes to illustrate with the human body. In *Gulliver* the Hobbesian body politic is made specific and concrete in the image of the giant and the little people who make it up (significantly separated here and set at odds). The generalization we can make is that images always become more solid, less fragmentary, less shifty, less poetic in *Gulliver*.

In *Gulliver* Swift imitates a highly disciplined form, with a specified and limited vocabulary, which must express the shades of change that go on in Gulliver's mind as he moves from experience to experience without drawing attention to itself. The *Tale* imitates a form which, we have seen, allows Swift the full play of his imagination without his

6. Williams, *Jonathan Swift and the Age of Compromise*, pp. 154–209.

stepping out of character; his speaker is a madman being carried along by his own rhetoric like a cork in the current. It can be argued that the greater discipline and thus perhaps the greater demand upon Swift's concentration make *Gulliver* a better example of his powers. Certainly *Gulliver* is a less ambiguous book, and its author, having himself been engaged in the world of politics since the writing of the earlier book, is by this time firmly committed and decided as to what is right and what is wrong, however difficult they may be to arrive at. Much of the savor has gone out of the Hack's skulduggery for him. But it can also be argued that Swift's real genius is a poetic one and that the *Tale*'s form, and its reliance on seventeenth-century modes, gives him a scope for his imagination which he never enjoyed again.

ADDITIONAL NOTES

NOTE A: Swift and the Polemical Tradition
(see above, p. 44)

The passage from which Swift quotes at the end of section 10 (187), concerning the passion of Acamoth, is a good illustration of Irenaeus' method of juxtaposing the imaginary and the real. Here is the whole passage:

> All things owed their beginning to her terror and sorrow. *For from her tears all that is of a liquid nature was formed; from her smile all that is lucent; and from her grief and perplexity all the corporeal elements of the world.* For at one time, as they affirm, she would weep and lament on account of being left alone in the midst of darkness and vacuity; while, at another time, reflecting on the light which had forsaken her, she would be filled with joy, and laugh; then, again, she would be struck with terror; or, at other times, would sink into consternation and bewilderment.

Irenaeus' critique, which is characteristic, follows:

> I feel somewhat inclined myself to contribute a few hints toward the development of their system. For when I perceive that waters are in part fresh, such as fountains, rivers, showers, and so on, and in part salt, such as those in the sea, I reflect with myself that all such waters cannot be derived from her tears, inasmuch as these are of a saline quality only. It is clear, therefore, that the waters which are salt are alone those

which are derived from her tears. But it is probable
that she, in her intense agony and perplexity, was
covered with perspiration. And hence, following out
their notion, we may conceive that fountains and
rivers, and all the fresh water in the world, are due
to this source.[1]

Despite a shaky physiology on his part, Irenaeus demonstrates the fact that when ideal or romantic figures do not
have a strong foundation in reality they are easily deflated
by a recourse to reality as a standard. The sensory nature
of a woman weeping, laughing, and perspiring tends to
destroy the abstraction she is meant to represent.

Irenaeus' treatment of the Gnostic practice of arbitrarily
yoking names and things is also, and perhaps more significantly, similar to Swift's. But, as usual, he tells us what
he is doing, leaving no chance for misapprehension. He
tells us that he is appalled at Valentinus' "audacity in the
coining of names." "It is manifest also," he adds, "that he
himself is the one who has had sufficient audacity to coin
these names; so that, unless *he* had appeared in the world,
the truth would still have been destitute of a name." He
is referring here to a passage attributed to Valentinus which
he reports in his usual dead-pan way:

> He [Valentinus] maintained that there is a certain
> Dyad (two-fold being), who is inexpressible by any
> name, of whom one part should be called Arrhetus
> (unspeakable), and the other Sige (silence). But of this
> Dyad a second was produced, one part of whom he
> names Pater, and the other Aletheia. From this Tetrad,
> again, arose Logos and Zoe, Anthropos and Ecclesia.
> These constitute the primary Ogdoad. He next states
> that from Logos and Zoe ten powers were produced,

1. Irenaeus, *Ante-Nicene Fathers*, *1*, 321. I have italicized the part Swift
quotes.

as we have before mentioned. But from Anthropos and Ecclesia proceeded twelve, one of which separating from the rest, and falling from its original condition, produced the rest of the universe [p. 332].

But then, noting the Gnostic doctrine that "nothing hinders any other, in dealing with the same object, to affix names after such a fashion," Irenaeus goes on to give his own version of it:

> there exists a power which I term a *Gourd;* and along with this Gourd there exists a power which again I term *Utter-Emptiness.* This Gourd and Emptiness, since they are one, produced (and yet did not simply produce, so as to be apart from themselves) a fruit, everywhere visible, eatable, and delicious, which fruit-language calls a *Cucumber.* Along with this Cucumber exists a power of the same essence, which again I call a *Melon.* These powers, the Gourd, Utter-Emptiness, the Cucumber, and the Melon, brought forth the remaining multitude of the delirious melons of Valentinus [pp. 332–3].

We do not want to press too far the idea that Swift gathered his method from Irenaeus alone, first because we have already shown Marvell and others to be practitioners in the same line, and second because the important consideration is not where Swift got his method but the lengths to which he took it, far beyond Irenaeus' intentions or scope. But what makes Irenaeus the important source is (as we suggested in Chapter 2) that he is in the patristic tradition of satiric attack on heretics, a tradition of which Swift wished the *Tale* to be a part. The *Tale's* sources are all, it should be noted, in the general religious tradition of controversial writing (Marvell and Parker being only two more writers in that tradition), rather than in the classical tradition of Augustan Rome.

In order to show the extent to which Swift was immeised in the polemical writing of his day on religious subjects I shall list a few echoes of this writing to be found in the *Tale*.

Eachard's metaphor of food, which we have noticed, finds echoes in the *Tale*; for example, his nut-cracking image may have suggested Swift's comparison of wisdom to "a *Nut*, which unless you chuse with Judgment, may cost you a Tooth, and pay you with nothing but a *Worm*"; and his reference to the "text . . . like a spiritual Sack-posset" suggests Swift's comparison of wisdom to a sack-posset.[2] The food Eachard refers to which must be *"hash'd* and *fricassed"* for "such nice and fashionable Stomachs" may have suggested Swift's *"Soups* and *Ollio's, Fricassees* and *Ragousts,"* which are for the man who "wants a Stomach and Digestion for more substantial Victuals." [3]

Marvell's *Rehearsal Transprosed* teems with images that are explored in the *Tale*. The analogy Marvell sees between rhetoric and embroidery that obscures the suit ("bedawbed with rhetorick, and embroidered so thick that you cannot discern the ground") [4] suggests the clothing imagery in section 2 of the *Tale*, where embroidery does just that. Marvell's "He scarce ever opens his mouth, but that he may bite; nor bites, but that from the vessicles of his gums he may infuse a venom" reminds us of Swift's "those whose Teeth are too rotten to bite, are best of all others, qualified to revenge that Defect with their Breath" or "do they think such a Building is to be battered with Dirt-

2. Eachard, *Some Observations*, pp. 1, 5, 62–3; G-S, p. 66.

3. Eachard, ibid., p. 63; G-S, pp. 143–4. Some other echoes of Eachard have been noticed by Robert C. Elliott, "Swift and Dr. Eachard," *PMLA*, 69 (1954), 1250–7.

4. Marvell, *Rehearsal Transprosed*, in *Works*, ed. Thompson, 2, 18.

Pellets however envenom'd the Mouths may be that discharge them." [5] Several of the *Tale's* central images are found in the *Rehearsal Transprosed:* the anatomical dissection, the oratorial machines (particularly the pulpit and stage), the tub itself, Peter (like Bayes) going mad with pride, and the chaos of new writing "posted fresh upon all Gates and Corners of Streets" (Marvell: "there was no post nor pillar so sacred that was exempt, no not even the walls of Paul's itself, much less the Temple gate, from the pasting up of the titles").[6]

Edward Stillingfleet is one of the divines whose polemical work Swift knew well. For example, Stillingfleet presents the image of a container heated but with no outlet for its vapor, which may have contributed to the theory of vapors: "Some vent must be given to a violent fermentation," Stillingfleet writes, "else the vessel might burst asunder; and I hope the good man is somewhat more at ease, since he purged away so much Choler." He also offers what may be a source for the discussion of indices, of entering a palace by the rear gate, of attacking armies from the rear, in the "Digression in Praise of Digressions": "he is a man of great courage indeed, that dares fall upon the reer, and begin to confute a Book at the end of it." [7]

To understand the source of some of these echoes, however, we must not restrict ourselves to one side of the controversy. In the case of the Marvell-Parker feud, Swift's

5. Marvell, 2, 262; G-S, pp. 49, 10.

6. Marvell, 2, 35, 290; 260; 311; 48; 260. G-S, pp. 123, 173; 58ff.; e.g., 39ff.; 114ff.; 34. Other echoes of Marvell in the *Tale* have been pointed out in G-S in the notes; by Pierre Legouis in *André Marvell, poète, puritain, patriote* (Paris, Henri Didier, 1928), pp. 385–6, 431; and by M. C. Bradbrook and M. G. Lloyd Thomas in *Andrew Marvell* (Cambridge Univ. Press, 1940), pp. 112–14.

7. *An Answer to Several Late Treatises Occasioned by a Book Entituled a Discourse Concerning the Idolatry Practised in the Church of Rome, and the Hazard of Salvation in the Communion of It* (London, 1673), *The First Part*, "The General Preface," pages unnumbered.

own sentiments were, we may suspect, on the less well-defended side. Parker is not, however, a man to be underestimated; he gave nearly as good as he got. We can trace Marvell's method in Parker himself, in his *Reproof*—a rather interesting example because he gets started the image of a tub which Swift was to pick up. This skirmish begins with Marvell's reference to the straight line which, if extended, becomes a circle: "as a straight line continued grows a circle, [Parker] had given [the government] so infinite a power, that it was extended into impotency." [8] Parker picks this up and quotes Marvell as speaking of the "unhoopable Jurisdiction" of an "unlimited Magistrate." [9] Parker remarks, alluding to the tubs used by dissenters as pulpits, that it is a

> Metaphor taken from a Tub, I suppose, because you find Power in your Book of Apothegms compared to liquor, for a certain Reason known to every body, though no body has exprest it so happily as your self, *viz.* because if *it be infinitely diffused or extended, it becomes impotency, even as a straight line continued grows a circle.* . . . But however for this reason it is necessary to *hoop up* the Authority of Princes, lest they too soon weaken themselves by too great a leakage of their Power; so that methinks according to your notion, there is nothing so patly emblematical of Soveraign Princes, as *Dufoy* in his Tub, or a Pig under a washbole, and if you would define them suitably to the conceit, they are nothing else but so many vessels of Authority, some Kinderkins [sic], some Hogsheads,

8. Marvell, 2, 146. Swift uses it in the same sense, saying that one who aspires too high and falls is "like a straight Line drawn by its own Length into a Circle" (158). Marvell uses it again on pp. 312–13. G-S points out the parallel, p. 158 n.

9. Samuel Parker, *A Reproof to the Rehearsal Transprosed, in A Discourse to its Author* (London, 1673), p. 11.

and some Tuns, according to the circuit or hoop of their Government. Though as you and your Puritan Coopers, or (as Mar-prelate words it) *Tub-trimmers*, have been pleased to contract their Power, all the Empire in the world might easily be contained in a pipkin or a quart pot, and he would pay dear for it, that should purchase the Kings Supremacy at the price of a jug of Ale [pp. 11–12].

He has learned his lesson well: from "unhoopable" he moves to ever smaller, more constricted tubs, until the obvious conclusion is that the Puritans would reduce the power of the government to a quart pot. Nor does he drop it there. His divisions of Marvell's arguments are "hoops and holas" (e.g., "Your last and lowdest hoop and hola is . . ."—p. 33). Marvell, then, answers that

whereas I only threw ["unhoopable"] out like an empty cask to amuse him, knowing that I had a whale to deal with, and lest he should overset me; he runs away with it as a very serious business, and so moyles himself with tumbling and tossing it, that he is in danger of melting his sperma ceti. A cork, I see, will serve without an hook; and instead of an harping-iron, this grave and ponderous creature may, like eels, be taken and pulled up only with bobbing.[1]

Swift, we shall see, uses both senses of tub, as a container and as a diversion. His development of the image of a tub, however, more closely follows Parker's, moving from the shape of a tub to "Vessels" and pulpits and "Tuns"—to lanterns, wells, and certain aspects of the human body.[2]

Again, Parker calls Marvell a "Coloss [sic] of Brass," and

---

1. Marvell, 2, 311. He goes on to accuse Parker of so much knowledge of "tubs, kilderkins, hogsheads, and their dimensions! that you might suspect him first to have served as gager of the Lambeth brewing."

2. See below, Ch. 4, sec. VII.

Marvell answers, "Brass upon brass is false heraldry," going on to refer "*Brazen-brow, Out-brazen, Brass-copper,* and I know not how many more of the same metal and statuary" to Parker. Swift picks this up in the critics' mirror of brass: "For, *Brass* is an Emblem of Duration, and when skilfully burnished, will cast *Reflections* from its own *Superficies,* without any Assistance of *Mercury* from behind." [3]

Thus it is not simply individual polemicists in which Swift finds inspiration, but the controversies in which they engaged. In fact, the images used in the *Tale* almost make up a polemic vocabulary for Restoration writers. The tub is one of these, cropping up in such works as L'Estrange's *The Dissenter's Sayings,* where attacks on him are "but as so many empty Casks thrown out to divert me from sinking the Rotten Barque they are Engag'd in." [4] The razor is another common image. Tillotson, in one of his rare moments of polemic, says that "Zeal is an Edg-Tool, which Children in understanding should not meddle withal; and yet it most frequently possesseth the weakest Minds." In Marvell the razor is an object which can be given the wrong function: "He never oils his hone but that he may whet his razor; and that not to shave, but to cut mens throats." *Tale:* "it is with *Wits* as with *Razors,* which are never so apt to *cut* those they are employ'd on, as when they have *lost their Edge.*" [5] Again there is the image of Puritans with large ears, which a note to *Hudibras* tells us was a reference to the roundheads' haircuts.[6] Butler calls them "asses ears"

3. Parker, p. 14; Marvell, 2, 321; G-S, p. 103.

4. Pt. I, "To the Reader," page unnumbered.

5. John Tillotson, "Sermon XIII, The Danger of Zeal, without Knowledge. Preached on November 5, 1682," in *Sixteen Sermons, Preached on Several Subjects and Occasions,* in *Works* (London, 1700), 2, 374; Marvell, 2, 31; G-S, p. 49.

6. Pt. I, Canto i, l. 10. *Hudibras* is full of images and phrases picked up by Swift. G-S has noticed a number of them in its footnotes, and so I shall only mention a few important ones: Mahomet's ass, Pt. I, Canto i, l. 232 (G-S, p. 264); the tailor, ibid., l. 466, and Canto ii, l. 22 (G-S, p. 76); the

and Robert South suggests another reason for using ears: the Puritan devotes so much time "to the hearing of sermons" that he has none left "to practice them. And will not all this set [him] right for heaven? Yes, no doubt, if a man were to be pulled up to heaven by the ears; or the gospel would but reverse its rule, and declare, *that not the doers of the word, but the hearers only should be justified*."[7] From the Puritan's point of view, Marvell says that Parker threatens him "with the loss of my ears, which however are yet in good plight, and apprehend no other danger, Mr. Bayes, but to be of your auditory. But it is no less than you have projected against all the Nonconformists, to the great prejudice of the nation, in wasting so unseasonably so much good timber to make whipping posts for them and pillories." Swift: the dissenter pulpit, "from its near Resemblance to a Pillory . . . will ever have a mighty Influence on human Ears"; and Jack founds an ear-cult in section 11.[8]

Many of these writers use the idea of "puffed up with pride," often associated with Puritan love of sermon making and claims upon the spirit.[9] One of the most suggestive is Joseph Glanvill's declaration that "mysterious, notional preaching . . . hath fill'd [the dissenter preacher] with air and vanity."[1] Another is in Eachard's *Second Dialogue* (1673): "speech is but words: and words are but motion:

lantern, Canto i, ll. 505ff. (G-S, pp. 36, 62, 192, 279, 282); canting through the nose, ibid., ll. 515ff. (G-S, pp. 28off.); Rosicrucianism, ibid., ll. 537ff. (G-S, e.g., p. 187); the reference to Darius' horse that neighed, Canto ii, ll. 137–8 (G-S, p. 282).

7. *Hudibras*, Pt. I, Canto i, l. 10; South, *False Foundations* in *Sermons*, 2, 347.

8. Marvell, 2, 318; G-S, p. 58. Jack's ear-cult is on pp. 200ff.

9. The image, of course, goes back at least to Job (e.g. 8:2, 15:2), and is commonly attached to the Gnostics by Irenaeus, p. 341, who speaks of their "inflated wise folly" and calls them "puffed up."

1. *Essay Concerning Preaching*, in *Critical Essays*, ed. Spingarn, 2, 275. He quotes I Cor. 8:1: "knowledge *falsly so called*, puffeth up" (p. 276).

and therefore that Divine that talks of Blasphemy or Heresie coming out of a man's mouth, whose heart is truly firm; he may as well gape for Blasphemy or Heresie at the spout of a pair of Bellows." [2] The latter may have contributed to the creation of the Aeolists. Marvell refers to "the extraordinary influx of God's Spirit," and South says the Puritan's preaching "is all but a jargon of empty, senseless metaphors; and though many venture their souls upon them, despising good works and strict living, as mere morality, and perhaps as popery, yet being throughly looked into and examined, after all their noise, they are really nothing but words and wind." [3] This last image, of South's, can be seen as a link with the tub Parker and Marvell squabbled over. First, it suggests the idea of the Grub Street productions which the men of Gresham and Will's accuse of being empty and which the Hack unwittingly proves to contain only maggots and worms (66); second, it suggests the tub itself, which is "noisy" but "empty"; third, it suggests the idea of the Aeolists who pump themselves full of wind, equating words and wind (153). Taken together, it links the metaphor of a container with the Aeolist's body.

Thus it is certain that Swift was steeped in the polemical writing of his day on religious subjects and that its vocabulary, as well as the techniques we have seen in section 1 of this chapter, inform the *Tale of a Tub*. [4] But more important, we have seen that Swift's echoing of these writers is not merely a memory of his reading but a conscious evocation of their quarrels and their tradition, going back to the Church Fathers, and a context of allusion which he could count on his readers' possessing.

2. P. 261; cited in Elliott, p. 1256.

3. Marvell, 2, 423; South, *False Foundations*, in *Sermons*, 2, 346.

4. C. M. Webster has demonstrated Swift's use of many of the themes of anti-Puritan satire: "Swift's *Tale of a Tub* Compared with Earlier Satires of the Puritans," *PMLA*, 47 (1932), 171–8.

NOTE B: Reassertion of Meaning in Nonscientific Style (see above, p. 64)

It should be made clear that the principle of semantics apparent in the scientists' failure to reform language can also be illustrated to some extent from the writings of other modern "Sects," "Societies," and "Fraternities."

We saw the same process at work in Milton's prose, where his imposed order of subordinating conjunctions suggests a kind of order and certainty which is contradicted by the freedom of association that actually guides the sentence. In the same way, the Hack draws himself up from time to time and makes a great effort at organization—backed up by assertions like "I know very well" and "it moves my Zeal and my Spleen" (31); but his mind is altogether unsuited to hold any two concepts together. For example, at the beginning of the "Dedication to Prince Posterity" he says, "I HERE present *Your Highness* with the Fruits of a very few leisure Hours, stollen from the short Intervals of a World of Business, and of an Employment quite alien from such Amusements as this: The poor Production of that Refuse of Time which has lain heavy upon my Hands, during a long Prorogation of Parliament, a great Dearth of Forein News, and a tedious Fit of rainy Weather . . ." (30). The passage is specifically a parody of the claims of writers like Sir Richard Blackmore that they write their epics in off hours,[1] and it is perhaps significant that the "Dedication to *Prince Posterity*" should parody the preface to *Prince Arthur*. The opening passage of Blackmore's preface is also being parodied, however, for a stylistic quirk:

1. See the preface to Richard Blackmore, *Prince Arthur, An Heroick Poem in Ten Books* (London, 1695), page unnumbered: *"Poetry has been so far from being my* Business *and* Profession, *that it has imploy'd but a small part of my* Time; *and then, but as my* Recreation, *and the Entertainment of my idle hours. If this Attempt succeeds . . . I shall think the* Vacancies *and* Intervals *that for about two years past, I have had from the* Business *of my* Profession . . . *have been very well imploy'd."*

> To what ill purposes soever Poetry has been abus'd, its true and genuine End is, by universal Confession, the Instruction of our Minds, and Regulation of our Manners; for which 'tis furnish'd with so many excellent Advantages. The Delicacy of its Strains, the Sweetness and Harmony of its Numbers, the lively and admirable manner of its Painting or Representation, and the wonderful Force of its Eloquence, cannot but open the Passages to our Breasts, triumph over our Passions, and leave behind them very deep Impressions. 'Tis in the power of Poetry to penetrate the inmost Recesses of the Mind. . . .[2]

The interminable genitive "of" phrases continue with "any sort of Affection" and "that of Athens" before the second page is reached. The main burden of Swift's parody is on Blackmore's use of the appositional genitive, in which one noun is abstract or both. But Swift has also hit upon the tendency of the language which underlies the pompous form. One term in the phrase enlivens the other, abstract one. "Delicacy," "Sweetness," and "lively" are the attributes of a young lady, "Poetry"; and though they do not succeed in bringing much life to "Strains," "Numbers," and "Painting," with "the wonderful Force of its Eloquence," they do appear distinctly incongruous when they "open the Passages to our Breasts, triumph over our Passions, and leave behind them [evidently as a result of the "Passages"] very deep Impressions." By a happy combination of clichés the concrete verb "open" joins the emphatic "deep" to activate "Impressions" and suggest tunnels and ruts.[3]

2. Ibid.

3. Elsewhere, Swift's moderns speak of words as being weighty and having gravity, or of impressions as being deep; thus words are "Bodies of much Weight and Gravity, and it is manifest from those deep *Impressions* they make and leave upon us" (60). By combining these two clichés—or by making them consistent with each other—he has created a little physical

In his parody, Swift uses the pomposity of the genitive groups to slip in a contradiction in the second clause: *short* becomes *long*, and fruits become refuse and dearth without the blink of an eye. The parisonic structure is shown to be no such thing; under the appearance of order is the rankest disorder. Because "stollen" activates "Fruits," making it a concrete fruit rather than abstract issues of consequences, "Refuse" has to be taken concretely also; and there is a tendency toward parallelism in the two nouns, given weight and substance by the following clause which has "Refuse . . . lain heavy upon my Hands." We are left with the image of fruits gone bad on the hands of the Hack. "Refuse" is also linked by one of the interminable "of's" with "Production." This word's abstract meaning of a literary work is hedged with the metaphoric meaning obtained from its connection with "Refuse of Time": it becomes "the total yield, produce, or proceeds" of "that Refuse of Time"; i.e. something growing out of refuse, which is good fertilizer. There is another way of reading the phrase too: it can be taken as a bringing forth or exhibiting of "that Refuse of Time," where the writing itself becomes refuse. It is only a step from here to the "Jakes, or an Oven," where writings end up later in the same chapter. The apparent inconsistency then comes to represent two scales of time or two ways of regarding time—as short and furious or as long and tedious, both of which appear to be contending in the Hack's mind.

The pompous mannerism, which, in the Hack at least, is a manifestation of his attempt at an appearance of order, is thus picked up by Swift and given a logic it was never

---

image of words sinking into the mind like footprints in the mud. Then, following the method employed by Eachard and Marvell, Swift goes on to "weighty" men, who aspire high but are pulled down by their physical weight, and "gravity" becomes the law of gravity which pulls them down (e.g., 32, 225).

intended to have. The passage as parody is a demonstration of the Hack's aspiration toward the false, of his attempt to put this false order on nature, and of nature's—or words' —refusal to let him.

NOTE C: Folly and Madness (see above, p. 187)

I have saved these notes on Erasmus' *Praise of Folly* until my last chapter because the relationship between Folly and the Hack is essentially one of different lights on a single solution to the problem of reality. Folly herself represents a refusal to face reality, and though she is very different from the Hack she illustrates what Swift saw to be the same error.

The distinction between the Hack and Folly is easy to draw—as I have suggested, the Hack is a sort of dark side of Folly. To see what I mean, we need only look at the expression of their similar views in their different vocabularies. Folly is opposed to the laborious definitions and divisions of the scholastic sermon, its logic and its rehearsed quality. But her own solution is to "speak 'whatever pops into my head.' "[1] Here is the "Christian simplicity" we encountered in Chapter 3: "whatever pops into my head" is an expression of complete subjectivity, no contact with other people being presupposed. But at the same time, it is expressed with vigor and is meant to imply a natural rather than artificial, or devious, response.

Now the Hack's expression of this idea is in terms of flint struck against metal: he says of moderns that they "strike all Things out of themselves, or at least, by Collision, from each other" (135). He is, however, speaking of moderns, whom he is imitating; when he speaks of himself, "what pops into my head" becomes a mechanical metaphor: "I have thought fit to make *Invention* the *Master,* and give

1. Erasmus, *Praise of Folly,* p. 9.

Method and *Reason,* the office of its *Lacquays"* (209). Thus
in *Praise of Folly* "simplicity" of this sort is expressed
simply, while in the *Tale,* when it is expressed as pomp-
ously as this, it takes on a more sinister quality; a meaning
which was perhaps latent in Folly is drawn to the surface.

The images which the *Tale* echoes from *Praise of Folly*
have undergone a striking transformation. For example,
there is Folly's stance on her platform, as well as her allusions to man's natural inclination to "prick up" his "ears"
"for mountebanks in the marketplace, for clowns and jest-
ers" (p. 8)—all of which is picked up by Swift: in the idea
of the oratorial machines which satisfy these needs (as opposed to the instruction of the sermon), even down to the
mountebank (46); [2] in his preoccupation with ears (re
pulpit, 58, or re enthusiasm, 200ff.); in his allusion to asses
and asses' ears (e.g., 35, 98–9, 192, 200). [3] All that Folly
praises here turns its ugly side to the reader.

It can even be argued that the *Tale* finds the general
outline of its argument (or, at any rate, the Hack's argument) in *Praise of Folly.* Folly begins by describing the
ills of the world: "Come, then, and suppose a man could
look from a high tower, as the poets say Jove is in the habit
of doing. To how many calamities would he see the life of
man subject! . . . the certainty of death is inexorable. Diseases infest life's every way; accidents threaten, troubles as-
sail without warning . . ." (p. 40). The Hack gives a similar account of the ills of existence for a modern in the
"Dedication to Prince Posterity"—writings vanish, all is
slippery and transient. [4] Folly then says, "But aided in part

2. See also ibid., p. 89.

3. Cf. ibid., pp. 11, 45, 52; the last—"he thinks he is listening to a fine
orchestra whenever he hears an ass braying"—is echoed in the *Tale,* G-S,
p. 257.

4. Cf. also a metaphor Pascal uses to express man's true condition: "We
sail over a vast expanse, ever uncertain, ever adrift, carried to and fro.
To whatever point we think to fix and fasten ourselves it shifts and leaves
us; and if we pursue it it escapes our grasp, slips away, fleeing in

by ignorance, and in part by inadvertence, sometimes by
forgetfulness of evil, sometimes by hope of good, sprinkling
in a few honeyed delights at certain seasons, I bring relief
from these ills; so that men are unwilling to relinquish
their lives even when, by the exactly measured thread of the
Fates, life is due to relinquish them" (p. 41). In the same
way, the Hack uses his introduction to show the ways one
can get above the ugliness and transcience of the world, by
senses or imagination, by pulpit, gallows or stage. The *Tale*
itself is a catalogue of these various solutions of the Hack's.
That Swift does not accept them is evident if we compare
another set of passages.

> Folly: The part of a truly prudent man . . . is (since
> we are mortal) not to aspire to wisdom beyond his sta-
> tion, and either, along with the rest of the crowd, pre-
> tend not to notice anything, or affably and companion-
> ably be deceived. But that, they tell us, is folly.[5]

> Hack: This is the sublime and refined Point of Felic-
> ity, called, *the Possession of being well deceived;* The
> Serene Peaceful State of being a Fool among Knaves
> [174].

Put simply, in the *Tale* "folly" becomes "fool" and, as William Empson has pointed out, here for the first time "fool"

eternal flight. Nothing stays for us . . . we have a burning desire to find a
sure resting place and a final fixed basis whereon to build a tower rising
to the Infinite; but our whole foundation cracks, and the earth yawns to
the abyss" (*Pensées*, No. 43, p. 25); this sums up the world of the "Dedication to Prince Posterity." Then, to see the other point of view we observe
in both Hack and Folly, turn to the Hack's introduction and compare it
with Lucretius' "well fortified sanctuaries serene, built up by the teachings
of the wise, whence you may look down from the height upon others and
behold them all astray, wandering abroad and seeking the path of life:
—the strife of wits, the fight for precedence, all labouring night and day
with surpassing toil to mount upon the pinnacle of riches and to lay hold
on power" (*De Rerum Natura*, Bk. II, ll. 7–13, pp. 84–5).

   5. Erasmus, p. 38. See also: "the more ways a man is deluded, the happier
he is" (p. 53), and p. 63.

has taken on its modern connotations and the "power" it derives "from a suggestion of nausea." [6]

Folly continues, "you will find no great exploit undertaken, no important arts invented, except at my prompting . . . for instance, is not war the seed-plot and fountain of renowned actions? Yet what is more foolish than to enter upon a conflict for I know not what causes . . . ?" (p. 30). In the *Tale* this folly has become madness: "For, if we take a Survey of the greatest Actions that have been performed in the World, under the Influence of Single Men; which are, *The Establishment of New Empires by Conquest: The Advance and Progress of New Schemes in Philosophy; and the contriving, as well as the propagating of New Religions:* We shall find the Authors of them all, to have been Persons, whose natural Reason hath admitted great Revolutions . . ." (162). Folly goes on to ask "What carried Quintus Curtius into that fissure, if not mere glory [i.e. folly]?" (p. 34). We have seen that in the *Tale* fortunate timing is all that separates glory from obloquy: "Upon so nice a Distinction are we taught to repeat the Name of *Curtius* with Reverence and Love; that of *Empedocles*, with Hatred and Contempt" (175). The whole "Digression on Madness" illustrates the difference between the view of illusion held by Folly and the Hack and that held by Swift. One makes it appear amiable, the only way to bear existence; the other treats it as a vicious cloak for knaves. [7]

There are, of course, many echoes of Erasmus in the *Tale* which show no particular alteration. Folly's recognition that "shame, infamy, opprobrium, and curses hurt only so far as they are felt" (p. 43) may be echoed by the *Tale's* "there is not, through all Nature, another so callous and

6. William Empson, *The Structure of Complex Words* (New York, New Directions, 1957), p. 110.

7. Folly, it should be acknowledged, distinguishes two kinds of madness, an amiable and an unamiable (Erasmus, p. 51); but I suspect Swift would have seen little difference.

insensible a Member as the *World's Posteriors,* whether you apply to it the *Toe* or the *Birch*" (48). The modern's love of whatever comes out of himself and the Aeolist's blowing himself up with wind find one of a host of possible sources in Folly's remark: "You will find that [practitioners of the arts] would sooner give up their paternal acres than any piece of their poor talents . . . the more unskilled one of them is . . . the more he will blow himself up, and spread himself" (p. 60).

Though the views of illusion may be different, the pictures of man's capacity drawn by the *Tale* and by *Praise of Folly* are alike in their pessimism. Folly exclaims: "And one can scarce believe what commotions and what tragedies this animalcule, little as he is and so soon to perish, sets agoing" (p. 70); and in the *Tale* Louis and Henry start wars for a whim. The difference between the two books lies in their solutions to the problems of reality.

INDEX